EDGAR CAYCE

In addition to his labors on behalf of the physically afflicted, the world-renowned prophet and psychic, Edgar Cayce, in a state of self-induced sleep, gave a series of 2,500 clairvoyant readings devoted to metaphysics, with reincarnation as their central theme.

This extraordinary book brings together the story of Jesus, as found scattered through these readings. EDGAR CAYCE'S STORY OF JESUS makes available for the first time the most challenging and thought-provoking contribution of America's "sleeping prophet."

" . . . these excerpts demonstrate the vitality of Cayce's subconscious mind."   —*Library Journal*

"Mr. Furst's book quotes at great length from the Cayce readings, and this should please the people who have been tantalized by very brief quotations in other, earlier books."   —*The Nashville Tennessean*

Berkley Books by and about Edgar Cayce

EDGAR CAYCE'S STORY OF ATTITUDES AND EMOTIONS
edited and arranged by Jeffrey Furst

EDGAR CAYCE'S STORY OF JESUS
edited and arranged by Jeffrey Furst

EDGAR CAYCE'S STORY OF KARMA
edited and arranged by Mary Ann Woodward

EDGAR CAYCE'S STORY OF THE ORIGIN AND DESTINY OF MAN
edited and arranged by Lytle Robinson

IS IT TRUE WHAT THEY SAY ABOUT EDGAR CAYCE?
Lytle Robinson

Most Berkley Books are available at special quantity discounts for bulk purchases for sales promotions, premiums, fund-raising, or educational use. Special books, or book excerpts, can also be created to fit specific needs.

For details, write: Special Markets, The Berkley Publishing Group, 375 Hudson Street, New York, New York 10014.

EDGAR CAYCE'S
STORY OF JESUS

SELECTED, ARRANGED AND
EDITED BY JEFFREY FURST

BERKLEY BOOKS, NEW YORK

If you purchased this book without a cover, you should be aware that this book is stolen property. It was reported as "unsold and destroyed" to the publisher, and neither the author nor the publisher has received any payment for this "stripped book."

EDGAR CAYCE'S STORY OF JESUS

A Berkley Book / published by arrangement with
Coward-McCann, Inc.

PRINTING HISTORY
Coward, McCann/Berkley Medallion edition / June 1976

All rights reserved.
Copyright © 1968 by The Edgar Cayce Foundation.
This book may not be reproduced in whole or in part,
by mimeograph or any other means, without permission.
For information address: Coward, McCann and Geoghegan, Inc.,
200 Madison Avenue, New York, New York 10016.

The Penguin Putnam Inc. World Wide Web site address is
http://www.penguinputnam.com

ISBN: 0-425-10327-7

BERKLEY®
Berkley Books are published by The Berkley Publishing Group,
a division of Penguin Putnam Inc.,
375 Hudson Street, New York, New York 10014.
BERKLEY and the "B" design
are trademarks belonging to Penguin Putnam Inc.

PRINTED IN THE UNITED STATES OF AMERICA

30 29

for the Master
who has never given up
on any one of us

CONTENTS

NOTE

Various Readings are indicated by number as indexed in the Cayce files. (This to preserve the individual's anonymity.) They are shown mostly verbatim with extracted passages occasionally shortened or underlined for emphasis. Explanatory or clarifying material is inserted in parentheses. Original questions are at times paraphrased in order to preserve the continuity of text.

Biblical quotations are taken from George M. Lamsa's Aramaic translation of *The Holy Bible From Ancient Eastern Manuscripts.*

INTRODUCTION

Any student of the Edgar Cayce materials must eventually come to a crossroads in thought (and belief) as concerns various criteria—(1) The essential validity of the information which came through the sleeping Cayce—(2) The source of that information from the standpoint of phenomenology—in how it was gathered or selected from the unconscious mind of Cayce. And finally (3), of utmost importance—What purpose or significance can be assigned to Cayce in relationship to Holy Scripture, especially as his (Cayce's) existence relates to the individual known as Jesus of Nazareth.

This latter question is one which will be pursued throughout these pages, and its answer can only be found within the minds of those who will openly approach all evidence in attempting a meaningful awareness or relationship with Creation as we come to know it.

Quite frankly, Cayce presents both an enigma and a paradox. The enigma is readily apparent as we scan the 14,246 clairvoyant Readings recorded during Cayce's lifetime, and at the same time make a study of his own personal life. Here we are constantly impressed by the consuming dedication which drove this man through four decades of continual effort in attempting to aid and assist others. Why else would a man endure putting himself in an unconscious state some fifteen thousand times during a span of over forty years, when on awakening he had no conscious recall of anything he ever said while asleep? Add to this his refusal to accept monetary returns beyond what was necessary for his modest immediate family

9

needs—plus having to endure a non-ending stream of investigators and abuse from various sources—and we see a man who certainly had attained a firm inner belief in what he was doing. And if Cayce's life does not rank as a well-stated example of the Christian ethic, then how else can it be appraised? Or, why else would he have done it? That, in addition to how he ever put up with everything concerned through all those years while still maintaining his sanity, is the enigma.

The paradox exists in the fact that much of the information which came through the sleeping Cayce was extremely alien to the awakened Edgar Cayce's manner of thinking—and especially contrary to his fundamentalist Christian background. This is the foundation of our discussion. As such, the paradox presented Cayce himself with both an unceasing burden and still an undeniable appeal for further search and enlightenment.

The sleeping Cayce never detracted from the Biblical Jesus of whom Edgar Cayce spoke with love and admiration in his Sunday school classes and followed affirmatively in his early readings of the Bible—yet so much was added to the dimensional concepts of Jesus through the sleeping Cayce that one can only wonder on the source, and ultimately, the purpose of Edgar Cayce's life. Was this man truly a prophet, or simply a well-intentioned phenomenon? How shall we consider the wealth of information which came through him?—As either the largest source of revelation given to the human race since the time of the Master—or as some fantastic cosmic accident? Or should we regard Cayce as inspired by demons or discarnate spirits?—But then surely we must consider the existence of Good, and the alternate possibility of Divine guidance throughout.

As a troubled seeker of Truth—this writer has wrestled at length with many of the basic questions which rankle the inner consciousness of man—does God truly exist in a relationship attainable by man's growth and understanding? Is the Holy Bible a consistent valid stream of Divine

Revelation? Did Jesus actually do all that was said of Him? Then too, what of such matters as the Virgin Birth? And finally, did He in fact arise from the dead?

To this, we add still another thought—Was Edgar Cayce as correct about Jesus as he was about so many other things? And if so, where do we as individuals fit in—or how?

Edgar Cayce, both asleep and awake, repeatedly stated that Jesus was the Light and the Way. However, during his sleep-state Cayce expanded considerably on what we would hope to understand of the Master and His purpose, especially as regards Creation and man's ultimate evolvement. It is in following That Light and That Way that this book is dedicated.

JEFFREY FURST
1968

PREFACE

WHAT IS A READING?

The following paragraphs contain some of the few recorded words of Edgar Cayce (in his conscious state) speaking on the subject of his clairvoyant discourses, or Readings.

This is included to both explain the Readings as he experienced them, and also to indicate some measure of the man in his awakened state.

For additional material, see Appendix A—"My Life and My Work."
> *(Talk given to Norfolk Study Group*
> *Open Meeting, February 6th, 1933)*

What is a reading?

It is rather hard to describe something which has become so much a part of me—almost like trying to describe what my face looks like. I can show you, but I can't tell you. I might tell you some of my experiences and thoughts concerning the readings; but as to what a reading is I can only tell you what others have said about them and what has come to me as I have studied the effect created in the minds of those receiving readings.

It would not be an exaggeration to say that I have been in the unconscious state (during which the readings are given) perhaps ten thousand times in the last thirty-one years; yet I myself have never heard a single reading. How can I describe one to you?

Many people who have never heard a reading have asked me just how I knew I could give one. I never did know it—don't know it yet—except by taking another person's word for it.

The first step in giving a reading is this: I loosen my clothes—my shoelaces, my necktie, my shirtcuffs, and my belt—in order to have a perfectly free-flowing circulation.

Then I lie down on the couch in my office. If the reading is to be a physical one, I lie with my head to the south and my feet to the north. If it is to be a life reading, it is just the opposite: my feet are to the south, my head to the north. The reason for this difference in "polarization", as the readings themselves call it, I do not know.

Once lying comfortably, I put both hands up to my forehead, on the spot where observers have told me that the third eye is located, and pray. Interestingly enough, I have unconsciously and instinctively, from the very beginning, adopted the practices used by initiates in meditation. This instinctive putting of my hands to the point midway between my two-eyes on my forehead is a case of what I mean.

Then I wait for a few minutes, until I receive what might be called the "go signal"—a flash of brilliant white light, sometimes tending towards the golden in color. This light is to me the sign that I have made contact. When I do not see it, I know I cannot give the reading.

After seeing the light I move my two hands down to the solar plexus, and—they tell me—my breathing now becomes very deep and rhythmic, from the diaphragm. This goes on for several minutes. When my eyes begin to flutter closed (up till now they have been open, but glazed) the conductor knows I am ready to receive the suggestion, which he proceeds to give me, slowly and distinctly. If it is a physical reading, for example, the name of the individual to receive the reading is given me, together with the address where he will be located during that period of time.

There is a pause—sometimes so long a pause (they tell me) that it seems I haven't heard the directions, so they give them to me again—after which I repeat the name and address very slowly, until the body is located, and a description of its condition is begun.

This, then, is how I give a reading. I am entirely unconscious throughout the whole procedure. When I wake up I feel as if I had slept a little bit too long. And frequently I feel slightly hungry—just hungry enough for a cracker and a glass of milk, perhaps. As to the validity of the information that comes through me when I sleep—this, naturally, is the question that occurs to everyone. Personally, I feel that its validity depends largely on how much faith or confidence the one seeking has in the source of information. Of course its validity has been objectively proved many hundreds of times by the results that have come from applying the advice.

With regard to the source of information, I have some ideas, naturally; but even though I have been doing this work for 31 years I know very little about it. Whatever I could say would be largely a matter of conjecture. I can make no claims whatsoever to great knowledge. I, too, am only groping.

But then, we all learn only by experience. We come to have faith or understanding by taking one step at a time. We don't all have the experience of getting religion all at once, like the man who got it halfway between the bottom of the well and the top when he was blown out by an explosion of dynamite. We all have to have our experiences and arrive at conclusions by weighing the evidence with something that responds from deep within our inner selves.

As a matter of fact, there would seem to be not only one, but several sources of information that I tap when in this sleeping condition.

One source is, apparently, the record that an individual or entity makes in all its experiences through what we call time. The sum-total of the experiences of that soul is "written", so to speak, in the subconscious of that individual as well as in what is known as the Akashic records. Anyone may read these records if he can attune himself properly.

Apparently I am one of the few who can lay aside their own personalities sufficiently to allow their souls to make this attunement to this universal source of knowledge—but I say this without any desire to brag about it. In fact, I do not claim to possess anything that other individuals do not inherently possess. Really and truly, I do not believe there is a single individual that doesn't possess this same ability I have. I am certain that all human beings have much greater powers than they are ever conscious of—if they would only be willing to pay the price of detachment from self-interest that it takes to develop those abilities. Would you be willing, even once a year, to put aside, pass out entirely from, your own personality?

Some people think that the information coming through me is given by some departed personality who wants to communicate with them, or some benevolent spirit or physician from the other side. This may sometimes be the case though in general I am not a "medium" in that sense of the term. However, if a person comes seeking that kind of contact and information, I believe he receives it.

Many people ask me how I prevent undesirable influences entering into the work I do. In order to answer that question let me relate an experience I had as a child. When I was between eleven and twelve years of age I had read the Bible through three times. I have now read it fifty-six times. No doubt many people have read it more times than that, but I have tried to read it through once for each year of my life. Well, as a child I prayed that I might be able to do something for the other fellow, to aid others in understanding themselves, and especially to aid children in their ills. I had a vision one day which convinced me that my prayer had been heard and would be answered.

I still believe that my prayer is being answered and as I go into the unconscious condition I do so with that faith. So I believe that if the source is not wavered by the desires of the individual seeking the reading, it will be from the universal. Of course if an individual's desire is very intense to have a communication from Grandpa, Uncle, or some great soul, the contact is directed that way, and that becomes the source. Do not think that I am discrediting those who seek in that way. If you're willing to receive what Uncle Joe has to say, that's what you get; if you're willing to depend on a more universal source, that's what you get. "What ye ask ye shall receive" is a two-edged sword. It cuts both ways.

(A talk given in Washington, D.C., February 3, 1935.)

On the subject of soul power I have nothing new to offer other than my understanding of what was presented by the man Jesus who became the Christ. For I am determined that as long as I live I will know nothing among men save Jesus Christ and Him crucified! For until we crucify our own personal desires we can never know whether we have a soul or not!

What is soul power?

Some years ago I had the privilege of meeting one of the world's best known scientists—a man considered throughout the world as an electrical wizard. He said at that time, "There isn't such a thing as a soul; it is purely the development of the race ideal."

Just a few days ago I had a communication from that same man. He said, "Cayce, I do not know whether I was right in what I said to you in 1910 or not. We do not know that man has a soul; we cannot prove it with our instruments; yet when we see the entire world seeking, seeking, seeking, there must be something. And I am convinced that when scientists go to work at studying God, just as they have undertaken to study how to make greater conveniences for mankind, we will learn something about the soul—if there is one."

Not long ago I had a letter from a writer I know, in which he told me statistics on all the wonderful things that have been accomplished lately—how many new trains set in motion, how many new airplanes, new this, new that and the other. But I am wondering if that is really civilization. We see so little about what good is being done for our fellowman; there's so little being presented! We as a people are so material-minded that we are thinking of the pleasures and satisfactions of the moment rather than of what we may learn about our inner selves.

I am reminded of what a physician asked me not long ago, in seeking a reading through me for himself. "Would you advise that I affiliate myself with some church so that I may increase my clientele?" he asked. I was very much struck by that question. Is that why most people go to church these days, that they may be well thought of, that they may improve their material status, rather than that they may truly worship by communing with God through their inner selves?

If we would truly find the soul, truly acquire soul power, we should let the motivating influence in us be the love of God as it manifests itself in our actions toward men. We and others can tell what our motivating influence is by what it makes us do toward our fellowman.

Jesus Christ said that the whole gospel is "Thou shalt love the Lord thy God with all thy heart, thy soul, and thy body, and thy neighbor as thyself". Then all the rest of the Bible is nothing but an explanation of that one sentence.

So whenever we begin to delve into the motivative

influence within our inner selves we will have to analyze
first our relationship to God, as it manifests itself in our
relationship to our fellow man.

We have been admonished by this one, that one, and the
other to develop our personality in order to be a power in
the world; but if we turn rather within ourselves, where
the kingdom of heaven is, what has been the promise?
"All these things shall be added unto you, in their place."
All that is necessary will be added, as we take step after
step; for as we use what we know, the next step is given to
us. We are all on our way for a development. What did the
Master say about our becoming aware of our souls? "In
patience possess ye your souls." How many of us are patient and know that we are patient with the fellow who
says or does something nice to us, because we immediately
begin to think he wants something from us. That's human
nature.

The soul is of God. If we love God and act like it, then we
express the soul power. But how many of us really act like
it? We say we believe that God is love, and that we should
love our neighbor and our enemy; but how many of us
really do? Until we do, how can we become aware that we
have a soul?

Let's not confuse the terms spirit and soul; for they are
not the same. I believe in the survival of personality, yes. I
believe it is possible for us to communicate with those
who have passed on; but I'm not preaching that we should
do it, no. I would prefer (hadn't you?) going to headquarters for orders, than to anyone lower. We had all rather
have our orders, our instructions, our promises, from
headquarters! Who is our headquarters? To as many as
have named His name, He is the headquarters. And His
promise has been, "If ye ask in my name, believing, that
shall I give unto you". Do we really believe that? If so,
then we would not be satisfied with anything else! It is
true, "He has given his angels charge concerning thee, lest
thou dash thy foot against a stone". But from whom do
we want our orders? And how may we receive them? We

may receive them through the awareness of that within us which is eternal—our soul! Only our soul!

What is the power of the soul, then? All that is within the infinite itself! All of that! It is ours! He has given it to us! What is every man's birthright? What did Esau sell for a mess of pottage? He sold that awareness that he might approach the throne of God itself! For what? To satisfy the cravings of the body for a moment! And that's what we're doing every day, isn't it? That is what keeps us from knowing our inner self. We are so pressed about by the things of the outer self, or outer world. What did the Master say about the seed that was sown in one place? The cares of this world came in and crowded it out, until there was nothing left. And that's what is the matter with most of us; that's why we are disturbed and wondering what it is all about. Can't we accept, and then live, the truth expressed in "In my Father's house are many mansions; if it were not so I would have told you; and I go to prepare a place for you, that where I am there ye may be also".

If we were as anxious about where we came from as we are about where we are going, we would be in quite a different position as to what we are doing with ourselves now, wouldn't we? And there is only one way that we can find out or know what the power of that influence is that carries on and on, and that is through the Divine within us as we give it expression in relation to someone else! We can't explain it to someone else; we have to experience it individually, through just doing a kindness to another, to someone perhaps who cannot do for himself, and then we experience it.

In a letter from an individual several thousand miles away whom I had tried to aid with the information coming through me as a channel, she said, "I have regained my health through following the suggestions you gave, but—most of all—my husband and I have found God. I am now ready to die any day, but—praise God—I'm living for something!" If you know what it is to bring that into the meaning of a person's life, you realize—as I cannot tell you—that there is such a thing as a soul. If you don't, just go out and do a kindness, a good deed. It makes something happen to you, and you feel good about it yourself! And the world looks a great deal better to you, no matter if you are hungry. "As ye do it unto the least of these my brethren, ye do it unto me!"

What is the soul? It is the God-Force in the weakest of our brethren, in the lowest of our fellow men. And when we do an unkindness to another individual we do not hurt the individual but we hurt God and ourselves. When do we dishonor God? When we do an unkindness, say an unkind word about our fellow man! What will make us aware of the soul? When we become God-minded and conscious of the fact that we are our brother's keeper! What was the excuse of the first man who did a wrong to another? "Am I my brother's keeper?" Many of us try to hide behind something, to prevent our own conscience from hurting, and say, "Well, I don't have to worry about that; that's his job." If he is a living being that is wandering, disturbed, then it is our job, when we come in contact with him, if we want to know God at all!

How may we use our soul power? By manifesting the fruits of the spirit, which are: kindness, patience, long-suffering; just doing those things we would like to have done to us. No matter how many fancy names we give to it, that's what is necessary when we come right down to facts. And if we seek first those fruits of the spirit, to manifest them in our lives towards our fellow man, all other things will be added unto us—and we will be expressing the soul power within us. "Know ye not that your bodies are the temples of the living God!" He has promised to meet us in our temple, within our inner self. In what condition is He going to find that temple? Whenever we remain in a prayerful, meditative state, asking Him to meet us there, we may gain that which if applied in our daily lives gives us the knowledge of the power of God in all its beauty.

Can we ever become aware of our soul power by finding fault with someone else? Suppose God found fault with us? Should we wonder that we suffer, when we consider how many hard things we have said about people? But what has He promised? "If ye will take my yoke upon you and learn of me, ye shall find rest unto your souls." He has promised to meet with us and talk with us, to bring to our remembrance all things even from the beginning, if we will only listen to that voice from within, using what we have today, and that necessary for tomorrow will be added in its due time. Today is the accepted time! If we will hear, we may become aware of the soul power within our inner self.

Many of us in our suffering have doubted the ability of the Christ Consciousness to arouse us to that necessary activity in our daily life. But the experience of the world has been from the very beginning, "Know, O Israel, the Lord thy God is One!" What destroyed the people in Atlantis, or in any nation of which we have any record? The attempt to promulgate the power of self alone. We are a power unto ourselves, but our individual self is the only thing that can keep us away from God. Those that would know God must first believe that He is, and then just act like it, and they will become aware of the God-Consciousness within themselves that makes all as one.

Then, those things that are spiritual must permeate the body, the mind, the soul, if we would make ourselves one with God—even as the Father, the Son, and the Holy Spirit are one. How great is the soul power? It is everlasting, for it is the gift of God to every individual.

Like begets like. We must love Him and keep His commandments if we would truly know Him and the soul power that is within each one of us.

Chapter One

FROM THE READINGS

Q. When did Jesus become aware that he would be the Saviour of the world?
A. When he fell in Eden. (2067-7)

Q. Does this mean that Jesus had been Adam?
A. Study the Book which tells of Him, JESUS, born of the Virgin Mary; (Then) know this is the soul-entity (Jeshua) who reasoned with those who returned from captivity in those days when Nehemiah, Ezra, Zerubbabel were factors in the attempts to re-establish the worship of God; and that (as) JESHUA, the scribe, translated the rest of the books written up to that time.

Then realize (also) that is the same entity, who, as JOSHUA, as the mouthpiece of Moses, who gave the law; and was the same soul-entity who was born in Bethlehem. The same soul-entity who, in those periods of the strength and yet the weakness of Jacob in his love for Rachel, was their firstborn, JOSEPH. As ZEND (father of Zoroaster)—this is the same entity. And this entity was that one who had manifested to Father Abraham as the prince, as MELCHIZEDEK, the priest of Salem, without father and without mother, without days or years, but a living human being in flesh, made manifest in the earth from the desire of Father-God to prepare an escape for man; as was warned by the same entity, as ENOCH; or, as in those days of ASAPHA, or AFFA, in those periods when those of the Egyptian land were giving those counsels to the many

23

nations, when there would be those saved of the physical
from their own making (or doing) in the physical. Or,
as the first begotten of the Father, who came as
AMILIUS in the Atlantean land and allowed himself to
be led into the ways of selfishness. (364-8) And this
was also the entity ADAM—and this was the Spirit of
Light. (5023-2)

These Readings came from the sleeping Edgar Cayce between 1932 and 1944. It should be remembered that prior
to 1923 Cayce spent over twenty years giving clairvoyant
"Readings" for hundreds of physically afflicted persons
with no mention at any time during that period of any
such items as biblical history, metaphysics, religious
philosophy, or especially the subject of reincarnation.

Then in Dayton, Ohio a man named Arthur Lammers
became interested in Cayce's work, and being a student of
philosophy and comparative religions, suggested some
non-routine questions be posed to the sleeping Cayce. The
answers which came through (in the 3744 series) proved
a major surprise for the Cayce family and served as the
basis for a new type of clairvoyant discourse—the "Life
Reading". A detailed story of this is chronicled in Cayce's
biography *There Is A River,* by Thomas Sugrue.

At that time (and subsequently) Cayce was a devout
Christian—a Sunday School teacher, who had no
background whatever in metaphysical or religious philosophy beyond his own fundamentalistic beliefs.

Consequently, the comments which came through the Life
Readings on such subjects as akashic records, planetary
sojourns, and past incarnations with their related karmic
implications, were decidedly alien to the awakened
Cayce's manner of thinking. Nevertheless, the Life Readings were pursued from 1923 onward and comprise a major portion of the material in the Cayce files.

Any study of the 2,500 Life Readings or the Metaphysical
Readings associated with them, provides the reader with

numerous references to Biblical history and the individual who wrote it and lived it.

Cayce would, in one breath as it were, rattle off direct quotes from both Old and New Testaments—sometimes paraphrasing them, sometimes interpreting; then mention persons well-known in Holy Writ alongside others whose names and relationships are lost in history other than as contacted (or revealed) through Cayce's unconscious mind.

Consider some of his statements concerning the Essenes, those offshoots of orthodox Jewry who were responsible for recording the Dead Sea scrolls.

Ye say that there were those periods when for four hundred years little or nothing had happened in the experience of man as a revelation from the Father, or God, or from the Sources of Light. What was it then, that made the setting for the place and for the entering in of that consciousness in the earth that ye know as the Son of man, the Jesus of Nazareth, the Christ on the Cross? Did the darkness bring light? Did the wandering away from the thought of such (light) bring the Christ into the earth? Rather, is this idea not a refutation of the common law that is present in spirit, mind, and body; that like begets like? As was asked oft, "Can any good thing come out of Nazareth?"

Isn't it rather that there were those that ye hear little or nothing of in thy studies—the Essenes—who dedicated their lives, their minds, their bodies to a purpose, to a seeking for that which had been to them a promise of old. Were there not individuals—men and women— who dedicated their bodies that they might be channels through which such influences, such a body might come? (262-61)

Then there were the diverse groups, as well as the Essenes, who had set themselves as a channel through which there was expected to be, in that particular period, the fulfillment of those promises indicated from the first promise to Eve unto the last, as had been recorded by Malachi. There were individuals who in their activities of daily life were in keeping with neither of the first indicated groups. (993-5)

Because of the divisions that had arisen among the peoples into sects, as the Pharisees, the Sadducees and their divisions, there had arisen the Essenes, who not merely had cherished the conditions that had come as word of mouth, but had kept the records of the periods when individuals had been visited with the supernatural, or out-of-the-ordinary experiences—whether in dreams, visions, voices, or what not. (1472-1)

Mt. Carmel (was) the original place where the school of the prophets was established. (By Elijah, Elisha, Samuel) (2520-1)

And these were students of what ye would call astrology, numerology, phrenology, and those phases of the study of the return of individuals, or reincarnation.

There were reasons why these proclaimed that certain periods formed a cycle—reasons which grew out of the studies of Aristotle, Enos, Mathias, Judy,* and others who supervised the school, as ye would term it in the present.

These individuals had been persecuted by leaders of the people, *and this caused the saying of which ye have an interpretation,* as given by the Sadducees, *"There is no resurrection" or "There is no reincarnation"—which is what the word meant in those days.* (5749-8)

Hence, there was the continued preparation and dedication of those who might be the channels through which this chosen vessel might enter—through choice—into

---

* Judy—unmentioned in Biblical texts, was, according to Cayce, one of the Master's early teachers. More of her story later.

materiality. Thus in Carmel—where there were the priests of this faith—there were the maidens chosen who were dedicated to this purpose, this office, this service. That was the beginning, that was the foundation of what ye term the church. (5749-7)

There were, then, twelve maidens in the temple, or of the ORDER of the Temple. And this entity was one of the twelve, associated with Mary in the preparations. (649-2)

The temple steps—or those that led to the altar, these were those upon which the sun shone, as it arose of a morning when there were the first periods of the chosen maidens going to the altar for prayer, as well as for the burning of incense. (5749-8)

On this day, as they mounted the steps, all were bathed in the morning sun; which not only made a beautiful picture, but clothed all as if in purple and gold. As Mary reached the top step, then, there were the thunder and lightning; and the angel led the way, taking the child by the hand before the altar. This was the manner of choice, this was the showing of the way—for she led the others on THIS particular day. (At this time Mary was between age thirteen and fourteen. The Conception came at sixteen.) (5749-8)

Q. Is the teaching of the Roman Catholic Church correct, in that Mary was without original sin from the moment of her conception in the womb of Anne?

A. It would be correct in any case. Correct more in this. For as for the material teaching of that just referred to, *you see, in the beginning, Mary was the twin soul of the Master in the entrance into the earth!* (5749-8)

Q. Was Anne also prepared for her part as mother of Mary?

Q. Only in general, not as specific as Mary after Mary's being pointed out. See, there was no belief in the fact that Anne proclaimed that the child was without father. It's like many proclaiming today that the Master was immaculately conceived; they say, "Impossible!" They say it isn't in compliance with the natural law. IT IS A NATURAL LAW, as has been indicated by the projection of mind into matter, and thus making of itself a separation to become encased in same—as did man (in the beginning.) Then, in that there had been an encasement *was* there a beginning. Then there must be an end when this must be—or may be—broken; and this began at that particular period. Not the only—this particular period with Anne, and then the Master AS the son—but the ONLY begotten of the Father in the flesh AS a son OF an immaculately conceived daughter! (5749-8)

Q. Then neither Mary nor Jesus had a human father?
A. Neither Mary nor Jesus had a human father. They were *one* soul so far as the earth is concerned. (5749-8)

Q. Did Mary's conception of Jesus take place in the temple at Jerusalem or in the Essenes at Mt. Carmel?
A. The Essenes' to be sure. Because of the adherence to those visions as proclaimed by Zacharias in the orthodox temple, he (Zacharias) was slain even with his hands upon the horns of the altar. Hence these who were being protected (Mary and Elizabeth) were in Carmel, while Zacharias was in the temple of Jerusalem. (5749-8)

Q. Was Zacharias, father of John the Baptist, an Essene?
A. As has been indicated, Zacharias at first was a member of what you would term the orthodox (Jewish) priesthood. Mary and Elizabeth were members of the Essenes, you see; and for this reason, Zacharias kept Elizabeth in the mountains and in the hills. Yet when there was the announcing of the birth (of Jesus) and Zacharias proclaimed his belief, the murder, the death, took place. (5749-8)

Q. It is difficult to grasp the concept of reality of the Immaculate Conception. Could you please clarify?

A. Neither is there much indicated in sacred or profane history as to the preparation of the mother for that channel through ' which immaculate conception might take place. And this—the immaculate conception—is a stumblingstone to many worldly-wise. (5749-15)

As the spirit was made manifest in the body purified by consecration of purpose in the lives manifested in the earth, so might the spirit—bring to the organs of (its own) flesh, a body through which the spirit may itself manifest in the earth (As its twin soul).

Remember those forms which have been given. First, He was created—brought into being from all that there was in the earth, as (Adam) an encasement for the soul of an entity, a part of the Creator; knowing separation in death. Then He was made manifest in birth through the union of channels growing out of that "Thought of the Creator" made manifest, but so expressed, so manifested as ENOCH as to merit the escaping of (physical) death—which had been the result of the law of disobedience. He was made manifest in MELCHIZEDEK by desire alone, not knowing body, not knowing mind—save its own; brought into materialization as of itself; passing from materialization in the same manner. Then there was perfected that period again in BODY when the other soul, or portion of self (Eve), was made manifest by the consecration of the mother (Mary); meeting self, then, by that same quickening power which had been made manifest in the beginning, or at first. (2072-4)

Here we come again to the mention of the Master having previously existed or manifested as both Enoch and Melchizedek—All of which gives John 8:56-58 and Genesis 14:18 a decided ring of truth regarding both Cayce and the thread of this discourse.

More of the Essenes later, but note the inclusion of

"Judy", an individual who is unmentioned elsewhere in the pages of history, and the fact that Cayce himself died in 1945, two years before the Dead Sea Scrolls were discovered (as he predicted they would be). The Scrolls' association with the early Essenes therefore makes for a rather startling and unmistakable tie-in with Cayce's overall commentaries on those times and the peoples who lived therein.

In these initial paragraphs we have outlined a summary of what Cayce stated again and again in the Readings from 1923 on as regards the story of Creation. It is a story that must be pieced together from literally hundreds of separate Readings, for different individuals, given over a period of two decades. Yet the story is amazingly consistent and inter-related throughout.

It has been said before that no man has a good enough memory to be a consistently good liar or fabricator of tales without being bogged down eventually in a sheer weight of detail. Consider then the hundreds of people that Cayce gave Life Readings for, along with their almost invariable inter-relationships during various past lives with others who also had Life Readings. In later Readings Cayce would often add to the story, or the relationship, but he never veered from his original statements regarding, say, the inter-involvement of several members of a family throughout previous periods where two or more had incarnated at the same time, and therein had been personally involved with one another. For Cayce to have fabricated all of these by reason of an active imagination or some other unknown source defies our logic and intellect. Certainly from somewhere he was picking up rather detailed personal information, neatly threading it together and reciting it forth, mostly without hesitation, as fast as a stenographer could take it down in shorthand. Then too, the individuals who received Readings seem generally agreed that the information that was given them somehow repeatedly struck an inner chord of awareness or understanding of themselves . . . as if that Reading had been truly given just for them.

And, Cayce never in all those years gave a Reading, physical or otherwise, for a person who didn't exist. A common ploy by investigators is to submit a fictitious name or set of facts to a psychic such as Cayce. This was apparently attempted on various occasions, at which time Cayce would announce that he could not find or locate such a person. Subsequently there would be no complaint from the person who had not secured the requested Reading.

Too, he would often be given a name, years after an initial Reading, then after stating, "Yes, we have had this body before", go into a lengthy discourse as if there had been no break in time whatsoever.

But consider again the initial paragraphs regarding the Master and the effect they must have had upon the awakened Cayce. Here was a traditional Christian, trained as a Fundamentalist Sunday School teacher stating not only that reincarnation was a fact, but also that Adam and Jesus were one and the same individual! And, to make matters more complicated, this same beloved Jesus was being referred to as Enoch, the scribe who some believe wrote the first books of the Bible; as Jeshua who later translated and brought those books up to date; as Joseph the son of Jacob, sold his brothers into captivity in Egypt; as Joshua, the companion of Moses who finally brought the children of Israel back to Jerusalem; and as Melchizedek, priest of Salem, who feasted centuries before with Father Abraham—giving rise apparently to the statements of Jesus, "Even before Abraham was, I AM". And, "Abraham knew my day, and was glad thereof".

Then too, we have an "Amilius"—referred to as "The first begotten of the Father"—coming to the Atlantean land! Shades of lost continents—and unknown, unrecorded names and relationships tied in with well-known names from the Old Testament! Surely the sincere and devout Cayce must have trembled fully inside upon hearing these accounts and then prayed long and hard concerning the source.

Or, consider the statements that he, as a Protestant Christian layman made, concerning the Virgin Birth, and the Roman Catholic claims in tracing their origins back to the temple on Mt. Carmel. A fascinating sidenote is that by an odd quirk of fate, the Roman Catholic church in Virginia Beach is located directly across the street from the old Cayce home and former A.R.E. headquarters. It is named for Mary—"Stella Maris" or "Star of The Sea". In Palestine the Carmelite monastery on Mt. Carmel is also named "Stella Maris"

Finally, there is the unmistakable fact that according to the Readings, from Genesis to Revelation the entity Edgar Cayce was repeatedly intertwined in the lives and purposes of the Master and His associates throughout numerous incarnations—from Atlantis to the present "New Age" or "Aquarian Age", however we come to phrase it.

Surely if the subconscious mind of Edgar Cayce created all this intricate detail as a work of fiction, then that fiction in itself must stand as a masterful accomplishment.

Chapter Two

IN THE BEGINNING—GENESIS

In the beginning was the Word, the Word was God, the Word was with God. "HE MOVED". Hence, as He moved, Souls, portions of Himself, came into being. (263-13)

The entity (2497) was in the beginning, WHEN ALL WERE IN THE SPIRITUAL FORCE, when the morning stars sang together in the glory of the coming of the Lord to make possible the developing of man's influence in the world.

The First Day

In the beginning God created the Heaven and the earth. And the earth was without form, and void; and darkness was upon the face of the deep. And the Spirit of God moved upon the face of the waters. And God said, Let there be light: and there was light. And God saw the light, that it was good; and God divided the light from the darkness. And God called the light day, and the darkness He called night. And the evening and the morning were the first day. Genesis 1:1-5

Before that the entity (341) was among those when the forces of the Universe came together, when upon the waters there was the sound of the coming together of THE SONS OF GOD—The morning stars sang together, and over the face of the waters there was the

voice of the glory of the coming of the plane for man's
indwelling. (341-1)

Read, first, five or six verses at the beginning of the
first chapter of Genesis, and in the third verse understand what it means that the knowledge is within thine
own self, the light necessary for yourself to be one of
the best men God ever created.

They are not foolishness, my friend! It's the law of the
Lord, and you must one day face it! (2879)

For thyself came not merely by chance. For the earth is
a causation world; in the earth cause and effect are as
the natural law. And as each soul enters this material
plane it is to meet or to give those lessons or truths that
others, too, may gain the more knowledge of the purpose for which each soul enters.

*For did the Master Jesus come by chance? Or was it not
according to the preparation made from the very foundations of the world?* For as another has indicated,
"Without Him there was not anything made that was
made." When ye, as a soul-entity, in the beginning
sought companionship with God, losing that companionship with God, losing by choice of that which
would satisfy or gratify a material desire only, ye, as the
Master did, entered again and again, ye come to fulfill
the law, the law that brought thy soul into being to be
one with Him. (3645)

Before that we find the entity (5056) was in the Atlantean land, and in those periods BEFORE ADAM was
in the earth. The entity was among those who were the
THOUGHT PROJECTIONS and a real musician on
pipes and reed instruments.

Ye (1857) were with him (Cayce) in the beginning.
Ye were both then, as it were (for comparison) as the
WIND upon the waters, that announced the glory of the
coming of man! Hence ye were both as SPIRITUAL

IMPORTS AND PURPOSES WHEN ADAM FIRST
WALKED IN THE GARDEN.

Among those who first came into the earth's sphere,
before it became habitable to human life. Only then, as
vision, did the entity view the earth's sphere, and passed
to the other spheres about the earth. (228-2)

Whether we concur or disagree with Cayce concerning the
story of Creation, we must necessarily go back to Genesis
and other books of the old Testament and also the legends
associated with the "Fall of The Angels" prior to the coming of Adam in order to fully interpret Edgar Cayce's
Story of Jesus. The story as reconstructed from the Readings is that there was, indeed, an initial fall in spirit by
numerous entities who came within the earth sphere.
These spirit entities, or souls, came and began "playing at
creation"—projecting themselves into the material earth
as "thought forms"—into the very rocks and trees—coex-
isting within various mineral and life forms, both animal
and vegetable. Here the souls eventually became so enmeshed, or hardened in the material diversions and creations of their own making, that they ultimately lost their
conscious identity of being creatures or creations of God.

In that particular experience there still were those who
were physically entangled in the animal kingdom, with
the appendages, with cloven hoofs, with four legs, with
portions of trees, with tails, with scales, with those
various things that Thought Forms had so indulged in
as to separate the purpose of God's creation of man as
man—not as animal. (2072-8)

According to the Readings these individuals became
known in the story of Genesis as "The Sons of Man".
Other souls, not trapped in the material earth, were aware
of this situation and chose to enter the earth plane in order
to aid the entities who had lost their identity and
awareness of the Creator. This second wave of souls
became known as "The Sons of God" and were led into
the earth by the entity we know as The Master, Jesus.

The Readings make numerous references to the "Sons of Man" as being entrapped in strange grotesque bodies—curiously reminiscent of ancient legends of centaurs and satyrs—of men with wings and feathers, hoofs or claws, half-fish or part-tree—of demonic spirits encased as dragons or reptiles and other weird, hideous beasts.

> The entity was among the children of the Law of One, those that were the SONS OF MEN, yet of the Daughters of the Lord—or those who had become purified of those entanglements in the animal forces that became manifest among many. (1066)

> Some brought about monstrosities, as those of its associations with beasts of various characters. Hence, those of the styx, satyr and the like; those of the sea, or mermaids; those of the unicorn, and those of various forms. (364-10)

Accordingly, the Sons of God set themselves to working at creation also (in accord with Divine guidance) and fashioned or evolved the flesh bodies which were intended to be the channels for man's eventual release from his material being. This was done by thought form projection . . . through the glandular centers of the higher developed species of primates that were chosen as the most advantageous of the animals then inhabiting the earth (for the purposes and problems involved).

> Then the earth brought forth seed in her season, and man appeared in five places at once—the five senses, the five reasons, the five spheres, the five developments, the five nations. (5748-1)

Q. Did the appearance of what became the five races occur simultaneously?
A. Occurred at once.

Q. Are the places designated for the beginning of the five races correct?

A. As we find—those in the Gobi, the yellow; the white in the Carpathians; the red in the Atlantean and in the American; the brown in the Andean; the black in the plain and the Sudan or in the African. (364-13)

This emergence of the five races was parcel to the essential plan whereby the Sons of God could assist the Sons of Man in a return to consciousness of being with and through the Creator. And so the stage was set for the entering into Atlantis of Jesus as Amilius—the At-Man or First Adam.

In the period then some 198,000 years before the entry of Ram into India, there lived in this land of Atlantis one Amilius, who had first noted the separations of the beings as inhabited that portion of the earth's sphere or plane of those peoples, into male and female as separate entities or individuals. As to their forms in the physical sense, these were rather of the nature of thought forms, or able to push out of themselves in that direction in which development took shape in thought—much in the way and manner as the amoeba would in the waters of a stagnant bay or lake in the present. (364-3)

Q. How is the legend of Lilith, the legendary first woman, connected with the period of Amilius?
A. In the beginning, as was outlined, there was presented that that became as the Sons of God, in that male and female were as in one, with those abilities for those changes as were able or capable of being brought about. In the changes that came from those things, as were of the projections of the abilities of those entities to project, this as a being came as the companion; and when there was that turning to the within, through the sources of creation, as to make for the helpmeet of that as created by the First Cause, or of the Creative Forces that brought into being that as was made, then—from out of self—was brought that as was to be the helpmeet, not just companion, of the body. Hence the legend of the associations of the body during that

period before there was brought into being the last of
the creations, which was not of that that was made, and
a helpmeet to the body, that there might be no change
in the relationship of the Sons of God with those relationships of the Sons and Daughters of Men. (364-7)

Q. What was meant by the Sons of the Highest in Atlantis and the second coming of souls to the earth, as mentioned in a Life Reading given through this channel
(Cayce)?

A. In this period or age, as was seen—there is fault of
words here to project that as actually occurs in the formation of that as comes about! There was, with the
will of that as came into being through the correct channels, of that as created by the Creator, that of the continuing of the souls in its projection and projection—
see? While in that as was of the offspring, of that as
pushed itself into form to satisfy, gratify, that of the
desire of that known as carnal forces of the senses, of
those created, there continued to be the war one with
another and there were then—from the other sources
(worlds) the continuing entering of those that would
make for the keeping of the balance, as of the first purpose of the Creative Forces, as it magnifies itself in that
given sphere of activity, of that that had been given the
ability to create with its own activity—see? And hence
the second, or the continued entering of souls into that
known as the earth's plane during this period, for that
activity as was brought about. Let's remember that as
was given, in the second, third from Adam, or fourth, or
from Amilius, there was "In that day did they call upon
the name of the Lord"—is right! And ever, when the
elements that make for littleness, uncleanness, are
crucified in the body, the Spirit of the Lord, of God, is
present! When these are overbalanced, so that the body
(physical), the mental man, the imagination of its
heart, is evil, or his purpose is evil, then is that war continuing—as from the beginning. Just the continued warring of those things within self as from the beginning;
for with these changes as brought sin into the world,
with the same came the fruits of same, or the seed as of

sin, which we see in the material world as those things
that corrupt good ground, those that corrupt the elements that are of the compounds of those of the first
causes, or elementals and pests are seen, and the like,
see? So does it follow throughout all creative forces,
that the fruits of that as is active brings that seed that
makes for the corrupting of, or the clearing of, in the
activative forces of, that being acted upon. (364-7)

Q. What was meant by "As in the first Adam sin entered, so in the last Adam all shall be made alive"?

A. Adam's entry into the world in the beginning, then,
must become the saviour of the world, as it was committed to His care, "Be thou fruitful, multiply, and subdue the earth!" Hence Amilius, Adam, the first Adam,
the last Adam, becomes—then—that that is given the
power over the earth, and—as in each soul the first to
be conquered is self—then all things, conditions and
elements, are subject unto that self? That's a universal
law, as may be seen in that as may be demonstrated
either in gases that destroy one another by becoming
elements of the same, or that in the mineral or the
animal kingdom as may be found that destroy, or
become one with the other. Hence, as Adam given—the
Son of God—so He must become that that would be
able to take the world, the earth, back to that source
from which it came, and all power is given in His keeping in the earth, that He has overcome; self, death, hell
and the grave even, become subservient unto Him
through the conquering of self in that made flesh; for,
as in the beginning was the Word, the Word was with
God, the Word was God, the same was in the beginning. The Word came and dwelt among men, the offspring of self in a material world, and the Word
overcame the World—and hence the world becomes,
then, as the servant of that that overcame the world!
(364-7)

Q. Please give the important incarnations of Jesus in the
world's history.

A. In the beginning as Amilius, as Adam, as Mel-

chiezdek, as Zend, as Ur, as Asaph, as Jeshua—
Joseph—(Joshua)—Jesus.

Then, as that coming into the world in the second coming—for He will come again and receive His own who
have prepared themselves through that belief in Him
and acting in the manner; for the Spirit is abroad and
the time draws near and there will be the reckoning of
those even as in the first so in the last and the last shall
be first; for there is that Spirit abroad—He standeth
near. Ye that hath eyes to see, let him see. He that hath
ears to hear, let him hear that music of the coming of
the Lord of this vineyard; and art thou ready to give account of that thou hast done with thine opportunity in
the earth as the Sons of God, as the heirs and joint heirs
of glory with the Son? Then make thy paths straight, for
there must come an answering for that thou hast done
with thy Lord! He will not tarry, for having overcome
He shall appear even as the Lord and Master. Not as
one born, but as one that returneth to his own, for He
will walk and talk with men of every clime, and those
that are faithful and just in their reckoning shall be
caught up with Him to rule and to do judgment for a
thousand years! (364-7)

In the above Reading Cayce ties in and relates the Al-
pha/Omega concept of Christ from Genesis to Revelation
in an extremely interesting and understandable manner.
Indeed, the entire series of Readings on the Book of
Revelation is in itself a worthwhile separate study.
Therein Cayce relates the Revelation of John as a symbolic allegory of the human body's structure and evolvement to the ultimate Christ Consciousness within—all
related to the promised second coming of The Master.

The Atlantean period as revealed in the Readings can also
well entail a full study of its own. Its significance within
our text is related to the references of Jesus as Amilius,
plus the over-all plan for soul development and the eventual return or at-one-ment of all souls with the Creator.

. . . In the days when the Sons came together in the first of the morning light by the earth's sun, this entity was among Those who gathered to worship the sun. (4543)

Here a rational basis for the sun-worship still current among some primitive groups is implied, with the sun as a symbol of the Creator.

Q. Please explain the statement given in Genesis, "In six days God made the heaven and the earth!"

A. That each may interpret this according to his own comprehension, let each become aware of the power of the Father in His manifestations in the earth. When it is considered (as was later given, or WRITTEN even before this was written) that "a thousand years is as but a day and a day as but a thousand years in the sight of the Lord," then it may be comprehended that this was colored by the writer's desire to express to the people the power of the Living God—rather than a statement of six days as man comprehends days in the present. Not that such was an impossibility, but rather that men should be impressed by the omnipotence of that they were called on to worship as God. (262-57)

The Seventh Day

Thus the heavens and the earth were finished, and all the host of them.

And on the seventh day God ended His work which He had made; and He rested on the seventh day from all His work which He had made.

And God blessed the seventh day, and sanctified it; because that in it He had rested from all His work which God created and made.

These are the generations and of the earth when they were created, in the day that the Lord God made the earth and the heavens." Genesis 2:1-3

Sure, it is indicated that He rested on the 7th day, to take stock, or to let His purpose flow through that which He perfected in itself. (3491)

Why shouldn't God withdraw and rest? God had given His Son the divine images, even the pattern for His own material body. Is it any wonder as Amilius looked about Him that He soon began to draw on that perfect image for a perfectly created man body?

This is the origin of our traditional concept that the seventh day is a holy day, to be sanctified as commemorating the day when all preparation was completed for the incoming of the first Son of God, and those of His brother souls that chose to come with Him into the earth. The Son's day became Sunday in our tradition.

The Atlantean epoch lasted over a period of some two hundred thousand years. It was in the early part of that evolution that the Son of God, as Amilius, drew from himself the human body.

As to the highest point of civilization (in Atlantis), this would first have to be determined according to the standard as to which it would be judged—as to the highest point was when Amilius ruled with those understandings. As to the one (Amilius) that understood the variations, or whether they become man-made, would depend on whether we are viewing from a spiritual standpoint or a purely material or commercial standpoint; for the variations, as we find, extend over a period of some two hundred thousand years. (364-4)

An over-all plan for soul development or evolution as taken from the Readings will be covered in the following chapter, along with some of the ramifications as they affect our understanding of the Christ Consciousness and our relationship to the earth plane. Meanwhile it should be noted that Cayce gave Life Readings wherein the individuals were stated to have lived upon the earth over ten million years ago—long before the developments which led up to Amilius and the bringing forth of the five races. This latter event occurred around one million B.C.— About the time that the continent of Lemuria became inhabited and was developed to a relatively high state of culture—much akin to what we now refer to as the Stone Age. In the Readings Lemuria was also referred to as Mu, Og, or the Land of Oz, and was said to have occupied an area west of the South American continent extending into Southern California and south-western U.S.A. It eventually broke up and submerged during three widely spaced periods of earth changes which overlapped the emergence of the Atlantean culture and the similar catastrophies that ultimately broke up and sank that continent.

The timetable for these various occurrences can be assembled thus. Not all dates were given in the Readings. Some approximations have been made for the more ancient periods.

1,000,000—800,000 B.C.	—Early Lemurian development.
500,000 B.C.	—Lemuria inundated by water, peoples scattered.
400,000-300,000 B.C.	—Lemuria inhabited and civilization advanced.
250,000 B.C.	—Second Lemurian catastrophy, possibly by fire.
200,000 B.C.	—Early Atlantean culture emerged.
80,000 B.C.	—First Atlantean disturbance. Final Lemurian submergence.
28,000 B.C.	—Second Atlantean disturbance. Recorded biblically as the Great Flood.
10,700 B.C.	—Final destruction and sinking of Atlantis.
10,390 B.C.	—Completion of The Great Pyramid in Egypt by the priests Ra-Ta and Hermes.

This last date is important in that it bridges the Atlantean culture to more recent times, and especially to structural evidences which are still available for archeological study.

Over 650 of the Life Readings given by Edgar Cayce touched upon the Atlantean and Lemurian periods leading up to the establishment in Egypt of much of the Atlantean culture. This period, dating back some twelve to thirteen thousand years ago according to the Readings, once again brought together the entities Cayce (as Ra-Ta the High Priest) and The Master, possibly, as the legendary Hermes.

But before going into that account, let us thread together some of the background or reasoning, as given in the Readings, as it concerns the subject of Soul Development—and therein the relationship to the universal Christ spirit or consciousness exemplified in the man Jesus, who through His sacrifice and acceptance of the Will of God became The Christ. This final achievement apparently, was the plan and pattern from the beginning.

Chapter Three

ON SOUL DEVELOPMENT

What has been given as the truest of all that has ever been written in Scripture? *God does not will that any soul should perish!* But man, in his willfulness, harkens oft to that which would separate him from his Maker! *. . . He has not willed that any soul should perish, but from the beginning has prepared a way of escape!* What, then, is the meaning of the separation? Bringing into being the various phases so that the soul may find in manifested forms the consciousness and awareness of its separation, and (a return to) itself, by that through which it passes in all the various spheres (stages) of awareness. Thus the separation between light and darkness. Darkness, that it had separated—that a soul had separated itself from the light. Hence He called into being Light, and awareness began. We look out and see the heavens, the stars, and, as the Psalmist has said: "The heavens declare the glory of God and the firmament sheweth His handiwork, as day unto day uttereth speech and night unto night sheweth knowledge". (262-56)

But when the Prince of Peace came into the earth, He overcame the flesh *and* temptation. So He became the first of those that overcame death in the body, enabling Him to so illuminate, to so revivify that body as to take it up again, even when those fluids of the body had been drained away by the nail holes in His hands and by the spear piercing His side.

45

Yet this body, this entity, *too* may do these things; through those promises that were so new yet so old, as given by Him. "Not of myself do I these things", sayeth He, "but God, the Father that worketh in me; for I *come* from him, I go to Him."

He came, the Master, in flesh and blood, even as thou didst come in flesh and blood. Yet as He then proclaimed to thee, there is a cleansing of the body, of flesh, of blood, in such measure that it may become illumined with power from on high; that is within thine own body to will: "Thy Will, O God; not mine, but Thine, be done in me, through me". (1152-1)

Q. Discuss the various phases of spiritual development before and after reincarnation in the earth.
A. This may be illustrated best in that which has been sought through example in the earth.

When there was in the beginning a man's advent into the plane known as earth, and it became a living soul, amenable to the laws that govern the plane itself as presented, the Son of Man entered the earth as the first man. Hence the Son of Man, the Son of God, the Son of the First Cause, making manifest in a material body. This was not the first spiritual influence, spiritual body, spiritual manifestation in the earth, but the first man—flesh and blood; the first carnal house, the first body amenable to the laws of the plane in its position in the universe.

For, the earth is only an atom in the universe of worlds! And man's development began through the laws of the generations in the earth; thus the development, retardment, or the alterations in those positions in a material plane.

And with error (sin) entered that as called *death,* which is only a transition—through God's other door—into that realm where the entity has builded, in its manifestations as related to the knowledge and activity respecting the law of the universal influence.

Hence the development is through the planes of experience that an entity may become one *with* the First Cause; even as the angels that wait before the Throne bring the access of the influence in the experience through the desires and activities of an entity, or being, in whatever state, place or plane of development the entity is passing.

For, in the comprehension of no time, no space, no beginning, no end, there may be the glimpse of what simple transition or birth into the material is; as passing through the other door into another consciousness.

Death in the material plane is passing through the outer door into a consciousness in the material activities that partakes of what the entity, or soul, has done with its spiritual truth in its manifestations in the other sphere.

Hence, as there came the development of that first entity of flesh and blood through the earth plane, he became *indeed* the Son—through the things which He experienced in the varied planes, as the development came to the oneness-with the position in that which man terms the Triune. (5749-3)

Q. When did the knowledge come to Jesus that He was to be the Savior of the world?
A. When He fell, in Eden. (1092)

The War of the Angels

Q. What is meant here by the war in heaven between Michael and the Devil?
A. As has just been given, as is understood by those here, there is first—as in the spiritual concept—the spiritual rebellion, before it takes mental form. This warring is illustrated there by the war between the Lord of the Way (Archangel Michael) and the Lord of

Darkness (Satan)—or the Lord of Rebellion. (281-27)

Q. Are angels and archangels synonymous with that which we call laws of the *universe*; if so, explain and give an example.
A. They are as the laws of the universe; as in *Michael*, the Lord of the Way, *not* The Way but the Lord *of* the Way, hence disputed with the influence of evil as to the way of the spirit of the teacher or director in his entrance through the outer door. (5749-3)

Banishment—Man's Will, not God's

Q. Is it the destiny of every spiritual entity to become eventually one with God?
A. Unless that entity wills its banishment. As with man: in giving him the soul there was given the will wherewith there might be manifested in the entity either the spiritual or the material.
With the will the entity—either spiritual or physical—may banish itself. Again it is a compliance with law. As given, hell was prepared for Satan and his angels. Yet God has not willed that any soul should perish. He gave the will to His creation, MAN, that man might be one with Him. As the meaning of destiny is law, the compliance with the law enables one to become the law. (900-20)

This reference to self-banishment is of considerable interest as it concerns the concept of an all-loving Creator—who thus would never conceivably condemn His creations to eternal punishment or damnation—and also in light of the Readings' astrological reference to Saturn as a sphere of re-moulding—as for a new beginning before returning to earth and its temptations. In fact, the Saturnian experience is decidedly reminiscent of Dante's *"Inferno"* and other tales of Hell or Purgatory.

Saturn

In Saturn we find the sudden or violent changes—those influences and environs that do not grow, as it were, but are sudden by change of circumstances materially—or by activities apparently on the part of others, that become a part of self by the very associations. Yet these are testing periods of thy endurance, or thy patience, or thy love of truth, harmony and the spirit that faileth not. From the combination of this with Uranus, we find the extremes; the material or mental environs in which the very opposites may be expected. Remember, only in Christ Jesus do extremes meet. (1918-1)

Each entity should know that every thought and act are the materials out of which they are building their very being. The sojourns in the various spheres are but the results of their own desires.

In the earth, matter takes all its various forms of presentation of energy or force as radiated from the various solar aspects. All force in the (earth) sphere assumes a three dimensional appearance.

In Jupiter, all ennobling influences are accentuated; whether they be from Earth, Venus, Mercury or Mars. *In Saturn, that (sphere) to which all insufficient matter is cast for its remoulding, preparation is made for returning or re-entering through those influences of the Uranian—which make for the extremes,* very good or very bad; and making for extraordinary condition in relationships . . . throughout other experiences, called in the earth plane occult influences. (311-2)

EC's experience during Reading 1671-1:

I thought I was on Saturn. The ring around it was like a shield, and it was a place where entities learned that they couldn't go all the way around the ring like they could on earth. They could go to this place (Saturn) but couldn't get around it—where the band was around it.

For the earth and Saturn are opposites, as it were . . . to Saturn go those who would renew or begin again; or who have blotted from their experience much that may be set in motion again, through other influences and environs that have been a portion of the entity's experience. (945-1)

Stages of Soul Development
As Represented by the Solar System

In the development, then, that man may be one with Father, (it is) necessary that the soul pass—with its companion, the will—through all the various stages of development, until the will is lost in Him, and he becomes one with the Father.

The illustration of this we find in the man called Jesus. This man, as man, makes the will the will of the Father; then becoming one with the Father, and the model for man. . . .

When the soul reached that development in which it reached earth's plane, it became the model in the flesh, as it had reached through developments in those spheres, or planets, known in the earth's plane, obtaining then the One in All.

As in Mercury pertaining of Mind.
In Mars of Madness.
In Earth as of Flesh.
In Venus as Love.
In Jupiter as Strength.
In Saturn as the beginning of earthly woes, that to which all insufficient matter is cast for the beginning.
In that of Uranus as of the Psychic.
In that of Neptune as of Mystic.
In Septimus (Pluto?) as of Consciousness.
In Arcturus as of the developing. (900-10)

With these Readings we have broached the subject of Planetary influences and Astrology in relationship to soul development. It is significant that of the 2500 Life Readings in the Cayce files, almost all refer to past lives or incarnations with specific astrological or planetary influences bearing on the present.

Past earth experiences, according to the Readings, express themselves through an individual's emotions—while at the same time the individuals' mental aspects are shown as being developed from indwelling in planes of consciousness (represented by planets) between earth lives. Planetary relationships are thus explained as being symbolic of these dwellings and the development achieved in the experience. Consequently, each individual varies considerably not only in mental and emotional traits, but also in the manner or degree that a given planet or planetary configuration affects that person.

Soul Development As It Relates To
The Akashic Records

In brief, planetary relationships are explained as being an integral part of the great plan for soul development. This plan calls for the individual soul-entity to experience creation in all its diversity, so that each may return as a companion with the Creator.

The record of this experience becomes that part of an individual known as the Akasha or soul record. It was these akashic records that the subconscious mind of Edgar Cayce was able to scan and comment upon through the Life Readings.

The record of planetary influences found in the Akasha was explained as being emblematic of how an individual had reacted to various mental and emotional situations in the past. This was shown to be a present and continually evolving relationship:

Then in giving the astrological influences, these would vary considerably from what would be seen from the spiritual or the . . . soul-experience in the earth's plane.

Were this entity's experiences given from the purely astrological science, as accepted in many quarters, they would vary entirely from this (record) which may be given here—or what is viewed from here.

For these are the Akashian records of the entity's or soul's development. As to how the present experience, with its environs, will be acted upon or influenced . . . there will be little influence from an astrological standpoint. The entity will be governed, rather, by earth's plane; by its appearance rather than by astrological influences. (566-1)

Each soul, each body, each individual is an individual entity. What is done and what is thought become a living record of the experience of that individual entity—in whatever sphere of consciousness this activity may have been recorded upon the skein of time and space. (1292-1)

As to whether a soul is developed or retarded during a particular life depends on what the person holds as its ideal, and what it does in its mental and material relationships about that ideal.

Life is a purposeful experience, and the place in which a person finds himself is one in which he may use his present abilities, faults, failures, virtues, in fulfilling the purpose for which the soul decided to manifest in the three-dimensional plane.

Know in thyself that there are immutable laws, and the universe about thyself is directed by laws set in motion from the beginning.

So, as ye condemn, so are ye condemned. As ye forgive, so may ye be forgiven. As ye do unto the least of thy brethren, so ye do it unto thy Maker. These are laws; these are truths; they are unfailing. And because He may often appear slow in meting out results does not alter or change the law. An error, a fault, a failure, must be met. Though the heavens, the earth, may pass away, His word will not pass away. His word is the way, the truth, the light. Each soul must pay to the last jot or tittle. (As phrased repeatedly in the Readings—here quoted from *There Is A River*)

In giving the interpretations of these records (of the entity) these are upon the skeins of time and space. Oh, that all would realize this and come to the consciousness that what we are is the combined result of what we have done about the ideals we have set. (1549-1)

It becomes quite personal to a startling degree when we realize that not a word we have spoken, not a thought we have harbored, nor any single act we have committed but what has been fully recorded in this "Book of Life".

Q. What is meant by the "Book of Life"?
A. The record that the individual entity itself writes upon the skein of time and space, through patience, and is opened when self has attuned to the infinite, and may be read by those attuning to that consciousness. (2533-8)

Remember, all ye may know of heaven or hell is within your own self. All ye may know of God is within your own self. (4035-1)

How Edgar Cayce arrived at that point in consciousness of another individual's soul record was explained in dream experiences which he had some twelve to fifteen times while giving Life Readings. Here is one such description. . . .

I see myself as a tiny dot out of my physical body, which lies inert before me. I find myself oppressed by darkness, and there is a feeling of terrific loneliness. . . . Suddenly, I am conscious of a white beam of light. As this tiny dot, I move upward following the light, knowing that I must follow it or be lost.

As I move along this path of light, I gradually become conscious of various levels upon which there is movement. Upon the first levels there are vague, horrible shapes—grotesque forms such as one sees in nightmares. As I pass on, there begin to appear on either side misshapen forms of human beings, with some part of the body magnified.

Again there is a change, and I become conscious of gray hooded forms moving downward. Gradually these become lighter in color. Then the direction changes, and these forms move upward—and the color of the robes grows rapidly lighter.

Next, there begin to appear on each side vague outlines of houses, walls, trees, etc., but everything is motionless. As I pass on, there is more light and movement, in what appear to be normal cities and towns. With the growth of movement, I become conscious of sounds —at first indistinct rumblings, then music, laughter and the singing of birds. There is more and more light; the colors become very beautiful; and there is a blending of sound and color.

Quite suddenly, I come upon a hall of records. It is a hall without walls, without a ceiling; but I am conscious of seeing an old man who hands me a large book—a record of the individual for whom I seek information.

Q.   What is meant by the Akashic Records?
A.   Those made by the individual. . . . (2533-8)

For the light moves on in time, in space; and upon that skein between them are the records written by each soul in its activity through eternity—through its awareness—not only in matter but in thought, in whatever realm the entity builds for itself in its experience, in its journey, in its activity. The physicist builds in the field of mathematics, the artist in the field of demonstration and color, the musician in sound, and so on. All are a part of the soul's ability, according to that field in which it has developed. (815-1)

The Problem of Man

The continuing problem of Man as expressed in the Readings is to combine mind and emotion, awareness and consciousness, with will and purpose in becoming again at one with the Creator. Until that time, we, as individuals, remain earthbound—or within the confines of our solar system. The ever-present stumbling block to this return to at-onement with God, is ego or self—self-interest, self-indulgence, self-purposefulness. And, according to the Readings—*all sin*, all error, all evil, indeed *the only sin, is self!*

Thus, as developing individuals we return to the earth again and again in order to gain experiences and to work at problems or purposes we have created in previous experiences. This pattern is set and exemplified by the Master—the path is as varied in complexity as there are individuals treading it. Each of us has arrived at any point in time through a separate set of circumstances and experiences, consequently each of us must return in our own separate way—yet each must return in *His way*—through the crucifixion of self.

The possibilities comensurate with this return to the Creator are what can be termed (with some inadequacy) as "God's grace".

Is God's hand short that there would not be all that each soul would require?

But hast thou conceived—or canst thou conceive—requirements of influence to meet all the idiosyncrasies of a single soul? How many systems would it require? (5755-2)

As such, the Universe was created for our awareness and coming to understanding of its design and purpose.

As has been indicated by some, ye are part and parcel of a Universal Consciousness, or God. And thus (part) of all that is within, the Universal Consciousness, or Universal Awareness: as are the stars, the planets, the Sun and the Moon.

Do ye rule them or do they rule thee? They were made for thine own use, as an undividual. Yea, that is the part (they play), the thought which thy Maker, thy Father-God, thinks of thee. For ye are as a corpuscle in the body of God; thus a co-creator with Him, in what ye think and in what ye do. (2794-3)

When the heavens and the earth came into being, this meant the Universe as the inhabitants of the earth know it. Yet there are many suns in the Universe—even those (suns) about which our Sun, our earth, revolves. And all are moving toward some place—yet space and time appear to be incomplete.

Then time and space are but one. Yet the sun that is the center of this particular solar system is *the* center; and as has been known of old, it (the Sun) is that about which the earth and its companion planets circulate or revolve. A beginning in understanding these (facts) and the influence upon the lives of individuals was thought out—or evolved, or interpreted—by those of old, who were without the means for observing which are considered necessary today, in order to understand.

Astronomy is considered a science, and astrology foolishness. Which is correct? One (the science) holds that because of the position of the earth, the Sun and the planets, they are balanced one with another in some manner or some way—yet that they have nothing to do with man's life, or the expanse of life, or the emotions of the physical being in the earth.

Then why and how do the effects of the Sun so greatly

influence other life in the earth—and not affect man's life and man's emotions?

Since the Sun has been set as the ruler of this solar system, does it not appear reasonable that it does have an effect upon the inhabitants of the earth as well as upon plant and mineral life in the earth? . . . Thus we find given in the Bible: "The sun and the moon and the stars were made also"; this being the writer's attempt to convey to the individual the realization that there is also an influence in their activity.

For remember: they . . . the sun, the moon and the planets . . . have their marching orders from the Divine, and they move in these. Man alone is given the birthright of free will. He, alone, may defy his God. (5757-1)

Planets were Created for Man's Development

Then rather than have the stars rule the life, the life should rule the stars. For man was created a little bit higher than all the rest of the whole universe; and is capable of harnessing, directing and enforcing the laws of the universe. (5-2)

The earth is the Lord's and the fullness thereof. The Universe He called into being for these purposes: so that individual souls who might be one with Him would have the influences for bringing this to pass—or so that this might come into the experience of every soul. For hath it not been given that the Lord, thy God hath not willed that any soul should perish? But He hath prepared with every temptation a means and a way of escape? Hence the period of the entrance (birth) is not ruled by the position (of sun and planets) but may be judged by the position, as to influences upon an entity's experience; (influences) because of the entity's application of self's abilities, relative to its position in the universal scheme of things. . . . (1347-1)

For when thou beholdest the glory of the Father in the earth, how orderly are all His glories! Hast thou watched the Sun in his orbit? How orderly are those places of the inhabitation of the souls of men—even in thine own understanding of this solar system! How orderly are brought into manifestation day and night, heat and cold, spring and summer. Canst thou, as His son, be more un-orderly than He, and expect His blessings? (440-14)

Planetary Sojourns

Thus as the soul passes from the aspects about the material environs of the earth, we find that the astrological aspects are represented as stages of consciousness; given names that represent planets or centers, or crystallized activity. Not that flesh and blood, as known in the earth, dwell therein; but in a consciousness, with a form and manner which befits the environ. (1650-1)

Also, during the interims between such (material) sojourns, there are consciousnesses or awarenesses. For the soul is eternal and it lives on—and it has a consciousness and awareness of that which it has built. (2620-2)

For it is not strange that music, color and vibration are all a part of the planets, just as the planets are a part—and a pattern—of the whole universe. (5755)

Then there are the sojourns in other realms of the solar system which represent certain attributes. Not that ye maintain a physical earth-body in Mercury, Venus, Jupiter, Uranus or Saturn. . . . There is, however, an awareness or consciousness in those realms, when absent from the body; and there is a response to the position those planets occupy in this solar system. . . .

Hence ye often find in thy experiences that places, peoples, things and conditions seem a part of self, as if ye had been in the consciousness of them. (2823-1)

In giving that which may be helpful to this entity in the present experience, respecting the sojourns in the earth, it is well that the planetary or astrological aspects also be given. It should be understood, then, that the sojourning of the soul in that environ (planetary), rather than the position (square, trine, etc, of planets at birth), makes for a greater influence in the experience of an entity or body, in any given plane.

This is not to belittle that which has been the study of the Ancients, but rather it is to give the understanding of same. And, as we have indicated, it is not so much (important) that an entity is influenced because the Moon is in Aquarius or the Sun in Capricorn; or Venus or Mercury in that or the other house or sign; or the Moon in Sun sign; or that one of the planets is in this or that position in the heavens. But rather because those positions in the heavens are from the entity having been in that sojourn as a soul!

This is how the planets have the greater influence in the earth upon the entity, see? For the application of an experience is what makes for development of a body, a mind, or a soul. (630-2)

Thus we find that the sojourns about the earth, during the interims between earthly sojourns, are called astrological aspects. Not that an entity may have manifested physically on such planets, but (have manifested) in that consciousness of that environ. And these (consciousnesses) have been accredited with certain potential influences in the mental aspect of an entity. (2144-1)

Being absent from the material body is manifested in what we call astrological aspects, which become a phase of each and every soul and are signposts along the individual way. For . . . all of these are a part of thy heritage, thy innate urge—that arise from and produce influences in the material experience in the present. (1745-1)

As to urges arising from astrological aspects, or sojourns and activities, when absent from materiality; we find these coming from the Moon, Mercury and Uranus. (2459-1)

Astrologically, then, we find the influences are not merely because of the position of a star or planet, Sun or Moon, or any of the astrological aspects or effects or influences. Rather, because . . . of sojourns and activities of the innate or soul-self through such environs. . . . The material sojourns find expression in the emotional portion of the entity's being. . . . But from the astrological, we find the influences innate. Some are to be cultivated so that they may grow and expand and become more of a portion of the influence. Just as others are to be curbed, and a lesson gained and applied—rather than allowed to drift. (1700-1)

As to the appearances in the earth, not all may be given, except as a pattern indicated in the personality and individuality of this individual entity. Personality is that which ye wish others to think and see. Individuality is that which your soul prays for, hopes for, desires. These (two) need not necessarily be one; but their purpose must be one, even as the Father, the Son and the Holy Spirit are one. So must body, mind and soul be one in purpose and in aim. (5246)

For the entity finds itself a body, mind, and soul: three. Or the earth consciousness is a three-dimensional plane in one. So man's concept of the Godhead is three-dimensional: Father, Son, and Holy Spirit. The communication or activity or motivating force, then we find, is three-dimensional: time, space, and patience. None of these exists in fact, except in the conception of the individual, as he may apply (self) to time, space or patience. (4035-1)

But what has all this to do with soul development?

Each entity is a part of the Universal Whole. Then all the knowledge and understanding which has ever been a part of the entity's consciousness has a part in the entity's experience. Thus unfoldment, in the present, consists merely in becoming aware of experiences through which the entity has passed, in any consciousness, either in body or in mind. (2823-1)

Soul Development

For without passing through each and every stage of development, there is not the correct vibration to become one with the Father. . . . Then in the many stages of development throughout the Universe or in the great system of the Universal Forces, each stage of development is made manifest through flesh—which is the testing portion of the Universal Vibration. In this manner, then, and for this reason, all are made manifest in flesh and there is the development through aeons of time and space, called Eternity. (3744)

Each planetary influence vibrates at a different rate of vibration. An entity entering that influence enters that vibration: (it is) not necessary that he change, but it is the grace of God that he may! It is part of the Universal Consciousness, the Universal Law. (281-55)

Hence the entity passes through those stages which some have seen as planes, some as steps, some have seen as cycles, and others have experienced as places. (5755-1)

As in the studies of the entity: it is seen that the soul of man is a mere speck in space; yet the soul is that vital force or activity which is everlasting. Though the earth or the stars may pass away; though there may be changes in the universe as to relative positions; these are (all) brought about by the combinations of those specks of human activity, in respect to the soul's expression in any sphere of existence. (1297-1)

In thyself, thou dost oft find one friend for that or this relationship—one for the prop, (support) another to arouse. Yet all are the work of His hand, and are thine to possess, thine to use.

Thus, though there may be many worlds and many universes, even solar systems greater than our own which we enjoy in the present; this earthly experience, or this earth, is a mere speck when considered as to our own solar system. Yet the soul of man, thy soul, encompasses all in this solar system, or in others. (5755-2)

Q. Are any of the planets, other than the earth, inhabited by human beings or animal life of any kind?
A. No. For only upon the earth plane, at present, do we find man is flesh and blood. Upon others, we find those (conditions) of his own making, in preparation for his own development. (3744)

Astrology—General Statements

The greater influence from any (planet) is from whatever one from which the soul-and-spirit return, to bring the individual force to the earth. As the spirit is breathed into the body, whence did it come? That is the influence; not the revolution-ideas given by those who study those planetary forces. (3744)

The inclinations of man are ruled by the planets under which he is born, for the destiny of man lies within the sphere or scope of the planets . . . but let there be understood here—no action of any planet, or the phases of the sun, the moon, or any of the heavenly bodies, surpasses the rule of man's willpower. (3744-3)

Or, as Cayce stated again and again in the Readings—*"Mind is ever the builder".*

In giving that which may be understandable, and that which may be helpful from the material angle at this time, as we find, *it would be well that all consider the varying aspects from that considered as astrological influence.*

As we have given through these channels, astrological influences are effective in the experience of each and every entity. However, when the activities of a soul-entity have been such as to cause or to form the appearance of the entity in a particular sphere of (planetary) activity, the position of the sojourn of the entity to the earth has the greater influence than just the adverse or benevolent positions of the planet or of a whole solar system upon the entity's activity!

Then it is as this: When the activities of an entity, a soul in the earth, have been such that its passage from the earth would become a birth into the realm of matter known as Mars, Venus, Jupiter, Uranus, Neptune, Moon, Mercury, Polaris, or any of these effective in the universal influence, you see, the sojourn there and the positions of any of the planets are more effective than the influence brought to bear because of a position in a certain place or portion of the universal forces. See?

Hence, as we find, these conditions are only as urges. (398-2)

As to those (influences) of the constellations or of the Zodiacal signs in the life of this entity, these are merely the wavering influences in the life . . . and not those directing forces ever present in the inner soul of this entity. These (facts), we find, are in opposition to much that is taught at present, or given in the earth plane. (8-1)

Yet may this entity be set apart: for through its experiences in the earth it has advanced from a low degree, to that which may not even necessitate a reincarnation in the earth! Not that it has reached perfection; but there are realms for instruction where the entity may go, if the entity will hold fast to the ideal. . . . Remember, there are material urges (here), and there are also materials in other consciousnesses, not alone in the three-dimensional. (5366-1)

Mind—As The Builder

Thus we find this entity in the present—as in each entity—the result of what has been applied, of Creative Influences, in every phase of its experience—thus making for what some call karma, others call racial hereditary forces.

Thus environment and hereditary forces (as generally accepted) are in reality the activities of the mind of the entity, in its choices, through its experiences in the material, in the mental and in the spiritual planes. . . .

There are then those accredited signs or omens—or indications of characteristics—in the innate and manifested activities of the entity. But these are irrespective of what the entity is to do, or will do, respecting same. In interpreting the records here, we find from the astrological aspects the entity is influenced not because of the position of the Sun, the Moon, or of the earth in its relationship to planets or Zodiacal signs or other influences. Yet all of these are recognized as part of the entity's environment. (1796-1)

For life is a continuous experience. And the mind, the soul and the will are the influences that act through material manifestations, for the improvement and development—or for retardment—in the whole of the experience.

For each soul enters each experience for development, that it may be prepared to dwell with that which it seeks as its goal. Hence the necessity for each entity to set its ideal in each experience.

Hence we find that the developments throughout the entity's activities, either in a material sojourn or through an astrological experience are but an evolution—or a making-practical. *For it is not what an individual entity may proclaim that counts; but what each soul—does about what it has set as its ideal, in relationship to other individuals around it!* (1235-1)

Astrological aspects may or may not become a part of the experience, physically, for the entity. For these are merely urges, and the will—that which designates God's creation of man from the rest of the animal world—rules as to what an individual soul does with his opportunities, in his relationship with his fellow man. (3340-1)

Then what are the Sun spots? A natural consequence of that turmoil which the sons of God in the earth reflect upon same (the Sun). Thus they oft bring confusion to those who become aware of them.

Know (then) that thy mind—thy mind—is the builder! As what does thy soul appear? A spot, a blot, upon the Sun? Or as that which giveth light unto those who sit in darkness, who cry-aloud for hope? (5757-1)

Mind As Related To Will

The strongest of such powers in the destiny of man is: first, the Sun. Then the planets closer, or those that are coming to ascendency at the time of birth.

But let it be understood here: no action of any planet or phase of the Sun, Moon or heavenly body surpasses the rulership of man's individual will power. For this is the power given by the Creator to man, in the beginning when he became a living soul, with the power to choose for himself.

The inclinations of man, then, are ruled by the planets under which he was born. To this extent, the destiny of man lies within the scope or sphere of the planets. Given a position of the solar system at the time of the individual's birth, it can be worked out—that is, the inclinations and actions (can be worked out), without regard to the power of the will, or without the will being taken into consideration. (3744)

(Female, age 22 yrs. Born 9/23/02, new York City.)
Yes, we have the conditions, the impressions are given here, with respect to will as thus far exhibited and without reference to the will as it is to be manifested in the present earth's plane.

. . . the soul's forces took its position in earth plane from the influences direct of Jupiter and of Venus and Mercury's influences, with those afflictions in Moon and Saturn with the better influences in Uranus and in Arcturus.

The effects then as manifested in this body, without the will's influences, are as these: for we find the birth comes in that position when the earth's change comes near the cusps. Hence one who has many conflicting emotions, yet with the purpose of the Jupiter influence, or ennobling in the extreme. (140-3)

Will . . . that factor which may be trained, even as may be the mental forces; will, that developer in the material force—being the balance (wheel) between influences innately built or of karmic influence; which makes for freedom of the mental being. For, in truth one finds freedom, and he who findeth truth is free indeed. (1719-1)

For will is the factor which affords the opportunity to choose what is for development or for retardation. As so oft has been indicated: "There is today, now, set before thee—before each and every soul-entity—that which is life or death, good or evil". Each soul chooses its manifestations. (1646-2)

Can Astrology Help?

Q. Is it proper to study the effects of the planets upon our lives, in order to understand our tendencies and inclinations better, as they are influenced by the planets?

A. When studied right (it is) very, very, very much worth while. Then how studied aright? By studying the influence (of the planets) in the light of knowledge already obtained by mortal man. Give out more of that knowledge—giving the understanding that the will must ever be the guiding factor to lead man on, ever upward. (3744)

Not that there are not definite helps to be found in astrology; but those who live by it are more often controlled than controlling. Astrology is a fact, in most instances, but astrological aspects are only signs and symbols. No influence is of greater value or help than the will of an individual. Use such directions (from the planets) as stepping stones and do not let them become stumbling stones in thy experience. (815-6)

In closing, let 3744-4 (given 2-14-24) continue our theme of soul development with planetary influences accorded their usual accompanying role:

Q. What are the laws governing relativity of all force?

A. In giving the manifestation of such a law, which does exist, we first must consider that, (which) is called force, and that force then in its relations, or the relativity of that force to all force.

There were set in the beginning, as far as the concern is of this physical earth plane, those rules or laws in the relative force of those that govern the earth, and the beings of the earth plane, and also that same law governs the planets, stars, constellations, groups and those that constitute the sphere, the space, in which the planets move. These are of one force, and we see the manifestation of the relation of one force with another in the many various phases as is shown, (here in the readings) for in fact that which to the human mind exists, in fact does not exist, for it has been in past before it is to the human mind in existence.

In this we see the law of the relations of conditions, space or time and its relation to human mind, as is capable of obtaining information upon the earth plane from a normal force or condition. Hence, we bring the same word, relativity of force, to prove its own self, and condition, for we have as in this:

The earth in its motion is held in space by that force of attraction or detraction, or gravitation, or lack of gravitation in its force, so those things that do appear to have reality, and their reality to the human mind, have in reality passed into past conditions before they have reached the mind, for with the earth's laws, and its relations to other spheres, has to man become a past condition. So it is reached only in the further forces as will show, and as is given, for man to understand in this developing, or this evolution from sphere to sphere, or from plane to plane, in this condition.

Hence, we find to the normal mind, there is no law as to relativity of force, save as the individual may apply same in the individual's needs of them. That is sufficient.

Then in a later paragraph the sleeping Cayce gave further insight to gaining awareness in relationship with the universal forces.

The study from the human standpoint, of subconscious, subliminal, psychic soul forces, is and should be the great study for the human family—for through self man will understand its Maker, when it understands its relation to its Maker. And it will only understand that through itself. And that understanding is the knowledge as is given here in this state. (3744-4)

The following reading (5749-14), was given to Thomas Sugrue as a basis for the philosophy chapter in *There Is A River*. It is here reproduced in its entirety:

You will have before you the inquiring mind of the entity, Thomas Sugrue, present in this room, and certain of the problems confronting him in composing the manuscript of *There Is A River*.

The entity is now ready to describe the philosophical concepts which have been given through this source, and wishes to parallel and align them with known religious tenets, especially those of Christian theology.

The entity does not wish to set forth a system of thought, nor to imply that all questions of a philosophical nature can be answered through this source—the limits of the finite mind preventing this.

But the entity wishes to answer those questions which will naturally arise in the mind of the reader of many of the questions which are being asked by all people in the world today.

Therefore the entity presents certain problems and questions, which you will answer as befits the entity's understanding and the task of interpretation before him.

Mr. C.: Yes, we have the inquiring mind, Thomas Sugrue, and those problems, those questions that arise in the mind of the entity at this period. Ready for questions.

Q. 1   The first problem concerns the reason for creation. Should this be given as God's desire to experience Himself, God's desire for companionship, or in some other way?
A. 1   God's desire for companionship and expression.

Q. 2   The second problem concerns that which is variously called evil, darkness, negation, sin. Should it be said that this condition existed as a necessary element of creation, and the soul, given free will, found itself with the power to indulge in it, or lose itself in it? Or should it be said that this is a condition created by the activity of the soul itself? Should it be described, in either case, as a state of consciousness, a gradual lack of awareness of self and self's relation to God?

A. 2　It is the free will and its losing itself in its relationship to God.

Q. 3　The third problem has to do with the fall of man. Should this be described as something which was inevitable in the destiny of souls, or something which God did not desire but which He did not prevent once He had given free will? The problem here is to reconcile the omniscience of God and His knowledge of all things with the free will of the soul and the soul's fall from grace.

A. 3　He did not prevent, once having given free will. For He made the individual entities or souls in the beginning. The beginnings of sin, of course, were in seeking expression of themselves outside of the plan or way in which God had expressed same. Thus it was the individual, see?
Having given free will, then—though having the foreknowledge, though being omnipotent and omnipresent—it is only when the soul, that is a portion of God, *chooses* that God knows the end thereof.

Q. 4　The fourth problem concerns man's tenancy on earth. Was it originally intended that souls remain out of earthly forms, and were the races originated as a necessity resulting from error?

A. 4　The earth and its manifestations were only the expressions of God and not necessarily as a place of tenancy for the souls of men, until *man was created to meet the needs of existing conditions.*

Q. 5　The fifth problem concerns an explanation of the Life Readings. From a study of these *it seems that there is a trend downward from early incarnations toward greater earthliness and less mentality. Then there is a swing upward, accompanied by suffering, patience and understanding. Is this the normal pattern* which results in virtue and oneness with God obtained by free will and mind?

A. 5 This is correct. It is *the pattern as it is set in Him.* (The Master)

Q. 6 The sixth problem concerns interplanetary and intersystem dwelling between earthly lives. It was given through this source that the entity Edgar Cayce, after the experience as Uhjltd, went to the system of Arcturus, and then returned to earth. Does this indicate a usual or unusual step in soul evolution?

A. 6 As indicated, or as has been indicated in other sources besides this one as respecting this very problem, Arcturus is that which may be called the center of this universe, through which individuals pass and at which period there comes the choice of the individual as to whether it is to return to complete there—that is, in this planetary system, our sun, the earth sun and its planetary system, or to pass on to others. This was an unusual step, and yet a usual one.

Q. 7 The seventh problem concerns implications from the sixth problem. Is it necessary to finish the solar system cycle before going to other systems?

A. 7 Necessary to finish the solar cycle.

Q. 8 Can oneness be attained—or the finish of evolution reached—on any system, or must it be in a particular one?

A. 8 Depending upon what system the entity has entered, to be sure. It may be completed in any of the many systems.

Q. 9 Must the solar cycle be finished on earth or can it be completed on another planet, or does each planet have a cycle of its own which must be finished?

A. 9 If it is begun on the earth it must be finished on

the earth. The solar system of which the earth is a part is only a portion of the whole. For, as indicated in the number of planets about the earth, they are of one and the same—and they are relative one to another. It is the cycle of the whole system that is finished, see?

Q. 10 This problem concerns the pattern made by parents at conception. Should it be said that this pattern attracts a certain soul because it approximates conditions which that soul wishes to work with?

A. 10 It approximates conditions. It does not set. For the individual entity or soul, given the opportunity, has its own free will to work in or out of those problems as presented by that very union. Yet the very union, of course, attracts or brings a channel or an opportunity for the expression of an individual entity.

Q. 11 Does the incoming soul take on of necessity some of the parents' karma?

A. 11 Because of its relationship to same, yes. Otherwise, no.

Q. 12 Does the soul itself have an earthly pattern which fits into the one created by the parents?

A. 12 Just as indicated, it is relative—as one related to another and because of the union of activities they are brought into the pattern. For in such there is the explanation of universal or divine laws, which are ever one and the same; as indicated in the expression that God moved within Himself and He didn't change, though did bring to Himself that of His own being, made, crucified even in the flesh.

Q. 13 Are there several patterns which a soul might take on, depending on what phase of development it is wished to work on—i.e., could a soul choose to be one of several personalities, any of which would fit its individuality?

A. 13 Correct.

Q. 14 Is the average fulfillment of the soul's expectation more or less than fifty per cent?

A. 14 It's a continuous advancement, so it is more than fifty per cent.

Q. 15 Are heredity, environment, and will equal factors in aiding or retarding the entity's development?

A. 15 Will is the greatest factor, for it may overcome any or all of the others; provided that will is made one with the pattern, see? No influence of heredity, environment or what not surpass the will; else why would there have been that pattern shown in which the individual soul, no matter how far astray it may have gone, may enter with Him into the holy of holies?

Q. 16 The problem which concerns the proper symbols, or similies, for the Master, the Christ. Should Jesus be described as the Soul who first went through the cycle of earthly lives to attain perfection including perfection in the planetary lives also?

A. 16 He should be. This is as the man (he was), see?

Q. 17 Should this be described as a voluntary mission (on the part of) One who was already perfected and returned to God, having accomplished His oneness in other planes and systems?

A. 17 Correct.

Q. 18 Should the Christ-Consciousness be described as the awareness within each soul, imprinted in pattern on the mind and waiting to be awakened by the will, of the soul's oneness with God?

A. 18 Correct. That's the idea exactly.

Q. 19 Please list the names of the incarnations of the Christ, as Jesus, indicating where the development of the man Jesus began.

A. 19 First, in the beginning, of course (as Adam or Amilius); Then as Enoch, Melchizedek, in the perfection. Then in the earth as Joseph, Joshua, Jeshua, Jesus.

Q. 20   Concerning the factors of soul evolution. Should mind, the builder, be described as the last development because it should not unfold until it has a firm foundation of emotional virtues?

A. 20   This might be answered Yes and No, both. But if it is presented in that there is kept, willfully, see, that desire to be in at-one-ment, then it is necessary for that attainment before it recognizes mind as the way.

Q. 21   A problem that concerns a parallel with Christianity. Is Gnosticism the closest type of Christianity to that which is given through this source? (Reincarnation)

A. 21   This is a parallel, and was the commonly accepted one until there began to be set rules in which there were attempts to take short cuts. And there are none in Christianity.

Q. 22   What action of the early church, or council, can be mentioned as that which ruled (out) reincarnation from Christian theology?

A. 22   Just as indicated (above)—the attempts of individuals to accept or take advantage of, because of this knowledge, see?

Q. 23   Do souls become entangled in other systems as they did in this system?

A. 23   In other systems that represent the same as the earth does in this system, yes.

Q. 24   Is there any other advice which may be given to this entity at this time in the preparation of these chapters?

A. 24   Hold fast to that ideal, using Him ever as *the* Ideal. And hold up that *necessity* for each to meet the same problems. And *do not* attempt to shed or to surpass (sidestep) or go around the Cross. *This* is that upon which each and every soul *must* look and know it is to be borne in self *with* Him. (5749-14)

Again—Mind and Free Will

Mind is the active force in an animate object; it is the spark or image of the Maker. . . .

. . . Mind is the Builder, being both spiritual and material; and the consciousness of same reaches man only in his awareness of his consciousness through the senses of his physical being. (826-11)

Q. Is the body at birth aware of the destiny of the physical body?
A. *God Himself knows not what man will destine to do with himself, else would He (not) have repented that He had made man!* He has given man free will. MAN destines the body! . . . Man may hold an ideal at the time of birth that would determine his destiny. (262-86)

. . . So soon as man contemplates his free will he thinks of it as a means of doing the opposite of God's will, though he finds that only by doing God's will does he find happiness. Yet, the notion of serving God sits ill with him, for he sees it as a sacrifice of his will. Only in disillusion and suffering, in time, space, and patience, does he come to the wisdom that his real will is the will of God, and in its practice is happiness and heaven. (2537)

Chapter Four

CONCERNING THE BIBLE

Q. What present printed version of the Bible gives the nearest to the true meaning of both Old and New Testaments?

A. The nearest true version for the entity is *that you apply* of whatever version you read *in your life*. It isn't that you learn from anyone. You may only have the direction. The learning, the teaching is within self. For where hath He promised to meet you? Within that temple!

There have been many versions of that which was purposed to have been written, and has changed from all those versions. But remember that the whole gospel of Jesus Christ is, "Thou shalt love the Lord thy God with all thy mind, thy heart and thy body; and thy neighbour as thyself. Do this and thou shalt have eternal life." The rest of the book is trying to describe that. It is the same in any language, in any version. (2072-14)

The story of the Bible and the story of Jesus in becoming the Christ are so inter-related within the body of the Cayce materials that it is extremely difficult to discuss one without getting involved in a sizeable side discourse on the other.

Since the entire framework of Edgar Cayce's story of Jesus is based upon reincarnation, it should be noted that according to the Readings The Master possibly had some thirty incarnations during His development in becoming

The Christ.* Only a third of these were elaborated upon in the Readings, which leaves a number of earthly existences unaccounted for. Cayce, for some reason, did not venture additional names and places in history where the Master had dwelt. Why, we may only speculate, but it does present possibilities for conjecture concerning additional historical personalities who just might have been an indwelling of The Master. Among these are three noteworthy ones in Egypt—Raai, who formulated "The Book of the Dead", or first Bible of that era. . . . The legendary Hermes, who according to the Readings was the architect of the Great Pyramid—And Amenophis IV, who proclaimed the One God and changed his name to "Akhenaten", which is variously translated as "Son of God", "Son of Man", and "Bearer or Giver of Life". Akhenaten, with his mate Nefertiti and brother Tutenkamen, poses an interesting possibility in the missing chapters of the lives of Jesus. Further, the claim to Akenaten's role as Founder of the Mystery Religions has been made by various sources. And, if we consider the current well publicized visions and predictions of Prophetess Jeane Dixon concerning Akhenaten and Nefertiti as truly forthcoming, we may be witnessing an added chapter in the developing.** Certainly the astrological conditions in early 1962 were ripe for the entering of an entity who could have a revolutionary effect upon the religions of the world. Raai, Hermes, and eventually the subject of The Great Pyramid also tie in with The Mysteries and their culmination in The Book of Revelation. Over a period of years numerous Readings were given on this last book of the Bible in conjunction with an interested study group of A.R.E. members.*** According to the Readings John the Beloved received his visions in deep meditation. Much of what he recorded is

* In one Reading an individual asked if he could gain perfection in this lifetime. (So as not to have to return to Earth again.) The sleeping Cayce flippantly replied, "Why should you expect to do in one lifetime what it took the Master thirty lives to attain?"

** A Gift of Prophecy—by Ruth Montgomery.

*** Readings on The Book of Revelation—A.R.E. Press.

described as a symbolic interpretation of the mysteries as
they relate to the spiritual development of the human
body—This in relation to the seven psychic centers, or
spiritual centers, associated with the body's endocrine
glands.

The message of The Revelation is that each of us, through
a proper approach to the body, mind, spirit principle of
the body as the Temple of the Living God, can attain the
Christhood even as He did. And that "Even greater things
shall we do" because He has prepared the Way to the
Father. (John 14:12)

It should be remembered that the Book of Revelation has
given Biblical scholars, theologians, and church communi-
ties in general a considerable amount of problems and
puzzlement throughout the centuries. As detailed by
Cayce, Revelation is not so quickly read or easily absorbed that one can digest it in an evening or two, but it
certainly is the most coherent and reasonable explanation
of the last book of the Bible that many students of this difficult subject have yet come upon. As such, Cayce's concepts of Revelation may or may not be the final word on
the subject, however we highly recommend their inclusion
by all students of Symbology or Meditation. In addition,
any study course on the Bible and comparative religions
should not pass them by without perusal.

Between Genesis and Revelation Cayce gave much of interest relative to the story of Man and The Master. According to Cayce many sections of the Bible were factual
while others were allegorical or symbolic, but in all
instances they were given so that Man could gain a better
understanding of his relationship and movement within
Creation. Then, as in Revelation 2:7, "He that hath an
ear, let him hear".

In Job 29:28 we find, "And to men he said, Behold, the
reverence of God, that is wisdom; and to depart from evil
is understanding". The Readings state that the Book of
Job was written by The Master (as Melchizedek) as an

explanation for the pattern of man in the earth. The characters are symbolic rather than actual persons who lived on the earth.

Interestingly, there is some question as to whether the incarnation of Jesus as Adam represents a single incarnation, or rather a series of incarnations through each of the five races of man, all lives finally being symbolized in the story of Adam as told in Genesis.

Such items as The Flood and the Tower of Babel are noted as factual by the Readings, and one woman who had a Life Reading in 1944 (5367) was told that in a previous existence she actually had been born on the Ark as a daughter of Japheth, son of Noah.

Another concept which comes out of the Readings is that we, as individuals, *are Israel* and that the twelve tribes and what they represent are all aspects of our spiritual selves. This interpretation is one which has a dual existence alongside the factual role of the physical or geographical Israel. Indeed, according to the Readings much of the Bible can be interpreted either physically, mentally, or spiritually, and often on all levels simultaneously. This three-dimensional theme recurs again and again throughout the Readings as a symbolic trinity representative of the earth plane.

The Covenants

Within the Bible we find a number of agreements or negotiations between God and Man which stand as rules and guidelines for how the relationship could be continued and brought to fruition. Theologians have listed seven of these covenants, the last of which was given through The Master at the Last Supper. The first of the covenants, of course, was between God and Adam in the Garden of Eden, whereupon they progress through Noah, Abraham and Moses to the Palestinian period with Joshua and finally David.

According to the Readings The Master was present during each of these periods, with the possible exception of Noah and the Flood where no specific mention was made of Jesus' presence.

Many theologians regard the covenants as indications of failure by man. However, the Readings take a more positive attitude, indicating that Man's development is continually upward and as such the covenants are more akin to a changing set of rules for groups, or individuals, who are progressing upward in steps from lower to higher grades in their schooling. In this manner too, the seven covenants can be likened to the seven spiritual centers of the body, or the seven seals in the Book of Revelation.

A Note on the Baptisms and the Law of Grace

Here we wish to insert an observation concerning a parallel aspect of Biblical symbology as it relates to the Stages of Man and the appearances of The Master in the earth. This thought has come about through the author's studies in astrological and symbolical materials relative to the Life Readings and those on soul development.

The key to this symbolic interpretation came about initially from a question which we had often entertained, but had never found a suitable explanation. Namely, "Why did Jesus have to be baptised?"

If we consider the story of Creation from the beginning, this baptism (which was necessary according to Cayce) could be the symbolic third Baptism of Man in a series of Four Baptisms—Earth, Air, Water, Fire. These four, as elements, are well documented and oft repeated both within and outside of the Readings; In the Zodiac, the Four Seasons, the four corners of the earth and sides of the square, the base of the pyramid, the four lower centers of the body, the Four Gospels, etc.

Briefly, the Four Baptisms could be conceived as follows:

I. *Earth*—The "Fall of the Angels". Spirits became so enmeshed in materiality that they totally lose their identity and awareness with God.

II. *Air*—Amilius, as Adam, leads the "Sons of God" to earth in order to help the entrapped "Sons of Man" back to awareness. Then God breathes air (spirit) into Adam and he becomes aware of God, though in a material flesh body.

III. *Water*—The practice of Baptism preceded Jesus (possibly through Zoroastrianism) as a symbolic means of purification—(again Spirit) washing away the original sin of Adam. When the actual Adam was so purified by John the Baptist, God's voice was heard to proclaim, "This is my first begotten Son, in whom I am well pleased." (Math 3:17) Then to, the fact that Jesus required baptism may further substantiate his role as Adam, since there, He had sinned.

IV. *Fire*—The promise of The Pentecost is the final baptism. There the Disciples received the baptism of The Holy Spirit, which came as tongues of flame from the heavens. Afterward they were able to perform miracles as The Master had throughout the balance of their lives in Palestine.

The promise comes from the New Covenant which Jesus proclaimed—that as we live through Him, we live under the Law of Grace rather than the Law of Karma. (Karma being the Old Testament's law of cause and effect—or "Eye for eye and tooth for tooth". As we interpret the Cayce Readings, the Law of Grace was always a potential for Mankind, but It wasn't until Jesus became The Christ—through accepting the crucifixion of self and then rising from the dead—that this New Covenant became a reality for everyone. Yet, in reality the Law of Grace still exists only as a promise to those who willingly follow His last admonition—"That we love one another, even as He has loved us." Otherwise we are still living under karma.

An example of the Law of Grace as it was originally taught might be found in this story attributed to Jesus, but not found in the present Gospels:

> The Master was seated one morning with some of his disciples at the gates of Jerusalem. They saw a wood-cutter come out of the city, singing on his way to work, and Jesus avowed, "There is a man who would not sing if he knew that he would be dead this evening." Evening came; Jesus was in the same place as the woodcutter returned and passed by, his axe over his shoulder, singing as before. The disciples murmured among themselves, in doubt over the prophet's words, and were about to desert him. The Master divining their thoughts, spoke to them gently, "That man *was* about to die, but he encountered in the forest a poor starving man to whom he gave half his bread. As a reward for this good deed God has spared his life. Go up to this man and open the bundle of wood he is carrying on his back." The disciples obeyed, and a poisonous serpent was found hidden in the bundle—Thus was the word of Jesus and the Grace of Providence verified to them.

Fire, as the final baptism of the three spiritual baptisms (along with water and air) is the one which now seems of vital concern for contemporary humanity. According to Cayce and others The New Age is upon us, with a forty year testing period from 1958 to 1998. Whether we cleanse ourselves by fire spiritually as did The Master (through Grace), or whether the earth is cleansed by fire of nuclear origin (material karma as in the days of Noah and lost Atlantis) is a matter for debate—by individuals and the Councils of Nations. Seemingly the situation as it now stands is in the balance. The world is apparently winding up for another weird potentially destructive confrontation with itself, and according to Cayce time is ripe for the promised second coming of The Master. But the time for His reappearance—so states the Readings—is not known, nor has it been known, from the beginning—even by the Master Himself.

In closing our chapter on the Bible we include a Reading pertinent to the New Testament which was given in 1938. Its significance in our story, aside from the obvious statements relative to the four Gospels, is the inclusion of the name Lucius. In the following chapters, as we trace the thread of Cayce and its interinvolvement with The Master through several incarnations, we should remember that the first reference to Lucius did not come through Cayce until 1937—many years after he had given himself his own first Life Readings.

Q. Who wrote the four Gospels?
A. These, we find, may best be determined by investigations of the records related to same . . . in the Vatican's own libraries.

MARK was first dictated, greatly by Peter. And this in those periods just before Peter was carried to Rome.

The next was MATTHEW, written by the one whose name it bears. As for the specific reasons—to those who were scattered into the upper portions of Palestine and through Laodicea. This was written something like thirty-three to thirty-four years later than MARK, and while this body that wrote same was in exile.

LUKE was written by Lucius* rather than Luke, though (Lucius was) a companion with Luke during those activities of Paul—and written of course, unto those of the faith under the Roman *influence.* Not *to* the Roman peoples, but to the provinces *ruled* by the Romans. And it was from those sources that the very changes were made as to the differences in that given by MARK and MATTHEW.

JOHN was written by several; not by the John who was

* Lucius is mentioned in the Bible as a teacher in Acts 13:1 and Romans 16:21.

the Beloved, but the John who represented, or was the scribe for, John the Beloved—and, as much of same, was written much later. Portions of it were written at different times and combined some fifty years after the Crucifixion. (1598-2)

Chapter Five

EGYPT

The subject of Egypt is exceedingly important within any overall study of the Cayce materials, for here we are dealing with visible remnants of history which Cayce dealt with in detail. However, his statements did not concern themselves with the past only, but in some extremely pointed predictions regarding the future, Cayce's subconscious mind laid his extensive psychic reputation on the block for the coming years to either uphold or refute.

Then too, Egypt is pivotal in our story of The Master, because in this period Cayce ties together the people of Atlantis with their heritage (in Genesis) directly through to Exodus and recorded history. Between was a period of many thousands of years, of which Cayce is rather specific. For example, he places the time of The Flood at 28,000 B.C., and the Exodus at approximately 5500 B.C.—much earlier than historians have believed. Additionally, he indicates that the Great Pyramid is some six thousand years older than modern authorities date it, stating that it was constructed over a one hundred year period from 10,490 to 10,390 B.C.

But regardless of how we attempt to gauge the passage of time through antiquity, the fact is that the Pyramid and Sphinx do exist. And according to the Readings they were constructed for specific purposes which tie in with the forty year period from 1958 to 1998 . . . and the earth changes that Cayce predicted would take place during these years. Moreover, Cayce placed himself solidly in the picture by affirming that he, in a previous existence, was the Priest Ra-Ta, who with Hermes supervised the erection of the Pyramid.

Again, it is well to let the Readings themselves relate much of the story:

Then, if it is practical to put activities of that period in present day language, or words: let's give a review of the happenings—what was attempted, what was accomplished, and what influence it had upon the souls.

Here we find, first, an individual with a desire and purpose, not for exploiting people, or individuals, or souls; but to build an influence within the experience of individuals in material life. This Priest (Ra-Ta) was not merely a director of spiritual counsel of the body of people who entered Egypt, but (director) of an activity in which all phases of man's endeavour were to be acted upon. . . . The Priest was an individual who had received inspiration from within. And realizing that such an influence might be imparted to others in their search for the reason and purpose of material life, he then sought out one who might foster such a study in materiality.

Thus from those places that were a portion of what is now called the Carpathias, he (Ra-Ta) came with a great horde (as to individual souls, numbering nine hundred) into the land now called Egypt.

Why Egypt? This had been determined . . . as the center of the universal activities of nature, as well as of the spiritual forces; and where there might be the least disturbances by convulsive movements which came about in the earth through the destruction of Lemuria, Atlantis and—in later periods—The Flood. When the lines about the earth are considered from (the standpoint of) the mathematical precisions, it will be found that the center is nigh unto where the Great Pyramid, which was begun then, is still located. Then there were (factors of) mathematical, astrological and numerological indications, as well as the individual urge.

Then the individual of that experience was not necessarily other than a soul or entity seeking knowledge as to the relationship of that which would sustain and gain for man certain abilities to continue not only physical evolution but spiritual or soul evolution also.

Such a one, then, was Ra, or Ra-Ta. (281-42)

The story of Ra-Ta's sojourn in Egypt is worthy of a separate book and treatment in itself. Accordingly, we will attempt to outline the situation briefly as it relates to the mainstream of our entire discourse.

Prior to Ra-Ta's coming Egypt was a weak nation beset with many internal turmoils. The first tribal rule was established in the fertile areas of the upper Nile, near what later became known as the Valley of the Tombs. The people were of the black race, who made early use of beasts of burden and lived in tents and caves. Before this the lands had been under the sea for nearly a quarter of a million years and the area was relatively free from the invasions of large wild animals which were causing considerable problems elsewhere in the world.

The second rule came under King Raai, a spiritually-minded leader who brought peace and a broad understanding of universal laws to the Egyptian tribes. Early in his reign he called together a meeting of the world's leaders—forty-four priests, seers and astrologers, who discussed methods for hastening man's development and the knowledge of the divine spirit dwelling within them. The theme of this council was "Spirit forces in man that make him supreme in the earth". Raai was the first to relate this power in man to a Higher Source, and his approach was through evidences of the sun's rays, along with influences of the moon and the waters in bringing forth life. His tents covered many phases of man's existence in the earth, as symbolized by the sun, moon, stars, and the elements. These were inscribed as spiritual laws upon tablets of stone which became the basis for *The Book of The Dead*. As such, it was not intended as a funeral ritual, though it later became so interpreted.

Raai's rule covered 199 years, and afterward he was worshipped as God's representative made manifest in the earth. With his companion Isai, they became revered as Ra and Isis—the original Gods of Egyptian mythology.

During Raai's reign (about 300 years before the last sinking of Atlantis and 11,016 years before the Nativity) Egypt was invaded by a large number of white men from the caucasian mountains, or land of Arart, led by a king of the same name (Arart) and guided by the priest Ra-Ta. King Raai surrendered almost immediately rather than become party to the shedding of his people's blood. Thereafter came a great deal of strife between the conquerors and the conquered, most of it being led by a native scribe of considerable power and influence.

The conquering King Arart then decided upon a bold and clever political move. He abdicated his throne in favor of a young son, Araaraat and appointed the troublesome scribe to a high office, with membership in the official family in the name Aarat. Rule over Egypt was thereupon turned over to a governing Troika, consisting of the young king Araaraat, the native Aarat, and the priest Ra-Ta. Another factor which helped to ease the tense internal situation was the attraction of the old king Raai to the maiden Isai, who was a daughter of one of the invaders.

Araaraat ruled for some eighty-eight years, during which time Egypt became a powerful, growing amalgamation of peoples, many of whom emigrated from India, Mongolia and Atlantis because of the eruptions and sinkings of their lands. This was not without problems, for

. . . the Atlanteans brought with them many "things",

or entities like automatons, and many Atlanteans looked on the native Egyptians as similar to these or in the class of these "things". (281-43)

Over the years, the High Priest Ra-Ta concerned himself mainly with the setting up of spiritual codes for conformity of worship of the One God and in building temples for physical and spiritual development of the masses. Frequently he made trips to Poseidia to study the methods of the Atlanteans who had remained faithful to the "Law of One". There Ra-Ta came in contact with the custodian and keeper of many of the secret religious tenets and rituals that had been handed down from generation to generation in Atlantis. The custodian, Hept-Supht, was anxious that the records and laws of the Children of One be preserved in Egypt, because of the impending submergence of the last portions of Atlantis. Also from Hept-Supht the Priest learned about the problems concerning the "Things"—as well as the "Sons of Belial", or materialists, who were followers of evil, and in continual opposition with the followers of the "Law of One".

Returning to Egypt, Ra-Ta planned and erected two new temples for the development of the subhuman mixtures— The Temple of Sacrifice, which was both a spiritual and physical hospital or health center—and the Temple Beautiful, which was concerned with advanced training in vocations, especially in Art and Music.

The body was worshipped then as sincerely as most of the . . . spiritual worship today; for bodies were changing in form as their developments or purifications were becoming effective in the temples. These bodies gradually lost, then, feathers from their legs . . . many lost hair from the body, gradually taken away. Many began to lose their tails, or protuberances in various forms. Many paws or claws were changed to hand and foot, so that there might be more symmetry of the body. Hence . . . the body became more erect, better shaped to meet the various needs.

Those who had achieved such transformation, to be sure, were considered to have the body beautiful—beauty as something divine, for the divine has brought and does bring such various beauties of form or figure to the body; for "the body is the temple of the Living God". (294-149)

The following Reading is both typical and informative of the Egyptian period.

Mrs. C.: You will have before you the life existence in the earth plane of (1223) born October 21, 1906, in Troy, N.C., and the earthly existence of this entity as Tek-Le-On, in Egypt; being among those purified in the Temple of Sacrifice for the bringing into the world of a purer, a better race. You will give a biographical life of the entity in that day and plane of earthly existence, from entrance—and how—into the earth's plane, and the entity's departure, giving the development or retarding points in such an existence, and the influences from same in the present. You will answer the questions that may be asked.

Mr. C.: We are given the record here of that entity now known as (1223). In giving a biographical account of the entity in the Egyptian experience as Tek-Le-On, it would be well that there be given for the entity—and much for the study of others—a background of the period; that there might be a more perfect understanding of the activities in the material sense in the earth's plane, of being purified in the Temple of Sacrifice for the propagation of a new race; also that it might be understood as to what are the sources of attraction to individuals with whom there may have been a connection in the material plane from experiences in the spiritual, or the application of an individual entity to the spiritual laws through an earthly existence in associations with others.

That entity, Tek-Le-On, was among the offspring of

those who were entangled in matter, yet with a spiritual import; yet having blemishes in the body that kept them—as individuals—from their associations with those of the race represented by the Priest in that experience.

Thus we find the entity was a daughter of those who were the children of that group so enmeshed. In the early experience, when the body was first presented by the mother to the Priest, the entity was among the first of the individuals to be offered in the Temple, called the Temple of Sacrifice, as ones who might be dedicated to the activities according to the theory or idea of the Priest as to how individuals might be prepared for the incoming of a different type, or a more perfect stature of man.

As there were then those activities which brought about this change, these brought hardships for the entity through its early experience; not only in its separation from its people but in its being regulated by ideas of an individual who had only ideas—though these in the light of the results might even in the present day be considered near to ideal, from a scientific point of view; yet from the purely mental and spiritual view might be called barbarous by some in the present.

Because, the limbs of this entity formed those activities that were part beast of the field, as would be called in the present. This not only to the Priest but to those helpers at the time offered the first problems, as to how—through mechanical as well as natural law as to cause and effect—there might not be reproduced such blemishes in the offspring of the body.

Thus in the experience for the first time there was found the eradication of that indicated in the flesh of the animal, in the lower or hind limbs or legs, that does not exist in the human being. While the expression is different in different animals, the projections through spirit projecting in matter, through the periods of the evolution, had NOT brought about the change of this gland—that is still existent in the animal in the material kingdom.

This was removed from the body—this body—by the operators, with the Priest, in that early stage of that group's interpretation of nature, as related to God's creation of man as a representative of the God-head, and as to what those of the kind had brought into existence.

These activities brought periods of disturbance, as these glands were removed and then the body was subjected to those relationships which would bring the deter-mining factor as to whether or not there had been the selecting or the correcting of that which had been deter-mined as the source of such variations.

Then these brought about those connections, asso-ciations and relations that were to the entity abhorrent; until there WAS the reproduction that was perfect in the body, as well as those that had not been inter-mingled with those of that phase of man's physical evolution.

Hence we find the close associations through that period of activity of the entity with those early actions that brought such a change in the race, or the peoples who were purified through the Temple, or the hospital, where—through their own volition—individuals were submitted to experimentation. However, it had not been the entity's own volition; yet this became the after development during the period, produced by the entity's own reactions when it aided others who later chose to be purified in that period of evolution, or change in relationships of groups in that particular period. As to that which causes the attractions or detractions when individual entities meet in any experience, it is because, as in body so in mind and spirit, like begets like. Where there has been the attraction in a given experience for individual activity that was creative in its nature, to bring a relationship of the individual entity or entities closer to the understanding of Creative Forces, or God, these are close and are attractions; and bring the closer relationships, seeking expression either in body or mind of Creative Influence in the relationships one to another.

Thus, as indicated in the relationships of this entity in that experience with the Priest, there comes to the entity the periods of close attraction, and others when there is almost a revulsion, toward other individuals with whom the entity experienced relationships through that particular period of its unfoldment.

As with the offspring there came the more perfect accord, so—as indicated for entity in the present—its activity in the home, and with the unfoldment of the lives of those of its own offspring, there is brought the greater understanding, the greater concept of man's true relationship to the Creative Forces as manifested in the Way, the Truth, the Light.

The entity spent practically the whole period of the experience in service in or about the Temple of Sacrifice; only in the periods when there was the regeneration of the Priest the entity aided in establishing its own home, when the dedicating of the Priest's service *after* that experience, brought a greater interpreting of those attempts of the Priest and associates to change, or to give to individual entities the OPPORTUNITY of being channels where and through whom the Sons of the Creative Energies MIGHT manifest.

As would be judged by the present day standards, the entity lived to be quite an elderly person—as it was two hundred and ninety-eight years (298). In those periods of regeneration there was brought joy throughout the latter portion of the entity's sojourn there.

Then how may the entity use such information in its
own experience today, as a practical aid?

Know that in patience, and in the consciousness that
comes as indicated in those glimpses of relationship,
there comes the growing in knowledge, in mercy, in
grace, in peace.

Then, keep that in thine heart, even as the Mother of
the Lord pondered these things and kept them in her
heart. (1223-6)

Ye ask, where is this now (the Temple Beautiful of ancient Egypt)? Disintegrated and in that sphere ye may
enter, and some have entered, where these are sealed as
with the Seven Seals of the Law in that these experiences now become as those of thine activities
among thy fellow men. (281-25)

According to the Readings various forms of therapy were
used in correcting both physical and mental deformi-
ties—Surgery, medicines, electrical therapy, diet, massage
and manipulation. Vibrations of music and color, singing,
chanting and dancing were also employed along with deep
meditation. There was also a purification process involving the use of flames from the altar fires.

Usually some six to seven years were required for a complete change or self-renewal, though in many cases the re-
juvenation was incomplete and several incarnations were
needed to complete the transformation. Within a few hundred years the mixtures disappeared entirely, leaving only
their memory as the basis for legends in years to come.

The following Readings are typical of many references
which touch upon those times and peoples, and the final
break up and sinking of Atlantis—

. . . in the Atlantean land when many were making
preparations for changes to other lands when calamitous
activities were imminent through the opposition of the

Sons of Belial to the Sons of the Law of One—(the entity was) an expert in handling the crafts of the day that made possible escape to the different lands, to the Pyrenees, to Yucatan and to Egypt. (815-2)

. . . In Atlantis when there was the breaking up of the land—entity came to what is now Yucatan—was the first to cross the water in the plane or air machine of that period—many people the entity knew went to the Pyrenees and to Egypt. (1710-3)

. . . in the Atlantean land when there were divisions between those of the Law of One and the Sons of Belial, and the offspring of what was the pure race and those that had projected themselves into creatures that became as the sons of man (as the terminology would be) rather than the creatures of God. (1416-1)

. . . In the Atlantean land during the period of egress before the final destruction—(the entity) coordinated departure activities—journeyed to Central America where some temples are being uncovered today—began practice of cremation—the ashes may be found in one of the temples prepared for same. (914-1)

. . . in the Atlantean land before Adam, a timekeeper for those who were called "things" or workers of the people—the entity felt need of change or reform so that every individual would have the right of choice or freedom—felt desire to improve conditions for the workers—felt need of God's hand in what evil had brought in the earth. (5249-1)

. . . in Atlantis during periods of the breaking up of the land. Set sail for Egypt, but ended up in the Pyrenees in what are now Portuguese, French and Spanish lands. In Calais may still be seen the marks in the chalk cliffs of the entity's followers as attempts (were made) to create a temple activity for the followers of the Law of One.

. . . the entity may be said to have been the first to

begin the establishment of the library of knowledge in Alexandria, ten thousand three hundred years before the Prince of Peace. (315-4)

The entity was in Atlantis when there was the second period of disturbance—which would be some twenty-two thousand, five hundred (22,500) before the periods of the Egyptian activity covered by the Exodus; or it was some twenty-eight thousand (28,000) before Christ, see? (470-22)

Ra-Ta's Banishment

An internal situation that had smouldered for many years eventually led to Ra-Ta's banishment from Egypt. This was brought about as a plot by a small group of the priest's enemies who wanted to mould the civilization to fit their own purposes. Central to this scheme was the maintaining of power over the natives and mixtures, keeping them as virtual slaves such as they had been in Atlantis. Also the masses could be held in oppression through ignorance and superstition if the Priest and his followers were conveniently removed from the scene. Ra-Ta fell into a trap subtly arranged by his detractors, whereupon there were loud cries for his removal. The King acquiesed.

Ra-Ta sought refuge in the Nubian land, (Now Abbysinia) along with over two hundred followers, many of them native Egyptians, and the venerable Hept-Supht who had meanwhile migrated from Atlantis. There they remained for nearly a decade.

There were begun some memorials in the Nubian land which still may be seen, even in this period, in the mountains of the land. Whole mountains were honeycombed, and were dug into sufficient to where the perpetual fires are *still* in activity in these various periods, when the priest then began to show the manifestations of those periods of reckoning the longitude (as termed now), latitude, and the activities of planets and stars, and the various groups of stars, constellations, and the various influences that are held in place, or that hold in place those about this particular solar system.

Hence in the Nubian land there were first begun the reckoning of those periods when the Sun had its influence upon human life, and let's remember that it is in this period when the *present race* has been called into being and the *influence* is reckoned from all experiences of Ra-Ta, as the effect upon the body physical, the body mental, the body spiritual, or soul body; and these are reckonings and the effects that were reckoned with, and about, and of, and concerning, in their various phases and effects.

These all were set, not by Ra-Ta—but *expressed* in the *development* of Ra-Ta, that these do affect—by the forces as set upon all—not only the inhabitant of a given sphere or planet, but the effect all has upon every form of expression in that sphere of the Creative Energies in action in that given sphere, and this particular sphere or earth—was the *reckoning* in that period. Hence arose what some termed idiosyncrasies of planting in the moon, or in the phases of the moon, or of the tides and their effect, or of the calling of an animal in certain phases of the moon or seasons of the year, or of the combining of elements in the mineral kingdom, vegetable kingdom, animal kingdom, in various periods, were *first*—discovered or first given, not discovered—first conscious of by Ra-Ta, in his first giving to the peoples of the Nubian land. (294-149)

Meanwhile the Egyptian kingdom was torn asunder by a series of rebellions and civil wars. Some of these uprisings were concerned with religious issues as well as political conflicts and ultimately involved even the King's own household.

Finally, in order to restore peace and conciliation among the various factions, arrangements were made for the Priest to return. The resultant reorganization and developments after his return, (along with his followers) led eventually to the building of the Pyramid, Sphinx, and the smaller Pyramid of Records.

Then with Hermes and Ra . . . there began the building of that now called Gizeh . . . that was to be the Hall of the Initiates of that sometimes referred to as the White Brotherhood. . . .

In this same Pyramid did the Great Initiate, the Master, take those last of the Brotherhood degrees with John, the forerunner of Him, at that place . . . as is shown in that portion when there is the turning back from raising up of Xerxes, as the deliverer from an unknown tongue or land; and again is there seen that this occurs in the entrance of the Messiah in this period—1998.

Q. What was the date of the actual beginning and ending of the construction of the Great Pyramid?
A. Was one hundred years in construction. It was begun and completed in the period of Araaraat's time, with Hermes and Ra.

Q. What was the date B.C. of that period?
A. 10,490 to 10,390 before the Prince entered into Egypt. (5748-5)

As the monument called the Pyramid of Gizeh was being built in the plains, this entity superintended building or laying the foundations. He figured out the geometrical position of the Pyramid with relation to the buildings which were put up or connected with the Sphinx.

The Sphinx was built in this manner: Excavations were made for it in the plains above where the temple of Isis had stood during the deluge which had occurred some centuries before. . . .

The base of the Sphinx was laid out in channels; and in the corner facing the Pyramid of Gizeh may be found the wording of how this was founded; giving the history of the first invading ruler and the ascension of Araaraat to that position. (195-14)

The Hall of Records, which has not yet been uncovered . . . lies between or along that entrance from the Sphinx to the temple . . . or the Pyramid, in a pyramid of its own. (2329-3)

Q. How was this particular Great Pyramid of Gizeh built?

A. By the use of those forces in nature as make for iron to swim. Stone floats in the same manner. This will be discovered (again) in 1958. (5748-6)

Here are several separate references from different Life Readings, given over a period of ten years, concerning Cayce's predictions of the discovery and uncovering of The Hall of Records.

. . . in Egypt during the building of many tombs that are being found today (the entity) aided in the construction of the Hall of Records yet to be uncovered. (519-1)

. . . in the Atlantean land when there was the knowledge, through the teachers and leaders of the Law of One, as related to the destruction of the Atlantean or Poseidian land, the entity journeyed from Atlantis or Poseidia first to the Pyrenees or Portugal land—later to the Egyptian land—during those periods after the recall of Ra-Ta, the Priest, when there were attempts for the correlation of knowledge, (the entity) was among the first to set the records that are yet to be discovered or yet to be had of those activities in the Atlantean land, and for the preservation of data that is yet to be found from the chambers of the way between the Sphinx and the Pyramid of Records. (1486-1)

. . . in Egypt, of the Atlanteans who set about to preserve records—(the entity) came with those groups who were to establish the Hall of Records or House of

Records and may directly or indirectly be among those
who will yet bring these to light. (3575-2)

Araaraat drew the people together and developed their
abilities so that they could be used for the benefit of the
masses, rather than classes. . . . Many titles were given
to him in the various dialects of the people. But
Araaraat is the one that will be found recorded, with
those of the other rulers. (341-9)

The entity Hept-Supht led in keeping of the records and
buildings that were put in their respective places . . . at
this time.

This was in the period, as given, of 10,500 years before
the entering of the Prince of Peace in the land, to study
to become an initiate in or through those same activities
that were set by Hept-Supht in this dedication
ceremony.

Q. Give in detail what the sealed room contains.
A. A record of Atlantis from the beginning of those
periods when the Spirit took form, or began the encase-
ments in that land; and the developments of the peoples
throughout their sojourn; together with the record of
the first destruction, and the changes that took place in
the land; with the record of the sojournings of the peoples and their varied activities in other lands; and a
record of the meetings of all the nations or lands, for
the activities in the destructions that became necessary
with the final destruction of Atlantis; and the building
of the Pyramid of Initiation; together with whom, what
and where the opening of the records would come, that
are as copies from the sunken Atlantis. For with the
change, it (the temple) must rise again.
In position, this lies—as the sun rises from the
waters—as the line of the shadow (or light) falls between the paws of the Sphinx; that was set later as the
sentinel or guard and which may not be entered from
the connecting chambers from the Sphinx's right paw
until the time has been fulfilled when the changes must

be active in this sphere of man's experience. Then (it lies) between the Sphinx and the river. (378-16)

These Readings thus state that records of Atlantis, presumably written ones, exist in an undiscovered structure near the Sphinx. Their discovery would constitute strong evidence of Atlantis' prior existence, as well as confirming the validity of the Cayce Readings. But Cayce did not stop with just this set of predictions. He tied them all together with other prophecies concerning vast earth changes, the reappearance of Poseidia, the beginning of a New Age—and the possibility of the promised return of the Master.

2000 to 2001 A.D.
Q. What great change or the beginning of what change, if any, is to take place in the earth in the year 2000 to 2001 A.D.?
A. When there is a shifting of the poles. Or a new cycle begins. (826-8)

1968-1969 A.D.
And Poseidia will be among the first portions of Atlantis to rise again. Expect it in sixty-eight and sixty-nine. ('68 and '69) Not so far away! (958-3) (June 28, 1940)

Yet, as time draws nigh when changes are to come about, there may be the opening of those three places where the records are one, to those that are the initiates in the knowledge of the One God; The Temple (on Atlantis) . . . will RISE AGAIN: also there will be the opening of the temple of records in Egypt; and those records that were put into the heart of the Atlantean land may also be found there. The records are one. (5750-1)

This, then (the Pyramid) holds all the records from the beginnings of that given by the Priest, Arart, Araaraat and Ra, to that period when there is to be the change in the earth's position; and *the return of The Great Initiate* to that and other lands, *for the fulfillment of those prophecies depicted there.*

All changes that occurred in the religious thought in the world are shown there; in the variations in which the passage through same is reached, from the base to the top—or to the open tomb and the top. These (changes) are signified both by the layer and the color and the direction of the turn. (5748-5)

In those conditions that are signified by the way through the Pyramid—as of periods through which the world has passed and is passing, in relation to religious or spiritual experiences of man—the period of the present is represented by the low passage or depression showing a downward tendency, as indicated by variations in the kind of stone used.

This might be termed in the present as the Crucitarian Age, or the age in which preparations are being made for the beginning of a new sub-race, or a change which—as indicated from astronomical or numerical conditions—dates from the latter or middle portion of the present fall. (1932)

In October there will be a period in which the benevolent influences of Jupiter and Uranus will be stronger and this—from an astrological viewpoint—will bring a greater interest in occult or mystic influences.

At the correct time, accurate imaginary lines can be drawn from the opening of the Great Pyramid to . . . Polaris or the North Star. This indicates it is the system toward which the soul takes its flight, after having completed its sojourn through this solar system. In October there will be seen the first variation in the position of the polar star in relation to the lines from the Great Pyramid.

The Dipper is gradually changing; and when this change becomes noticeable, as might be calculated from the Pyramid, there will be the beginning of the change in the races. There will come a greater influx of souls from the Atlantean, Lemurian, La, Ur or Da civilizations. These conditions are indicated in this turn in the passage through the Pyramid.

Q. What is the significance of the empty sarcophagus?
A. That there will be no more death. Don't misunderstand or misinterpret! The interpretation of death will be made plain. (5748-6)

As to the changes physical again: The earth will be broken up in the western portion of America.

The greater portion of Japan must go into the sea.

The upper portion of Europe will be changed as in the twinkling of an eye.

Land will appear off the east coast of America.

There will be upheavals in the Arctic and in the Antarctic that will make for the eruption of volcanoes in the Torrid areas, and there will be the shifting then of the poles—so that where there have been those of a frigid or semi-tropical will become the more tropical, and moss and fern will grow.

And these will begin in those periods in '58 to '98, when these will be proclaimed as the periods when His Light will be seen again in the clouds. (3976-15)

. . . in Atlantis in the period of the first upheavals and destruction that came to the land, as must in the next generation come to other lands. (3209-2)

These changes in the earth will come to pass, for THE TIME AND TIMES AND HALF TIMES ARE AT

AN END.* and there begin those periods for the read-justments. For how hath He given? "The righteous shall inherit the earth." HAST THOU, MY BRETHREN, A HERITAGE IN THE EARTH? (294-185)

For He hath given: "Though the heavens and the earth pass away, my word shall not pass away." This is often considered just a beautiful saying or a thought to awe those who have been stirred by some experience. But let us apply these words to conditions existent in the affairs of the world and the universe at present. What holds them together—what are the foundations of the earth? The Word of the Lord. (416-7)

What is needed most in the earth today? That the sons of men be warned that the day of the Lord is near at hand, and that those who have been and are unfaithful must meet themselves in those things which come to pass in their experience. (5148-2)

Q. What is meant by "the day of the Lord is near at hand"?
A. That as has been promised through the prophets and the sages of old, the time—and half-time—has been and is being fulfilled IN THIS DAY AND GENERA-TION, and that soon there will again appear in the earth that one through whom many will be called to meet those that are preparing the way for His day in the earth. The Lord, then, will come, "even as ye have seen him go".

Q. How soon?
A. When those that are His have made the way clear, PASSABLE, for Him to come. (262-47)

* ". . . where she (Earth) is nourished for a time, and times, and half a time. . . ." (Rev. 12-14) ". . . until a time and times and the dividing of time" (Dan. 7:25) ". . . it SHALL be for a time, times, and a half . . . all these THINGS shall be finished (Dan. 12:7)

As to times and places and seasons—as indeed has been indicated in the greater relationships established by prophets and sages of old—especially as given (by) Him: "As to the day and hour, who knoweth? No one, save the Creative Forces." (416-7)

Chapter Six

PERSIA

Of the world's great religious leaders, Zoroaster (or Zarathustra) is probably the least documented from an established historical standpoint. The time and place of his birth are unknown, as are the societies where he dwelled and the kinds of people he was associated with. Historians in general believe that he lived in eastern Persia somewhere prior to 500-600 B.C.

The scriptures of Zoroastrianism are inscribed in the Book of Zend or Zendavesta. They stress the individuality of man and his moral responsibility within the universe of his existence. Here man chooses to ally himself either with good or evil, and in the after life reaps a heaven or hell according to his actions on earth.

According to Zoroaster the Good God created all that is true, constructive, healthy and beautiful- -while all that is false, destructive, unhealthy, or ugly is the work of the Evil Being. In the Zendavesta the name of this evil being, Anti-Theos, is taboo and never mentioned. The great command to all who would follow Zoroastrianism is to fight for good over evil with all one's will and resources. In this way Good will ultimately triumph over the Evil One—but the task remains as man's responsibility.

Possibly a million adherents to the religion are alive today, mostly in India and Iran.

According to the Edgar Cayce Readings the entity Zend was father to the first Zoroaster, there being numerous subsequent individuals with the same name. Then too, as we have previously noted, Zend was mentioned as having been one of the incarnations of the Master.

Here again Cayce placed himself squarely in the middle of religious history by stating himself to have been the tribal chieftain Uhjltd (Yōo-It) who, in turn, was the father of Zend. It was also stated that in this particular lifetime Cayce, as Uhjltd, developed much of his psychic ability and powers of medical diagnosis which became so evident in the twentieth century.

As in other incarnations where Cayce and the Master were associated together, they brought with them a large throng of fellow souls. For, of the twenty-five hundred individuals who received Life Readings from Edgar Cayce, over four hundred were mentioned to have had incarnations during that period of history. Most of these were stated to have been directly or indirectly associated with the activities of Uhjltd and Zend. (All of which gives an added indication of the fantastic amount of interwoven information that came through the sleeping Cayce. For to research and relate the lives of those covered by this one chapter alone could fill several volumes.)

Briefly, this is the story:

After the building of the Great Pyramid and establishment of the library at Alexandria, Egypt emerged as the cultural center of the civilized world. The Persian and Arabian lands meanwhile were inhabited by tribes of primitive desert nomads. They were warlike and uncultured people, torn by disorder and dissension among many small kingdoms. All travel through their lands was hazardous, since any caravan was regarded as a prize for the first raiders to reach it. Their preoccupation with piracy and internal warfare hindered any social growth or material progress within the tribes for many centuries.

During this time, the strongest and richest ruler of the Persian-Arabian combine was legendary Croesus II, one of a long line of kings who resided in a lavish, well-guarded fortress. Therein he maintained a training school for noblemen's daughters, which served as the only semblance of culture and education in the land.

Eventually, numerous skirmishes with Bedouin tribesmen developed into a war which led to the defeat of Croesus and end of his rule. Raids by the Bedouins upon small kingdoms in the area continued until they were finally put down by the leader Uhjltd. With his wife Ilya, a niece of Croesus, they established the city of Toaz, or Is-Shlandoen, referred to in the Readings as "The City of the Hills and the Plains". It was built at the beginning of the foothills around an oasis in the Arabian desert on the remains of a village abandoned generations before by some of the offspring of Cain.

Toaz grew rapidly as a trade center between East and West, with many forms of social and commercial advancement being attributed to it. This was under the direction of Uhjltd who, though from Iran, had been trained in Egypt and followed Egyptian spiritual concepts. Civil laws and courts with judges came into existence. Hospitals were established and cleanliness was stressed among the people. Family relationships between husband and wife were of a higher standard than in any (then) current society, and emissaries were exchanged with other nations. Eventually even a school for prophets was established.

But most pertinent to our discussion was the spiritual awakening fostered by Uhjltd and his sons Ujndt and Zend. The sons were given special mental and physical training in their youth and became spiritual counsellors among the people. Along with a number of initiates from the secret societies of Egypt, religious emissaries were sent to many parts of the world, teaching the fatherhood of the One God for Universal Force, and the brotherhood of man.

With this hearkening and awakening to soul development there came a better understanding in the relationship of man to himself and to his Creator. In this manner the forerunners of Zoroastrianism taught that the powers which manifest through all creation, and in nature itself, are the gifts or manifestations of the One God or Universal Force. This was demonstrated to all the peoples by their dependence upon the elements which make for and sustain their physical bodies and emotional well being.

Indeed, many of the Zoroastrian tenets and rituals which have passed down through the ages and are known in the present bear a curious pre-Christian tinge. They practised baptism, circumcision, and a sacrificial mass with a communion of bread and wine. Their prophecies included the coming of a Messiah . . . who would be born of a virgin and visited by three Magi, or Zoroastrian wise men, who would predict His birth by astrological and numerological forecasts. (Cayce indicated that the Magi who arrived in Bethlehem came because of such predictions, and that they were Zoroastrian.)

However, the growth and abundance of Toaz and its populace attracted covetous attention from other groups, a number of whom sought to gain political and economical control in that part of the world. The Grecians in particular became a problem in this respect.

The following readings (briefed in May 1948 by young Mr. 826, visiting A.R.E.) re-create much of the flavor of those times as well as indicating the type of information that came from the unconscious mind of Edgar Cayce in such profusion and detail. (Note that Zend is sometimes referred to as Zen, Zan, San or Sen in these original extracts.)

Named Ujndt, he was an offspring of Uhjltd and Ilya in the city in the hills and plains, when attempts were made by peoples from Greece, Persia, and Chaldea to overcome the authority in that city; and he carried on and brought the influences which made it possible for the Zoroaster reaction to come into being. He made a study of the conditions of man: of nomads who sought only daily existence, self preservation, and satisfaction of the body appetites; of merchants and tradesmen from India, Egypt, and Indo-China or Hun land; and of worshippers of the Sun in the Gobi land. This study was for the purpose of bringing hope, cheer, and understanding in the mental, material, and spiritual spheres. Thus, through karma from that time, his greater abilities now lie toward universal welfare.

Interpreting the records of this entity will give a history of the city in the hills and plains during the middle and latter portion of Uhjltd's experience, and the effects of the divisions which arose after the invasion of the Grecians.

Then, to give the biographical outline, we find Uhjltd with the companion (and companions later) who began the activities, with their varied experiences in dealing with the groups that journeyed that way between the countries. The beginning of Ujndt's activity was during the time when negotiations had just been completed with the various nomad tribes of which Uhjltd had been a leader. Also, the turmoils with the Persian king were near completion as a result of the warlike activities of Uhjltd's former associates. Now, the environ was more of a commercial nature, and one in which the healings and spiritual welfare were sought. Into this environment, Ujndt came as the son of Uhjltd and the companion who had been responsible for saving Uhjltd from the disturbing influences during Uhjltd's healing.

Under these circumstances, Ujndt had the opportunity to see and be a part of the development of the city in the hills and the plains, which grew from a mere stopping place for caravans from the East to the West, or from Egypt to Persia, India, and the Mongoloid and Indo China land. Hence the City gradually became a place of exchange, or commercial center, as well as a religious center, and was a place where healings of many of those afflicted in various lands took place.

In the beginning, this brought confusion to Ujndt; yet with the changes wrought, more and more responsibility was gradually placed upon him. This assumption of responsibility was not merely because of circumstances, but because of the import of the entity himself; for he was one to whom many came more and more for assistance and direction in their association and activities with the varied groups.

As the universality of body, mind, and soul were considerations. so were land areas, vegetation, minerals, and products of nature and the soil made a part of the mental, spiritual, and material developments under Ujndt's direction. For it was a basic principle with him that, not only should land areas be made to produce, but also it was their privilege to produce, and that the provision of such opportunity should be a part of the activity of those who reside in such areas. Through karma, that principle is latent and manifest in his present experience.

In the latter part of Uhjltd's sojourn in that period, Uhjndt or Ujndt reached manhood at the age of 31 years, and had to cope with the activities which were just beginning from the Grecian land. First, the Grecians used groups of young women, and by their form of entertainment and associations, they attempted to undermine the activities in the city in the hills and the plains.

As a result of these attempts by the Grecians, differences grew between Ujndt and his brother Zend with respect to spiritual and material activities. Gradually, because of those disturbances, a division grew between the two brothers in the latter days of Uhjltd. Zend held to the theory that only spiritual passiveness should be the activity of man, while Ujndt held that there should be practical application of spiritual, mental and material needs to meet the law of the nature of man.

These divisions gradually increased so that there became adherents to each group, not only in the land about the city in the hills and the plains, but also in groups that were fostered by the teachings in Egypt, northern Persia, India, the land of On in the Mongoloid land, and in Tau in Indo-China. All of these groups had their part in producing the divisions which eventually brought the undermining of those who held to the principles of the one, and to the purposes and principles of the other.

Ujndt believed that spiritual influences were for practical application in the mental and material life, and that they were a part of every individual to be applied by him in connection with his associates, or to those with which he came in contact, such as the attempted invasion and military expedition from Greece. He desired to defend the city, not in a warlike nature; but he desired a spiritual, mental and material defense against the invasion.

On the other hand, the groups of Zend (later known as the Zoroastrian groups) withdrew from the city and its divisions.

However, Ujndt held to the principles which had been demonstrated when groups of maidens were sent from Greece as an undermining influence in the City, and for the most part they were made to become a determining factor for good. In the same way, as a leader and director of the activities, he turned the earlier portion of the attempted invasions to good. This was not done in appeasement by departure from principles, but through coordinating the physical, mental, and spiritual abilities, as had been taught by Uhjltd.

At the time of the departure of Zend and his followers from the City, which coincided with the passing (or death) of Uhjltd, many changes came in the activities of Ujndt. Instead of being a counsellor, the obligations and opportunities of leadership fell upon him. These brought a period of deep responsibility. Through karma, they are now reflected in his sincerity of purpose, and in the selflessness which may not be too highly spoken of.

Through his activities, lands which are often called barren lands were made productive, and an oasis was created from otherwise non-productive soil. Through karma, there is innate and manifested in him in the present an interest in lands, minerals, and the action of the elements of air upon vegetation in its development of products for the sustenance of man. Also, from that sojourn comes his ability to direct the activities of individuals and groups, and to counsel, and to instruct by writing.

In Egypt, (in a previous incarnation) the entity was rather of a passive nature, while in Persia he was more progressive and determined with a purpose and ideal. In Egypt, conditions were accepted; in Persia, he attempted to influence groups and masses. In the present, the Egyptian period shows what he should not be; while the Persian period shows what he should be. The truths should be applied, not merely as something that is ideal in the mental field, but as may be applied in the practical, every day life for good. (2091)

Named Esdena, he (826) was in the Arabian and Persian land when many came to the city in the hills and the plains to the leader who brought a new hope and a new vision of brotherly love in the earth and in those environs.

He was one who came to be the right-hand man of the leader Uhjltd. Having come from Uhjltd's own people, and being healed by Uhjltd in body, he was strong in the activities which brought material, mental and spiritual gains to many. Many attempted to supersede or bring about crosses between Uhjltd and Esdena who was of Uhjltd's mother's own people; for Esdena was also among the initiates of Egypt who came to an understanding of the activities begun there in that land where many of the teachers in and throughout the earth had been trained. Through karma from the sojourn, he now has the ability and inclination to become a recorder of fact, of fiction, and of things worthwhile, as well as to be a judge among his fellow men. He gained in soul development through the experience.

In interpreting the experience of Esdena, it is necessary to review the conditions which existed then. With the establishing of a Center, many of Uhjltd's people were gradually attracted to the surroundings. Among those of Uhjltd's father's tribesmen was this young man, Esdena, who was a cousin of Uhjltd, being of the family of Uhjltd's father's brother.

At the age of 12 years, he came under the influence of Uhjltd, being healed of desert or malarial fever.

He lived in surroundings of much the same character as many live in now. Tents were made of goatskin and of other animals from the desert and hills. Being in straits owing to the breaking up of the tribesmen by the revolt of Estrides and others who were pursued by the kings of Persia, Mesopotamia, and Chaldea, Esdena sought first the comforts of material existence. After being healed, he became one of the household of Uhjltd, and was trained by the leader who joined Uhjltd in the activities which gradually grew into the city in the hills and plains.

He showed the greatest aptitude in gathering data from the various groups who came for one purpose or another to that Center. For the varied groups brought the fruits of their individual lands, in exchange for that given out there in the form of healings, teachings, counsel, advice, and the awakening of possibilities which would arise in the experience of individuals and groups.

The cooperative forces were the things which were of the greatest interest to him, and he began a diary of the

happenings in and about that City. This pertained especially to the character of advice and counsel given by
Uhjltd; to the manner in which the various groups
depended upon the elements in the soil, air, sun, and
water to sustain the body forces; and as to how the
minds were developed by individuals who applied themselves in activities relating to the Universal or Creative
Forces. Men and women of the groups were co-
workers.

The type of relationships between the head of the
household and his helpmeet arose from Zan and
Zoroaster. These relationships differed from those in
existence in India, Mongolia, and Egypt during the
same period. Although they were naturally based on
conditions in these other lands, the relationships in this
City came closer to the ideal presented by Him who was
the representative and Son of the Maker of heaven and
earth, than in other countries.

This diary by Esdena was begun upon the advice of the
leader Uhjltd, who aided in recalling the varied incidents, and in classifying the groups from the various
lands. Commodities were divided into those from the
vine, the fig tree, corn, the fruits of the fields, the herds,
and those used by individuals such as adornments of
body, spices of preservation, condiments in food, cos-
metics in adornment, and money in exchange. These
were all included in the activities set for the different
groups; and later, under the supervision of others, there
was opened a place of exchange to be used by individuals and groups from varied lands, when there was
begun the collection of commodities.

So he rose gradually in authority and power wherein
more reliance was placed in what he gave with respect
to the activities in the City and the varied lands. Thus,
he ultimately became what might be termed "the right-
hand man" of the leader Uhjltd.

As to the spiritual, mental, and material advancements,

these came about as a natural growth; and he progressed in development until the time of the invasions by the lovely Grecians. Then he began to make overtures for peace; but when the attempts for peace failed, he reverted to the activities of his forefathers who had been trained in physical self defense. Yet never did he resort to aggression, or to the manner of warfare which had been the early training of him and his people. For he adhered more to the policy of watchful waiting, as it has been termed by those who rejected that as presented by the spirit of the Son of Man, in Him that once ruled or governed this land in which Esdena then sojourned.

In attempting to secure aid for the defense of the City, and for its restoration after destruction was wrought, he traveled to various lands, first to Egypt, then to the Caucasion land, thence to India. And in India he experienced those things which brought the first turning away or retarding influences in that sojourn. For using many of the opposite sex as a defense brought turmoil between Uhjltd and Esdena. This brought a temporary division in their activities. But when the periods came when Uhjltd made the last of his admonitions to the people, Esdena returned to the City, and reverted to the tenets of his early experience in that land, although there had been implanted that which brought a breaking up in the third and fourth generation.

His transition from the earth in that sojourn was at the age of 178 years; for the diets and clean living with respect to the soil, air, sun, and water were a portion of the tenets presented by him during that sojourn. And he passed as one honoured when there had been the change from the activities of the Grecians to the activities under Zan, and later Zoroaster. (826)

Named Inxa (538), she was one of the nomads, or Bedouins, in the outer edge of the Arabian deserts, and was the most beautiful of her group. *She ruled many by subjugating their minds through the power of her eye; and through Karma she now has that power.*

With the breaking up of the tribes of Zu and Ra by invasions from Lydian or Persian countries, she (538) came to the lands under the Pharaoh rule to the camps of Oujida (195) who led the raids. She and her people were persecuted from place to place, and finally sought succor in the city in the hills and plains. As a virgin damsel, she arrived there about two moons after the supervision of Edssi (437) was established, and she was healed from emaciation and want by the leader. She was the most beautiful in that environ, especially in the hair and eyes, and exerted a wide and helpful influence in dispensing information.

Many of the hardships experienced by her resulted from her feeling, knowing, that her very life existence depended upon her hate. Gradually, there awoke within her the desire to aid in the understanding of an ideal. Thus, she became a leader among the younger people, and her counsel was a helpful influence to the rising generation, or teen-age individuals. Through karma, the activities of the younger generation are appealing to her now.

In that sojourn, she was healed by Uhjltd (294), was closely associated with him. At 24 years of age, she married Xuni who rose as leader with the departure of Uhjltd in that experience. In that experience, she suffered much from mental disturbance until there awoke within her the purpose, aim, and desire to manifest her better self, rather than disturbing forces. As has been given, the fruits of life, or of the spirit, are love, longsuffering, patience, understanding, brotherly love, preference of others before self, and the like; while hate, contention, and such are destructive, and all should refrain from such.

With this mental change in her came the desire to put the change into effect; and with her companion Xeno she went about aiding the younger ones as an instructor and companion to them. In this respect, there was assigned to her the physical and mental training of Zan, of the leader's household, whose promise was to bring much to these people.

After the demise of the leader Uhjltd, oppression came, and she suffered from seeing her companion gradually drawn into relationships with the invaders who had killed various of the leaders, and the leader's household; yet she and her companions saved the two boys who became leaders in re-establishing the forces which brought peace and harmony.

In the latter portion of that experience, she increasingly developed her ability to control by the eye and by prayer others who could not be conquered in any other manner. She remained in that environ and gradually won back the companion, but he was never trusted by her or the leaders. At that time places of refuge or schools for the prophets were established. She lived to be 120 years old, retaining her vitality to the end. Ultimately, she chose to give over her activities to those who had been trained; then, she simply closed her eyes and rested.

Zan who became leader was trained physically and mentally by her, and closely associated with her. He is not in the earth plane at present, but came again as the Son of Man, or Saviour of the World. In the reappearance, many that were among those will be called blessed; for their place has been prepared, if they will but remain faithful. As He gave, "Who is my mother, my brother, my sister? He that doeth the will of my Father, the same is my mother, my brother, my sister." (538)

Named Ilya (288), she was in Persia and among the forces under Croesus. In her studies and education, she was closely associated with the adopted daughter (369) of the ruler, although they were of different households. Later, she lost her life through the invading forces from the South and East; and through karma she is averse to cutting instruments, for it was in that manner that bodily destruction came. Her greatest soul development came in the plain country. Though suffering hardships, she learned the lessons of the indwelling of spiritual forces. Through karma, she now seeks knowledge of every nature.

In that sojourn, she (288) developed her psychic abilities so that she could interpret to others their abilities.

The attitude towards Inxa (538) was that of protection against either mental or physical injury. These may be cultivated so that she and Inxa may be a helpmeet one for the other.

Her activities were with (Uhjltd) the one who became the leader, teacher, and healer during that experience; and she was closely associated with him as his companion after the escape from the Croesus stronghold in a portion of the Persian frontier. The activity was taken up in conjunction with others later who were the sons of Shem, in the city in the hills and the plains which had been abandoned by some of the offspring of Cain. The activities were begun which resulted in a general commercial center at that point.

The association was with varied groups consisting of natives, of Persians, and of those who made treks from various portions of the country, and the center gradually became known as a place of refuge and of teaching.

There was such a pronounced difference in the activities carried on by men in this City compared to men in other places, that eventually most of Ilya's time was spent with aiding Uhjltd with their offspring. Only two children did Ilya have in that period, both of whom were sons and became rulers or leaders in the activities which arose from that City. One was Zend, and the other (2091) brought expansion of the various activities through other lands.

Her principal associations were with groups from
Greece, Persia, the land of Said or India, the Car-
pathian, Tibet, and Chaldean lands, and those much
farther to the East. The Grecians attempted to undermine their activities so as to make the City a
stronghold for Grecian ideas, although the people called
Grecian then were a different type of individuals from
the Grecians today.

She (288) aided in educating the various ones of the
groups to carry on the activities of healing,
hospitalization, segregation for cleanliness, as well as
for teaching. In the latter part of that sojourn, she suffered disappointments because of the uprisings there;
but she lived to see her own offspring well established,
although in some respects not according to her own
ideas. One (Ujndt) (2091) turned out to be somewhat
of a nationalist, and the other (Zend) followed
theological activities; yet these proved most satisfactory
throughout the experience. She lived to an old age.

Her sojourn paralleled the period of Cushi in Biblical
history. That history did not refer to Zend. The city in
the hills and the plains was referred to in that history as
a place of sojourn of some of the children of Cain, combined later with some of the children of Shem. Consider
the faults of individuals in that experience, and know
that you are having the same problems with the same
individuals now.

Her present experience parallels the activities that were
carried on then, and there is a continuation of the associations which may be manifested now. All of the individuals indicated as being a part of those experiences
were associates of Ilya. Some were helpers, and to such
she may appeal in such a way as to find them helpers in
the present. Some attempted to undermine, and in such
she will find the same conditions existent. Being
forewarned, you will not allow your own house to be
broken up. (288)

Uhjltd's escape and sojourn upon the plains was his developing period; *it was the first instance of anyone developing psychic ability in the present earth plane.* It was the continuation of the development received in his sojourn, just previous, as Ra-Ta, the priest, in Egypt. The developing in that time was with the suffering of bodily ills from injuries received in the escape from the force which connived with the weaknesses of the physical to make Uhjltd a slave in bondage. (294)

Named Bestreld, he was in Persia, and was the *keeper of the wealth for King Croesus, consisting of gold, precious stones, metals, spices, and herbs. His name may still be found when they will be uncovered in the upper Chaldean country.* He gained in soul development in the ability to serve in many ways the people of his own and other lands, and even in the persecution by those who destroyed much of the storehouse; but he lost in storing or hoarding which caused the destruction by the hordes from the hill country to the South. Through karma from that sojourn, it is now of interest to him how goods may be preserved from outside influences. (1734)

The entity came from Egypt to the Arabian or Persian land to establish accord in the understanding of their religious cults and educational factors. The entity gained throughout the experience in soul development, yet it caused much turmoil by preventing marriage of those having bodily disorders. This brought dissension. The activities carried out later in Greece when beauty of body was almost worshipped, were begun by the entity in the hill city near Shuster, Arabia or Persia. The methods for preserving bodies may be found in the tombs there. These are in tablets, and *the sign or symbol that should be worn may be found, taken from the Maltese cross, then called Yahama.* (500)

Named Esdern, he was in Persia just previous to his Athenian or Grecian sojourn, for he made a quick return to that land. He was a Bedouin or Arab, and was a descendant of the people of the Hivite land, or of Japheth. He was active in the early portion of building the city in the hills and plains, and was opposed to the leader. He gained in soul development, but also lost a great deal through attempting to impose upon his fellows to satisfy his self. Turn more and more to those imports that are spiritual, including the admonishments of Moses, Joshua, Samuel, David, Asa, Habakkuk, Malachi, and Jesus. *Read John 14, 15, 16, and 17, and know that they apply to self.* (1927)

Named Su-She-Un, the entity was an astrologer or soothsayer in Persia, giving counsel to people of many lands and assisting in the teachings of the day, but rather in opposition to things taught by Uhjltd. Through karma from that sojourn, the entity is now confused as to intents and purposes. The entity has been associated with its present nephew in England when there was wantonness in the court, and in Persia when the nephew was healed by resorting to applications used by Uhjltd. (2328)

Named Abiduel, he was in Persia in the city of hills and plains when the teacher of the nomads had arisen to power and accomplishments among the Egyptians, Indian, Persian, Caucasians, and Mongoloids. These names designate merely their position, for each country save Egypt bore different names then. *He was town clerk, and made the records, which are now among the treasures in the caves and city outside of Shuster, Arabia.* He gained in soul development through understanding of the Law of One, which was greater then than now. Through karma from that experience comes the ability to interpret relationships as to sects, individuals, groups, nations, and cities and their environments. (892)

The entity was a member of caravans journeying between Egypt and the Far East, and he came to the city in the hills and plains in Persia after the city had become established as a center. *He was one of the first to apply pigment to cloth to make a variation in colors,* and he took the dyes from the sea, the soil, and from plants and herbs. He gained in soul development throughout; for he came in close association with Uhjltd, and brought much of the lessons to his own people in Egypt. (1467)

Named Illeon, she came from the isle of Crete to Arabia when there was a gathering of people to understand the relationships of the material and spiritual forces. She gained in soul development, for she became an emissary and gave out of the mental and spiritual abilities attained. *She later became known as "the prophetess of the hills", and many came to her for counsel, advice, understanding, and knowledge.* She dwelt in the hills and caves where the home may still be found near the Ilex hills. (268)

Named Elia, she was in Persia when the nomads captured many as hostages for the tribes; and she was King Croesus' daughter, and was taken captive by Uhjltd, the leader in the raid, who held her until she was taken from him by the next in charge. Through karma from that sojourn, she has a horror of being forced into any action, whether physical, mental, or political, subject to another's will. *She lost in soul development, for she took her own life to satisfy self, not in defense of principle, self, country, or position;* yet she gave much in many ways in the early portion of her life. (369)

Named Slumdki, she was a nomad in Persia, and *was mother of the ruler Uhjltd* who conquered Persia. She gave much to Uhjltd in counsel and advice, and came to the aid of, and taught, those who were subdued. Though there were condemnations and misunderstandings as to the purpose of the raids, she held little against the people, and became ruler or Queen of Persia. Through karma from that sojourn, she now has psychic ability through meditation, and business ability to direct and control groups, servants, or rulers. In the quietude of self's study of the experiences through the earth's plane, the psychic abilities will be opened, as they were in Arabia; and as they are opened, use them, not as self's satisfaction, nor of controlling lives, but as of service to those who seek to see His face. (2708)

Named Shasum, he came with one of the first caravans to the city in the hills and plains in Persia when it was a Mecca for those of many lands. He became a healer; hence, through karma, *blue-green is the color or vibration for him.* Also, many bangles, fancy things, wavy lines, and music of a particular nature raise his vibrations; and *if he will apply himself, he may become a healer by laying on of hands.* The whole duty of man in any experience is to show forth the love the Father has shown, in the manner and in the way as to bring hope to those that, from the material things, have lost sight of the promises to the children of men. He gained in soul development. (1469)

Named Uhilda, she was Uhjltd's older sister, and during the turmoils and raids, she increased the turmoils of the tribespeople; but with the establishing of the city in the hills and plains, she aided much in the activities there, especially in the healing of those blinded by the sands and glare. *She was among the first in that experience to protect the eyesight by shades or glass imported from Egypt and India.* Through karma, she now has ability as a teacher or director. (259)

Named Iahn, he was in Persia when the leader Uhjltd was destroyed and the land overrun by the Athenians. He attempted to stay the tide of destructive influences, and *aided in assisting Zoroaster and Zan in reestablishing a place for refuge in another portion of the land,* under the guidance of one who rose as ruler. He gained, lost, and gained in soul development. (333)

Named Ujdelda, she was a sister of Uhjltd who was much older than him, and was in Persia in the city in the hills and plains, when *he taught men to put away petty feelings, and petty hates, and that love, rather than might, makes right.* She assisted Uhjltd in his ac-

tivities, and stood with the people against the rebellions
of the nomads, and again when the Grecians and some
Persians brought turmoils. These activities brought her
joy and happiness in that sojourn, and may do so again
in the present. (1567)

Named Eblem, he was in the city in the hills and plains
in Persia, and was an apothecary or dealer in incense,
spices, gold, silver, and things for adornment as well as
for services of worship. *He was the first to use propaganda or advertising in the sale of materials.* (2077)

Named Xenia, he was second in command of the
Bedouins during the war between the Grecians and the
people of the plains. *The plains people brought consternation to the invaders by turning hornets loose among
them,* which brought Xenia power, and in the end
proved his undoing. Through karma from that sojourn,
he now has a love of the outdoors and of the mysteries
of nature. (2213)

Named Schar-Chestah, he was of the teaching class in
Persia, became closely associated with the commercial
life between Persia, and the city in the hills and plains,
he was keeper of the counsel, or adviser to the King,
and was of the household called the "House of Gold".
He was closely associated with the teacher in that City,
and helped in distributing the foundations for the
teacher who later arose. *One of his descendants was
among the Wise Men.* (1378)

Named Joyel, she was of the household of the leader in
the city in the hills and plains in Persia; and she gained
in soul development, *for the music was begun by her,
which became a portion of the call to worship of the
Moslems and East Indians,* and has given to many a
means of giving expression materially to the promptings
from within. Through karma from that sojourn, tolling
music and weird sounds have an influence on her now.
(324)

Named Ajhdltn or Hjltdn, he was in Persia, in the city in the hills and plains, now called Shuster; and he came from Persia, was healed in body by Uhjltd, and became his scribe. *Through karma, he now has a peculiar interest in the teachings that arose through the grandson of Uhjltd, or Zoroastrianism.* He was a recorder of the things which might aid people in attaining a more harmonious life in their particular environ, whether they were from the East, West, India, Egypt, Arabia, Iran, Mongolia, the Carpathians, or from the sea. (991)

Named Philos, he was the son of the king of Persia when there were questions as to the activities of the leader in the city in the hills and plains. He was the keeper of the records of the king, and of trade, commerce, and associations with other lands. When he knew of the great lessons of truth, physical help, mental counsel, and spiritual awakening which came to so many, he journeyed to that city, and made a compact. Under the ruins of the third city under that in Ur may be found many of the records made by him. He gained and lost in soul development, gaining when the tenets of the teachings from the hills were applied among his own people for preservation of moral influences and care of the body. The first of baths were instituted by him, and that there might be all temperatures of the bath. From that sojourn comes the tendency now for the preservation of physical activity for all people. His father was the first of the Croesus' kings about 8058 B.C. (870)

. . . In the Persian and Arabian land, when there were those activities from same in which there was the spreading of the tenets of truth by the teachings in the "city in the hills and the plains". The entity then was among the emissaries sent to the English land. There the entity made contributions for the gatherings of groups for definite service, aiding in the creating of groups for a common defense, a common cause. Thus the entity made its contribution to creative influences, during those early settlings in the land, not only of the Norse people but of the Huns as well, that became a part of that trying period in the early portions of that land's activity. (2625)

. . . as the Roman, or coming FROM what is now called the Roman land into the Persian and Arabian land; when there were those journeyings of the many owing to the settlings about the "city in the hills and the plains". There the entity exercised self in the early portion of its activity to that of coordinating the languages and the mathematical reactions.

And it may be said that the decisions by many to use numbers of the nature as arise in the use today were from a portion of the entity's experience with the young; though it lived to be . . . only sixteen years of age. (1505)

Named Ixelto, he was among the keepers of the treasury during the first and second Croesus in Persia, about 7,000 to 10,000 years B.C. This was when many came to the city in the hills and plains for the mental and spiritual good. He rose to pomp and power which was not always used properly, but in the latter portion, he sponsored those things given out by the leader in that City, although some considered them disturbing or producing discord. He gained and lost in soul development. Through karma from that sojourn, he now desires things with an oriental touch, such as hangings, draperies, or rugs. (962)

Q. Have I known any of the people in a former life with whom I have come in contact in this life?
A. Most (of those) we meet. We meet few people by chance, but all are opportunities in one experience or another. We are due them or they are due us certain considerations. (3246)

You were incarnated in Persia during the time of the

Master's previous incarnation there. And you were in the household of the leader (Uhjltd) through whom came the greater understanding. However, that sojourn does not influence you in this incarnation as much as the one when you were with the Master, Mary, and Martha and (as Mary Magdalene) were loved by the Master. (295)

From a reading for Uldha, daughter of Uhjltd:

Q. Have I in any experience through the earth plane been associated with Jesus Christ before He became the world teacher? If so, where?
A. In this same (Persian) experience, that of the brother . . . for He became then the leader in those lands, and much is still gained in thought from those of the Persian efforts in this direction; or, as is termed, in the present day, the Persian philosophy.

Q. What was His name at that time?
A. Zend. (993)

The Persian period brings to a close the Readings' major comments on Pre-History prior to the early Essenes and birth of Jesus. It is a sad and frustrating fact that the interim period was never probed by those who posed questions to Cayce. For example, the entire subject of the Jews bondage in Egypt on through the Exodus was only lightly commented upon in asides throughout the Readings—And whereas Jesus was indicated to have incarnated as both Joseph and Joshua during those periods, no questions were ever asked with an eye toward filling in more detail concerning the Biblical accounts of their individualities. In similar fashion little if anything was ever asked concerning Zend's over-all existence or place in history.

However, it is suspicioned that Cayce was inclined to elaborate on historical times mostly where he himself had incarnated—and especially along with the groups which accompanied the Master in His returning to Earth. As such, a large number of the individuals who received Life

Readings (including Cayce) were said to have lived in Palestine around the time of the Master. In the following pages their story is as intricately interwoven as it is enlightening of those times and events which shook the world 2,000 years ago.

Chapter Seven

PALESTINE—THE ESSENES AND MT. CARMEL

The Old Testament closes with Malachi 4:5-6:

> Behold, I will send you Elijah the prophet before the
> great and dreadful day of the Lord;
> And he shall turn the heart of the fathers to the children
> and the heart of the children to their fathers before I
> come to smite the earth to ruin.

Later, in the New Testament (Matthew 17:1-8), Elijah is
seen by Peter, James and John during the Transfiguration
of Jesus upon the mountain. There they viewed Jesus
speaking with both Moses and Elijah. . . .

> And as they were going down from the mountain, Jesus
> commanded them, saying, Do not speak of this vision in
> the presence of anyone until the Son of man rises from
> the dead.
> And his disciples asked Him, Why then do the scribes
> say that Elijah must come first?
> Jesus answered, saying to them, Elijah will come first,
> so that everything might be fulfilled.
> But I say to you, Elijah has already come, and they did
> not know him, and they did to him whatever they
> pleased. Thus also the Son of man is bound to suffer
> from them.
> Then the disciples understood that what He had told

them was about John the Baptist. (Matthew 17:9-13).

Here in a few short passages are summarized several of
the psychic experiences that characterize the Bible
—Prophecy by Malachi; precognition and prophecy by the
Master concerning His death and resurrection; the reincarnation of Elijah as John the Baptist; visions of discarnate entities by Peter, James and John; and finally a voice
from the heavens proclaiming, "This is my beloved Son, in
whom I am well pleased; hear him".

It was through these and many similar episodes recorded
in the Bible that Edgar Cayce came to accept the origin
and validity of his own psychic experiences and abilities.
Most pertinent to our story is the role of Elijah rein-
carnated as John the Baptist and his relationship with the
Essenes of Palestine. Cayce, as early as 1939 was refer-
ring to people in Life Readings as having been Essenes in
previous lives—even though Cayce himself had no conscious knowledge of this early pre-Christian sect.

The story of the Essenes as pieced together from
numerous Life Readings is one that again fits the pattern
and purpose for which The Master and his group again
came into the earth. In similar fashion to the Persian
period of Zend and Uhjltd, over 250 individuals who had
Life Readings were said to have incarnated at the time of
Jesus—many of them then being personally associated
with Him.

Especially important to the Readings concerning the
Essenes and the Temple on Mt. Carmel is the fact that
Cayce predicted that written records of this group would
soon be found, which indeed they were—if we accept the
Dead Sea Scrolls as coming from these same Essenes—for
the first of the Scrolls were discovered in 1947, two years
after Cayce's death.

Again, let us repeat the Readings' description of these
times:

Ye say that there were those periods when for four hundred years little or nothing had happened in the experience of man as a revelation from the Father, or God, or from the Sources of Light. What was it, then, that made the setting for the place and for the entering in of that consciousness in the earth that ye know as the Son of Man, the Jesus of Nazareth, the Christ on the cross? Did the darkness bring light? Did the wandering away from the thought of such (light) bring the Christ into the earth? Rather, is this idea not a refutation of the common law that is present in spirit, mind and body; that like begets like? As we asked oft, "Can any good thing come out of Nazareth?"

Isn't it rather that there were those that ye hear little or nothing of in thy studies—the Essenes—who dedicated their lives, their minds, their bodies to a purpose, to a seeking for that which had been to them a promise of old. Were there not individuals—men and women— who dedicated their bodies that they might be channels through which such influences, such a body might come? (262-61)

Q.　What is the correct meaning of the term "Essene"?
A.　Expectancy.

Q.　Was the main purpose of the Essenes to raise up people who would be fit channels for the birth of the Messiah who later would be sent out into the world to represent their Brotherhood?
A.　The individual preparation was the first purpose. The being sent out into the world was secondary. Only a very few held to the idea of the realization in organization, other than that which would come with the Messiah's pronouncements.

Q.　Were the Essenes called at various times and places Nazarites, School of the prophets, Hasidees, Therapeutae, Nazarenes, and were they a branch of the Great White Brotherhood, starting in Egypt and taking as members Gentiles and Jews alike?
A.　In general, yes. Specifically, not altogether. They

were known at times as some of these; or the Nazarites were a branch or a THOUGHT of same, see? Just as in the present one would say that any denomination by name is a branch of the Christian-Protestant faith, see? So were those of the various groups, though their purpose was of the first foundations of the prophets as established, or as understood from the school of prophets, by Elijah; and propagated and studied through the things begun by Samuel. The movement was NOT an Egyptian one, though ADOPTED by those in another period—or an earlier period—and made a part of the whole movement. They took Jews and Gentiles alike as members, yes. (254-109)

Eunice (1602) was in the promised Land when there were great expectations among the people of which she was a part in Galilee and Judea where she lived. And she was a friend of the wife of Zacharias, the mother of John. And during the visiting and association with the mother of the Master, she became acquainted with those who were taken by the edict of Herod.

These brought great disturbances and troubled periods to the entity, as it was questioned whether or not consideration was given by those who were said to have brought protection to Mary and to her Son, the Master. For the willingness to follow easier paths became too prominent in that experience. Yet, in the latter portion of the sojourn, her experiences came in good stead. For in her association with the data gatherers of the Romans for taxing, she enlightened some who became friends of those who accepted the Master's teachings, when there were questionings by those in authority. Hence, at present, she is interested in people in high places. Not that she is a social climber, but she is naturally attracted to people in high positions through her own innate abilities.

In Galilee, where Eunice lived, as she became aware of the changes which had come about, there was less of orthodox Jewry. This was the adherence to the tenets which had been established with the return of the people to Palestine from Persia. Yet, she was among the people who had united with the remnant left in Zebulon during the captivity. Thus, according to theology, they were a mixture of the Jews and the Samaritans.

However, the entity's family embraced the ideals and tenets of the Essenes, which was a religious order within Jewry. In her early years, this was for her a problem. For there were continued reports of incidents which were handed down as a part of the family records. These reports were by word of mouth rather than by books, and referred to occurrences in the Promised Land, and the promise to preserve a people, although they were in captivity. They told of the interference of Providence in returning one portion of the people to the Land of Promise, and how that portion had been preserved throughout the changes which had come about.

Then, as a result of the tenets of the Essenes, there was the looking for the Saviour, and the expectancy that she would see, know, and hear of this fulfilling of the promise in her own lifetime. Following this expectancy, there was the betrothal, and the birth of the Son who was to be especially endowed with the abilities which were to bring an awakening to the people. Through the association of the entity with Elizabeth, the mother of John, and the friendships with Mary and Joseph, all of this was a part of the conversation and thought of the entity.

And then there came the counseling of the Wise Men and their conversation and convocation with the king. This was followed by the edict of the king which robbed all the mothers of that particular portion of the land, and then the destruction. These events brought to Eunice a feeling of hurt within herself, and of hate towards those who, according to her, had caused the loss of the sons of so many during that period. As a result, she has within her now, little jealousies and little disputations that are to be eliminated if there would be the full knowledge of, and at-onement with, the Creative Forces. (1602)

The Essenes were a group of individuals sincere in their purpose and yet not orthodox as to the rabbis of that particular period. (2067-11)

The entity was closely associated with the priests who were active in the Carmelian area, where there had been the early teachings established years ago by Elijah, Elisha, Samuel; that taught the mysteries of man and his relationships to those forces as might manifest from within and without. (2520-1)

It is well that something of those activities through the land be given here, that there may be an understanding of the background.

. . . There were those various groups that held to what might be called the determining factors or principles. As would be termed in the present: there was the group which held to the orthodox Jewish belief—holding to the law and the prophets as the way of acceptance and grace in the spiritual sense.

(Then) there was a mixed group—as the Samaritans who, as far (as edification was concerned), were as well versed in the law as were those of the more orthodox belief in that particular period, but differed as to the manner in which there was more oft the interpreting of the laws by the ministers and teachers in the synagogues of the day. Also the adherents of the Samaritanic law felt that they were just as well (correct) in keeping the days, the seasons, the moons, the various activities, as were those of the more orthodox groups.

The only factor dividing these was a differing as to place of worship; yet the orthodox had little of that in common with other groups. (993-5)

. . . Then there were the divers groups, as well as the Essenes. . . . There were those of the Grecian and Roman faiths, who held to that idea of glorifying the body itself as a channel through which there might be sought manifestation by the Divine—if there was a choice made by the Divine, or if there were the Divine (according to their reasoning).

. . . This entity then came into activity in that heterogeneous or conglomerate thought—in the name then Ulai. The parentage of the entity was one Archaus—a close adherent of the Essenes' thought, yet of the orthodox group—and of one (the mother) who was a close associate of the mother of Martha, Mary and Lazarus, in the name Josada.

Then, *the entity was brought up in the tenets or schools of thought that had attempted to be a reconstruction of the former activities established by Elijah in Mount Carmel.*

Hence, coming under the influence of ALL of these tenets, the entity was greatly confused through its early experiences. The entity had the greater teachings, or was acquainted with the greater teachings of the Carmelites—now the Essenes—and of the orthodox groups that held to the service in the Temple and the close associations with those of the students and exponents of the Roman and Grecian people. It was to these latter mentioned teachings that the entity turned more, in its early years.

Thus, (in later years) when there were the first presentations to the entity of the thought as to the teachings of the Nazarene, and the entity having rejected John (The Baptist) as a disciple or even a forerunner, these appeared as mysteries to the entity.

Hence oft in its activities the entity grew cold, and again very enthusiastic as to the varying forms of activities—both as to the social and as to the more strict religious groups. (993-5)

For in those days there were more and more of the leaders of the people in Carmel—the original place where the school of prophets was established during Elijah's time and that of Samuel—these were called then Essenes; and those that were students of what ye would call astrology, numerology, phrenology, and those phases of study of the return of individuals—or reincarnation.

These (studies) led to a proclaiming that a certain period was a cycle; and these had been the studies then of Aristotle, Enos, Mathesa, Judas (not Iscariot), and those that were in the care or supervision of the school—as you would term it in the present.

These (ideas) having been persecuted by those leaders, (the) Sadducees, (who taught) there is no resurrection—or there is no reincarnation, which is what resurrection meant in those periods.

(Then) with those changes that had been as promptings from the positions of the stars—that is the common vision of our solar system and Sun, and those from without the spheres—or as the common name, the North Star—this began the preparation—for the 300 years, as has been given, in this period.

In these signs then was the new cycle—the beginning of the Piscean age, or that position of the Polar Star or North Star as related to the southern clouds. These made for the symbols, as would be the sign used, the manner of the sign's approach and the like.

These then were the beginnings and these were those that were made a part of the studies during that period.

Then there were again . . . the approach of that which had been handed down and had been the experiences from the sages of old—that an angel was to speak. As this occurred when there was the choosing of the mate (Mary) that had—as in only the thought of those so close—been immaculately conceived. These brought to the focal point the preparation of the mothers.

Then when there were those periods when the priest Zacharias, was slain for his repeating of same in the hearing of those of his own school, these made for those fears that made the necessary preparations for the wedding, the preparations for the birth, for those activities for the preservation of the child; or the flight into Egypt. (5749-8)

Hence, there was the continued preparation and dedication of those who might be the channels through which this chosen vessel might enter—through choice—into materiality. Thus in Carmel—where there were the priests of this faith—there were the maidens chosen who were dedicated to this purpose, this office, this service. . . . That was the beginning, that was the foundation of what ye term The Church. (5749-6)

There the entity was as the companion of the scribe, Ezra; making those activities which brought into the experiences of the young what might be called the reestablishing of the school that had been a part of Elijah's experience in Mt. Carmel. (2444-1)

Much might be given as to how or why and when there were the purposes that brought about the materialization of Jesus in the flesh.

In giving then the history: There were those in the faith of the fathers to whom the promises were given that these would be fulfilled as from the beginning of man's record.

Hence there was the continued preparation and dedication of those who might be the channels through which this chosen vessel might enter—through choice—into materiality.

Thus in Carmel—where there were the priests of this faith—there were the maidens chosen that were dedicated to this purpose, this office, this service.

Among them was Mary, the beloved, the chosen one; and she, as had been foretold, was chosen as the channel. Thus she was separated and kept in the closer associations with and in the care or charge of this office. . . .

Then, when the days were fulfilled that the prophecy might come that had been given by Isaiah, Malachi, Joel and those of old, she—Mary, espoused to Joseph—a chosen vessel for the office among those of the priests, the sect or group who had separated and dedicated themselves in body, in mind, in spirit for this coming—became with child.

Then, as the record is given, that is the common knowledge of most, there was born in Bethlehem of Judea that entity, that soul Jesus.

There was the period of purification according to the law, and then the days in the temple and the blessing by Anna and by the high priest.

And these made for those days of the beginning of the entity called Jesus—who becomes the Christ, the Master of Masters—in the days when there was the return to Nazareth and then the edict that sent them into Egypt that the prophecy was fulfilled, "My son shall be called from Egypt".

There five years were spent, as ye term time—by the mother, Joseph and the child. (5749-7)

Mary had fulfilled all things that God had required of her *and later fulfilled her physical karma by bearing three other children by Man.* In bringing perfection by balancing the spiritual, mental and physical in her own activities she made it possible for all women to have that opportunity. The chains of transgression slipped from all womankind, and from that day forward they have been a guiding influence in the civilizations of the world. (1904-2)

Anna lived in the Promised Land preceding and just following the entrance of the Prince of Peace into the earth. And she was a member of an organization which attempted, through the mysteries of the sages, to interpret time and place according to astrology and numerology.

Her interpretations were much sought by the leaders in the group. However, because some individuals were inclined to interpret and apply the knowledge for material benefits, difficulties arose between Anna and the leaders of the Essenes. Thus the study of the religious principles of various cults, groups, and lands has been and is an object of her search (in her present life); yet at times she feels afraid of this.

She was not in the Temple. But she chose the twelve maidens who were to be channels that might know truth so thoroughly that they could be moved by the Holy Spirit. (2408)

This entity was in the Promised Land when young girls were being prepared for the entrance of the Holy One, the man called Jesus. And she was among the first chosen, among the twelve maidens who ascended and descended the stairs upon which Mary was selected. She was of the Essenes of the household of Joseph—not of the Joseph who was chosen later, of course, but *a kinsman in the direct line from David.*

. . . There should not be merely the aggrandizement of an earthly or body passion. Each should give their bodies and there is a necessity for training, even as there was a training in that experience of the twelve girls, in the fitness of their bodies, and of their fathers and mothers.

In the present this is called eugenics, which is the preparation for the entrance of souls that make the earth better in material and spiritual ways. For God is not mocked; and whatever ye sow that must ye also reap. (1479-1)

Q. How were the maidens selected and by whom?
A. By all of those who chose to give those that were perfect in body and in mind for the service . . . each as a representative of the twelve in the various phases that had been, or that had made up, Israel—or man.

Q. Please describe the training and preparation of the group of maidens.
A. Trained as to physical exercise, first; trained as to mental exercises as related to chastity, purity, love, patience, endurance. All of these by what would be termed by many in the present as persecutions, but as tests for physical and mental strength; and this under the supervision of those that cared for the nourishments by the protection in the food values. These were the manners and the way they were trained, directed, protected.

Q. Were they put on a special diet?
A. No wine, no fermented drink ever given. Special foods, yes. These were kept balanced according to that which had been first set by Aran and Ra Ta. (5749-7)

Q. Could you name some of the 12 maidens?
A. Andra (649); Sophia (2425); Edithia (daughter of the Innkeeper in whose stable the Babe was born) (587); Mary (referred to as the Other Mary, or The Lady Elect) (2946); and 1981 (who later became the wife of James, son of Zebedee) was in the house of lodgement of the maidens, and third on the stair when the choice was made of Mary. (1981) (Note—others were named in later Readings.)

Q. Does the immaculate conception, as explained (see p. 29), concern the coming of Mary to Anne—or Jesus to Mary?

A. Of Jesus to Mary.

Q. Was Mary immaculately conceived?

A. Mary was immaculately conceived.

Q. How long was the preparation in progress before Mary was chosen?

A. Three years.

Q. In what manner was she chosen?

A. As they walked up the steps!

Q. How old was Mary at the time she was chosen?

A. Four, and as ye would call, between twelve and thirteen when designated as the one chosen by the angel on the stair. (5749-7)

Q. Give a detailed description for literary purposes, of the choosing of Mary on the temple steps.

A. The temple steps—or those that led to the altar, were called the temple steps. These were those upon which the sun shone as it arose of a morning when there were the first periods of the chosen maidens going to the altar for prayer; as well as for the burning of incense.

On this day, as they mounted the steps all were bathed in the morning sun; which not only made a beautiful picture but clothed all as in purple and gold.

As Mary reached the top step, then there was thunder and lightning, and the angel led the way, taking the child by the hand before the altar. This was the manner of choice, this was the showing of the way; for she led the others on this particular day.

Q. Was this the angel Gabriel? Was there ever any appearance of the angel Gabriel in the home?

A. In the temple when she was chosen, in the home of Elizabeth when she was made aware of the presence by being again in the presence of the messenger or forerunner (John). Again to Joseph at the time of their union. Again (by Michael) at the time when the edict was given. (Flight to Egypt)

Q.   Was this the orthodox Jewish temple or the Essene temple?

A.   The Essenes, to be súre. Because of the adherence to those visions as proclaimed by Zacharias in the orthodox temple, he (Zacharias) was slain even with his hands upon the horns of the altar. Hence, those as were being here protected were in Carmel, while Zacharias was in the temple of Jerusalem.

Q.   Was Mary required to wait ten years before knowing Joseph?

A.   Only, you see, until Jesus went to be taught by others did the normal or natural associations come; not required—it was a choice of them both because of their own feelings.

But when He was from without the roof and under the protection of those who were the guides (that is, the priests), these associations began then as normal experiences.

Q.   Were the parents of John the Baptist members of the band which prepared for Jesus?

A.   As has just been indicated, Zacharias at first was a member of what you would term the orthodox priesthood. Mary and Elizabeth were members of the Essenes, you see; and for this very reason Zacharias kept Elizabeth in the mountains and in the hills. Yet when there was the announcing of the birth and Zacharias proclaimed his belief, the murder, the death took place.

Q.   Where was the wedding of Mary and Joseph?

A.   In the temple there at Carmel.

Q.   Where did the couple live during the pregnancy?

A.   Mary spent the most of the time in the hills of Judea, and a portion of the time with Joseph in Nazareth. From there they went to Bethany to be taxed, or to register—as ye would term.

Q.   Who assisted as midwife?

A.   This has been touched upon through these sources (Readings); and as the daughter of the Innkeeper and those about assisted and aided, these have seen the glory, much, in their experiences. (5749-8)

Q. Please describe the membership of the women in the Essene brotherhood, telling what privileges and restriction they had, how they joined the Order, and what their life and work was.

A. This was the beginning of the period where women were considered as equals with the men in their activities, in their abilities to formulate, to live, to be channels.

They joined by dedication—usually by their parents.

It was a free will thing all the way through, but they were restricted only in the matter of certain foods and certain associations in various periods—which referred to sex, as well as to the food or drink.

Q. How did Mary and Joseph first come in contact with the Essenes and what was their preparation for the coming of Jesus?

A. As indicated, by being dedicated by their parents. (254-109)

For the entity Eloise then was in that capacity as one of the holy women who ministered in the temple service and in the preparation of those who dedicated their lives for individual activity during that sojourn.

The entity was then what would be termed in the present in some organizations as a Sister Superior, as an Officer, as it were, in those of the Essenes and their preparation. Hence we find the entity, then, giving, ministering, encouraging, making for the greater activities; and making for those encouraging experiences oft in the lives of the Disciples; coming in contact with the Master oft in the ways between Bethany, Galilee, Jerusalem. *For, as indicated, the entity kept the school on the way above Emmaus to the way that 'goeth down toward Jericho' and towards the northernmost coast from Jerusalem.* The entity blessed many of those who came to seek to know the teachings, the ways, the mysteries, the understandings; for the entity had been trained in the schools of those that were of the prophets and prophetesses, and the entity was indeed a prophetess in those experiences—thus gained throughout. (1391-1)

Q. Tell of the work, the prophecies, the hopes of Phinehas and Elkatma, Judy's parents, at Carmel, as Essenes.

A. These were those activities that may be illustrated very well in the ministry of the parents of the strong man—that a parallel may be drawn; as to how first there was the appearance to the mother, and the father, as to what should be the ministry, the activity of the entity (John the Baptist) that was to lead that group, and aid in the early teachings of the prophecies of the life of the child Jesus, as well as of John. For, John was more the Essene than Jesus. For Jesus held rather to the spirit of the law, and John to the letter of same. (2067-11)

When there first began those of John's teachings we find the entity then joined rather those of the Essene group. For John (the Baptist) first taught that women who chose, might dedicate their lives to a specific service. Hence, not only the brothers (James and John), but those employed by the brothers, Peter, Andrew, Judas (not Iscariot), joined in the activities. (540-4)

For Zebedee first was a follower of John, then of those that separated themselves from the Jewish Sanhedrin, the Jewish Law, and of the head of the Essenes in those studies to which both John the Baptist and the Master came first as teacher, and as instructors. (1089-3)

Q. Please describe the process of selection and training of those set aside as holy women such as Mary, Edithia, and others as a possible mother for the Christ. How were they chosen, and what was their life and work while they waited in the Temple?

A. They were first dedicated and then there was the choice of the individual through the growths, as to whether they would be merely channels for general services. For these were chosen for special services at various times; as were the twelve chosen at the time, which may be used as an illustration. Remember, these came down from the periods when the school had begun, you see.

When there were the activities in which there were to be the cleansings through which bodies were to become channels for the new race, or the new preparation, these then were restricted, of course, as to certain associations, developments in associations, activities and the like. We are speaking here of the twelve women you see—and all of the women from the very beginning who were dedicated as channels for the new race, see?

Hence the group we refer to here as the Essenes, which was the outgrowth of the periods of preparations from the teachings of Melchizedek, as propagated by Elijah and Elisha and Samuel. These were set aside for preserving themselves in direct line or choice for the offering of themselves as channels through which there might come the new or the divine origin, see?

Their life and work during such periods of preparation were given to alms, good deeds, missionary activities—as would be termed today.

Q.	Please tell of the contacts of Thesea, Herod's third wife, with Essenes; her meeting with one of the Essene Wise Men?
A.	There was the knowledge of same through the giving of information by one of those in the household who had been so set aside for active service. Through the manner and conduct of life of that individual, and the associations and activities, the entity gained knowledge of that group's activities.

Q.	Please describe the Essene wedding, in the Temple, of Mary and Joseph, giving the form of ceremony and customs at that time.
A.	This followed very closely the forms outlined in

Ruth. (Reading for Ruth.) It was not in any way a supplanting, but a cherishing of the sincerity of purpose in the activities of individuals.

When there was to be the association, or the wedding of Joseph and Mary—Mary having been chosen as the channel by the activities indicated upon the stair, by the hovering of the angel, the enunciation to Anna and to Judy and to the rest of those in charge of the preparations at that time—then there was to be sought out the nearer kin, though NOT kin in the blood relationships. Thus the lot fell upon Joseph, though he was a much older man compared to the age ordinarily attributed to Mary in the period. Thus there followed the regular ritual in the temple. For, remember, the Jews were not refrained from following their rituals. Those of the other groups, as the Egyptians or the Parthians, were not refrained from following the customs to which they had been trained; which were not carried on in the Jewish temple but rather in the general meeting place of the Essenes as a body-organization. (254-109)

The following is an added montage from the Life Readings which characterize the richness of detail that Cayce brought through concerning the Palestine period.

Notice that he continually weaves in historical Biblical scenes along with personal experiences, mental attitudes and emotional relationships, from these past existences—much of it as it now relates to the present—then at the same time includes warnings, encouragements and pronouncements for the individuals receiving the information. Also notice Cayce's fascinating knack for constantly coming back to a given subject or person—again and again—without changing or ignoring his original past statement regarding the situation. (And many of these Readings were given years apart from one another.)

This was the period from which *Elizabeth, the mother of John the Baptist,* might expect the greatest hope. For she was the mother of him of whom the Master said,

"Among them that are born of women, there hath not risen a greater than John the Baptist".

As she was then a chosen channel for the one who proclaimed the day of the Lord to be at hand, she may now remain a channel. And she may arouse the consciousness in the minds of many to the fact that the day of the Lord is at hand.

For whosoever will may come and take of the cup, even as He. He has promised to stand in the places of those who are discouraged, disconsolate, or have lost a vision, or lost hope. In the same way, this entity may be a channel through which many may take hope and be aroused to the awareness that the Lord is near, and that He stands at the door of thy consciousness so that ye may be awakened.

Then (later in time) *the entity was Saint Cecilia*—or as Celia the entity was first known, and then known for its abilities in the teaching and ministering to those in the various stages of man's expression and development there—in the Roman activity and experience of the early Church; for the entity brought hope, patience, understanding.

Thus we will find hours in the present oft when music—that is of the nature that brings into association those forces of the celestial as well as the mental and spiritual—will be the greater channel in which the entity may enable, or be enabled, to give the expressions of those messages, those lessons that will be so much a help, and bring hope, in the minds of others. (2156)

When the Master walked in the earth, Jochaim was of noble birth, being one of the sons of the priests of the land. Thus, he had a knowledge of music, art, and those things which would enable individuals to express themselves. Illustrations of these were the songs of the shepherds, and the songs of those who watched upon the mount for visions of that which had been proclaimed.

He was closely associated with Zachariah who was the announcer of things to come in the experience of the people. He followed these closely; and like Zachariah, he lost his life in defense of the principles for which he stood. (2167)

Anna was the waiting maid with Elizabeth and Mary when they each were heavy with child. This was during the activities which brought the Prince of Peace, the Christ, Jesus, into the earth. At their meeting when they had both become aware of what was to occur, she blessed them and made the prophecies as to what would be the material experience of each in the earth.

She helped the maidens prepare and consecrate their lives during their periods of expectancy. Hence, she was known as a seeress or prophetess. At present, she often hears innate experiences coming through voices, through sounds like music, or through the rushing of mighty winds. But know, oh my child, their source when such things come to pass.

She is able now to counsel and interpret experiences of every nature pertaining to the soul. Hold not to things of the flesh or of the earth, but do that which you did then in helping the young mothers and other young women and maidens of that day. For your counsel helped many people. Abide in that strength which may keep you, and which may aid you in counseling others. (1222)

Simean lived in the Palestine period during the preparation for the coming of the Master, and during His early activity. And he was well acquainted with and associated with the people of the hills who were having political and factional meetings then. He was also familiar with the activities of Zachariah, his persecution, and his death as he took hold of the altar, as well as the activities of the Holy Family in their flight into Egypt. (1643)

Margil was in Palestine when the Master walked in the earth. She was very close to both Elizabeth and Mary when there were preparations and confusions in the minds of individuals. This was as to who would be channels to the world, and to the hearts of men and women, for that which would arouse them to their relationships with the Creative Forces. It was also with relation to the manner in which it might be expressed, which is, only as we deal with our fellow men.

She was the midwife for both Mary and Elizabeth. While this was not from a personal standpoint, she counseled with them as to the purpose for which each had been chosen as the channel for the manifestations. Is it any wonder then that she is interested in what the home and young will mean in the lives of people who are just beginning to build a home. Yet she has been denied so much of these that she has an intense longing to be in a position where the minds of the young might be directed by her.

This explains her work now in directing the minds, hearts, purposes and ways of them who counsel in their individual channels or places of service. *For the people of the present are responsible for that which they create in the minds and hearts of the children who are to become the mothers and fathers of future generations. In the parents rests the responsibility for what the thoughts and actions of the children are to be. In the same way, she counseled the mothers then, as Margil.* (1648)

Sister Duene was in the earth when the holy women were made heads of the church, or counselors. They were not deaconesses, nor were they what we call today sisters of mercy or sisters superior. They took the Veil in order that they might better prepare themselves to be

channels through which greater blessings might come,
and to attain greater abilities for teaching. They
separated themselves from their families and homes so
that they might become channels of blessings to others.

She gained in soul development through her abilities as
a nurse, teacher, reader, song giver, and one who read
poetry. This will be a natural talent in the present, being
not merely rhymes, but also stories with lessons which
are a part of the experience of the listeners. She will be
inclined to give these stories during ordinary conversation. (2308)

Philo's experience at that time may become the key to
his present sojourn. For when the Master walked in the
earth, he was among the Essenes who made the predictions and the preparations for His entering in that
period. And he kept the records for the temple service
where the men and women were taught the law pertaining to material things, and the tenets relating to
spiritual matters. (1450)

Sophia lived in the Promised Land when individuals
looked forward to the channels through which the
Messiah was expected to come. And she was among the
group chosen to present themselves as channels worthy
of acceptance. Hence, during both her girlhood and
motherhood, she knew many of the people who were
active in some way in connection with this definite
religious experience.

She was a member of the sect or group called the
Essenes. And she was of the house of David, but had
little kinship to Joseph or Mary, although she belonged
to the same group. She gained in soul development.
However, like many who were of definite groups that
set meters and bounds in relation to groups, masses, or
even individuals, there were times when she doubted.
Nevertheless, as the works advanced to fulfillment,
relating to all phases of the material, mental, and spiritual phenomena, she was a believer. *And she was*

among those on the last day, who stood at the Cross.
(2425)

In giving the biographical life of the entity Josie, much of those activities might be indicated that brought about those later relationships with Mary, the mother of Jesus.

As has been outlined from here, there were those special groups of individuals who had made some preparations for the expected activities that were to come about during that particular period, especially those of the Essenes who had chosen the twelve maidens to indicate their fitness. This choice was to be made by those selections indicated by the spirit, and Josie was the daughter of Shem and Mephibosheth that was among those.

This entity, Josie, was close to Mary when the selection was indicated by the shadow or the angel on the stair, at that period of consecration in the temple. This was not the temple in Jerusalem, but the temple where those who were consecrated worshipped, or a school—as it might be termed—for those who might be channels.

This was a part of that group of Essenes who, headed by Judy, made those interpretations of those activities from the Egyptian experience—as the Temple Beautiful, and the service in the Temple of Sacrifice. Hence it was in this consecrated place where this selection took place.

Then, when there was the fulfilling of those periods when Mary was espoused to Joseph and was to give birth to the Saviour, the Messiah, the Prince of Peace, the Way, the Truth, the Light, soon after this birth there was the issuing of the orders first by Judy that there should be someone selected to be with the parents during their period of sojourn in Egypt. This was owing to the conditions which arose from the visit of the Wise Men and their not returning to Herod to report, when the decrees were issued that there should be the destruction of the children of that age from six months to two years, especially in that region from Bethany to Nazareth. (1010)

Edithia (587) was in the Holy Land when the Master walked among men. It was during the periods of denunciations when people questioned. And they wondered whether the Mother had escaped into Egypt or not, and whether she had fled in time for the child to be saved from the edict of Herod.

This individual was one of the household to which Mary, the Mother, had come when the Babe was born. Since that time, she has held the vision of that experience, not only the words of the Wise Men, but also the events which took place at the Inn. In the latter portion of that sojourn, she became closely associated with the people who held to the tenets which had been taught; and she gained in soul development.

At present, in the evening when the lights are low, she has often seen visions of lights, and heard sounds of voices which she heard then, and which are ringing in the spheres. And her heart grows heavy or glad when she turns within to the wonders of those experiences through which she passed. And it brings to her inner self the peace, joy, and harmony that she experienced when her understanding and awakening came during that sojourn.

Edithia was in a household, and of a lineage, where the men had been set aside for a definite service among the people of that day. This was not in the manner understood today with respect to Israel, but rather *that which was understood then by the meaning of the word, "Israel". It referred to those called by God for service among their fellow men.*

Then, the group or sect to which the household of Edithia belonged, had been prepared through study, experience, longing, and desire. And the time had come when there was to be a change in the order of things.

Man had been looked upon as the only correct line of understanding or application, and woman as an individual was only to obey the master of the house. And there had been the understanding of that which had been promised from the beginning of man's interpretation of his relationships to a Creative Force or God, that is, with a correct interpretation of, "and the seed of the woman shall bruise his head".

Then, certain ones were selected from that Brotherhood, so that one might be chosen by the Lord for the channel through which there might come the beloved Son, who would make the paths straight and bring man out of darkness into light. *And it was to be understood, through the very expression of that Being in the earth, that the law was written in the hearts of men rather then upon tables of stone, and that the Temple, the Holy of Holies, was to be within.* This was that which had been given as a pattern to those who had heard the voice in the wilderness, and was for the people who were scattered like a flock without a shepherd. And behold, the day, the hour, the time had come when that Shepherd must lead forth His flock, His brethren, into the light of the countenance of an All-Merciful Father.

This entity, Edithia, was among the daughters who were chosen to dedicate and consecrate their bodies, their minds, and their service to become a channel (one of the twelve maidens). And they were chosen in their early youth. Hence, the entity's thought and activity at that time was directed to that environment and atmosphere of expectancy and promise. And then the one was chosen, as though a gift from on High. At that time, this entity knew Mary, Martha, those of the households of Cleopas, of Anna, and of Joseph, and those of the brotherhood of the order called the Essenes in that particular land.

Afterward came the time when the law (Herod) demanded that the sons should be destroyed. But it was provided that the ones who were consecrated might be more abused than others by the Romans. For the Romans had been given by that brotherhood as the authority from which man was to be cleansed. Therefore, it was in that environment and under those conditions that Edithia lived in her early years. Also, during the years of preparation of the Master, there were again the years of longing, and of fear and doubt. At the same time, there were more and more attempts by those in authority to disband the members of the brotherhood.

Then, there was proclaimed by the son of Elizabeth that he had, through the prayers and activities of consecrated souls, become capable in the flesh of renouncing the priesthood, and of becoming an outcast, that there might be made known what had been promised by those of old. It was that he should be as the voice of one crying in the wilderness. "Prepare ye the way, for the day of the Lord is at hand". Edithia was one who aided in those preparations, and was a follower of the Lord during the periods of preparation, and during the persecutions that scattered the individuals chosen for offices.

Is there any wonder that she now has doubts and fears with respect to those in authority. And she feels that there should arise some one who would defy custom, authority, and even the things which keep harmony. And the day will arrive, even as it arose then, when he who separates himself will become the one that declares to all.

She has often found herself contemplating the face of the Master, as He was on that day when John (Baptist) declared, "Behold the lamb of God that taketh away the reproach of his people". This brings to her an awakening in the present. And she should hold to the experiences which arise from those that walked and talked with Him as a man. *For His activity changed, as it were, the course of the stars in their movement about the earth.* And it becomes in the hearts and souls of men that hope which quickens as the water of life; it heals as does the touch of His hand upon the brow; and it awakens as does the kind word spoken to those who are in doubt and fear. For this is His teaching, "As ye do it unto the least of my brethren, ye do it unto me".

Edithia lived during the periods of waiting when many doubted. She was in the presence of Him, as he increased. She was there when many of the disciples of John became doubtful because Herod slew him to appease a selfish desire, and because John had spoken against that which aggrandized a fleshly lust. The day came when Edithia was with the crowds that cried, "Hosanna! Ye come in the name of the Lord!" And although the days of trouble came, when He too was taken from His loved ones, Edithia remained with the Holy Women who acted as mourners for Mark. For the latter had been her companion when she dedicated herself, her abilities, and her body for those services.

These experiences become in the present, then, as lights or halos done in the body to show forth His love to His brethren, until it is fulfilled and He comes again.

Jesus was born in Palestine, in Bethlehem of Judea, *in a grotto which is not marked at present, but is called a stable.* It was in the den where shelter was to be had that the entity looked upon the child Jesus.

He was born on the nineteenth day of March. By the Julian Calendar, it was in the year four. From the Hebrew or the Mosaic calendar, it was in the year eighteen hundred and ninety-nine. (See p. 164 re dates.)

This entity was among the first chosen to be presented before the Lord as possible channels through which those great blessings were to come. So, when the birth came, the natural associations attracted the entity to the parents. Then, the Wise Men of the East, from India, Egypt, and the Gobi, came to Jerusalem where the

members of that consecrated group had been gathered.
And this was the fulfillment of that which had been impressed upon Edithia in the years of her preparation. In
the present, this action of the Wise Men influences her
thoughts towards the Son.

With respect to the shepherds, they came to the stable
because all nature, all the heavenly hosts, had proclaimed that glorious period for man. As the Wise Men
came to do honor and to give of their substance, she
realized that in body and mind, she had been dedicated
to that service to man in order that she might be a channel of blessing. And her soul awakened to the praise of
the shepherds who had experienced that cry of the
heavenly hosts, "Behold a son is given, and his name is
wonderful counsellor!" Then she realized, as she does
now, how all nature, the face in the water, the dew
upon the grass, the tint and the beauty of the rose, the
song of the stars, and the mourn of the wind, all proclaimed the mighty words of a merciful and loving God.
(587)

At her last reading, Edgar Cayce saw a mentor. This
was a holy experience. Keep inviolate, my child, those
things that must shortly come to thee, if ye will but
harken to the voices within. This again is him who proclaimed that the day of the Lord is at hand, John. It is
indicated in the manner of his garb—and his raiment
shall be white as snow, and they whose sins have been
as crimson shall be washed and as wool.

His feet are not of clay; his feet are not as brass, but as
of gold. That relates to the endearing messages which
may be brought to thee and thine. And thou may now
fulfill that for which thou then dedicated thy life, that
he through thine efforts in flesh may proclaim the wondrous year of the Lord for men.

John (the Baptist) was then, and is now, one of the
leaders of the White Brotherhood.

The meaning of the spinning sphere which she saw, indicates that the awareness within has come of the nearness of that proclaimed from the beginning, "Know the Lord thy God is one!" And who is his mother, his brother, his sister? They that do the will of the Father. What is the will? The law and love expressed in the words which the Master gave, "Love the Lord thy God with all thine heart, thine body, thy soul; and thy brother as thyself." (587)

Chapter Eight

THE NATIVITY

Here begins the Christmas story itself:

This Reading (5749-15) was given by Edgar Cayce at Virginia Beach, Va., June 22, 1941, at the Tenth Annual Congress of the Association for Research & Enlightenment, Inc.

Mrs. C.: You will have before you the enquiring mind of the entity Thomas Sugrue, present in this room, who seeks a continuation of information given on the life of the Master and its history in the material world, given in Readings of June 27, 1937 (5749-7 and 5749-8). Because of the purpose for which this information is to be used, he asks at this time for a description of a literary nature of certain events in the life of the Master which are known to us in outline but not in detail. You will give these as presented—first the birth of the Master at Bethlehem beginning with the arrival of Mary and Joseph at the Inn. You will include such details as weather, time, conversation with Innkeeper, number of people at the Inn, types they represented, recreations and occupations engaged in during the evening, what was being eaten and drunk, whether the guests knew the Child was being born, actual time of birth, etc.

Mr. C.: Yes, we have the information that has been indicated respecting some of the events surrounding the birth of Jesus, the Son of Mary, in Bethlehem of Judea.

The purposes are well known, for which the journey was made in the period. The activities of Joseph are well known. The variation or difference in their ages is not so oft dwelt upon. Neither is there much indicated in sacred or profane history as to the preparation of the mother for that channel through which immaculate conception might take place. And this, the immaculate conception, is a stumblingstone to many worldly-wise.

The arrival was in the evening—not as counted from the Roman time, nor that declared to Moses by God when the Second Passover was to be kept, nor that same time which was in common usage even in that land, but what would NOW represent January sixth.

The weather was cool, and there were crowds on the way. For, it was only a sabbath day's journey from Jerusalem. There were great crowds of people on the way from the hills of Judea.

The people were active in the occupations of the varied natures in that unusual land. Some were carpenters—as those of the house of Joseph, who had been delayed, even on the journey, by the condition of the Mother. Some in the group were helpers to Joseph—carpenters' helpers. Then there were shepherds, husbandmen, and the varied groups that had their small surroundings as necessitated by the conditions of the fields about Nazareth.

In the evening then, or at twilight, Joseph approached the Inn, that was filled with those who had also journeyed there on their way to be polled for the tax as imposed by the Romans upon the people of the land. For, those had been sent out who were to judge the abilities of the varied groups to be taxed. And each individual was required by the Roman law to be polled in the city of his birth.

Both Joseph and Mary were members of the sect called the Essenes; and thus they were questioned by those not only in the political but in the religious authority in the cities.

Then there was the answer by the Innkeeper, "No room in the inn", especially for such an occasion. Laughter and jeers followed, at the sight of the elderly man with the beautiful girl, his wife, heavy with child.

Disappointments were written upon not only the face of Joseph but the Innkeeper's daughter, as well as those of certain groups about the Inn. For, many saw the possibilities of an unusual story that might be gained if the birth were to take place in the Inn. Also there was consternation outside, among those who had heard that Joseph and Mary had arrived and were not given a room. They began to seek some place, some shelter.

For, remember, many of those—too—were of that questioned group; who had heard of that girl, that lovely wife of Joseph who had been chosen by the angels on the stair; who had heard of what had taken place in the hills where Elizabeth had gone, when there was the visit from the cousin—and as to those things which had also come to pass in her experience. Such stories were whispered from one to another.

Thus many joined in the search for some place. Necessity demanded that some place be sought—quickly. Then it was found, under the hill, in the stable—above which the shepherds were gathering their flocks into the fold.

There the Saviour, the Child was born; who, through the will and the life manifested, became the Saviour of the World—that channel through which those of old had been told that the promise would be fulfilled that was made to *Eve;* the arising again of another like unto

Moses; and as given to David, the promise was not to depart from that channel. But lower and lower man's concept of needs had fallen.

Then—when hope seemed gone—the herald angels sang. The star appeared, that made the wonderment to the shepherds, that caused the awe and consternation to all of those about the Inn; some making fun, some smitten with conviction that those unkind things said must needs be readjusted in their relationships to things coming to pass.

All were in awe as the brightness of His star appeared and shone, as the music of the spheres brought that joyful choir, "PEACE ON EARTH! GOOD WILL TO MEN OF GOOD FAITH".

All felt the vibrations and saw a great light, not only the shepherds above that stable but those in the Inn as well. To be sure, those conditions were later to be dispelled by the doubters, who told the people that they had been overcome with wine or what not.

Just as the midnight hour came, there was the birth of the Master.

The daughter of the Innkeeper was soon upon the scene, as was the mother of the daughter, and the shepherds that answered the cry—and had gone to see what was come to pass.

Those were the manners, and the ones present soon afterwards. For through the period of purification the Mother remained there, not deeming it best to leave, though all forms of assistance were offered; not leaving until there was the circumcision and the presenting in the temple to the Magi, to Anna and Simeon.

Such were the surroundings at the period of the birth of Jesus. (5749-15)

Q. In what manner was Joseph informed of his part in the birth of Jesus?

A. First by Mathias or Judah. Then as this did not coincide with his own feelings, first in a dream and then the direct voice. And whenever (comes) the voice, this is always accompanied with odors, as well as lights; and oft the description of the lights is the vision, see?

Q. Was he disturbed when Mary became with child while yet a virgin?

A. Owing to his natural surroundings and because of his advanced age too, (in comparison with) that of the virgin when she was given; or as would be termed in the present; because of what people say. Yet when assured, you see, that this was - the Divine, not only by his brethren but by the voice and by those experiences, he knew. For you see . . . from the time of the first promise—while she was still yet in training from the the choice—there was a period of some three to four years; yet when he went to claim her as the bride, at the period of, or between sixteen and seventeen, she was found with child.

Q. How old was Joseph at the time of the marriage?
A. Thirty-six.

Q. How old was Mary at the time of the marriage?
A. Sixteen.

Q. Were Mary and Joseph known to each other before the choosing for them to be man and wife?

A. As would be chosen in a lodge, not as ye would term of visitations; neither as only chosen by the sect or the families. In those periods in most of the Jewish families the arrangements were made by the parents of the contracting parties, you see; while in this (case), these (two) were not as contracting parties from their families. For Anne and her daughter were questioned as belonging to any (family), you see! Then it was not a

choice altogether, as if they were appointed by the
leaders of the sect, or of the group, or of the lodge, or
of the church—for this is the church that is called the
Catholic now . . . and is the closest.

Q. Who were the parents of Joseph?
A. That as recorded by Matthew, as is given, you see
one side recorded by Matthew, the other by Luke; these
on various sides, but of the house of David—as was also Mary of the house of David.

Q. Do we celebrate Christmas at approximately the right
time?
A. (There is) not a great variation; for there have been
many changes in the accounting of time, or accounting
for the periods from the various times when time is
counted—not far wrong; twenty-fourth, twenty-fifth of
December, as ye have your time now. (5749-7)

Q. In one reading we are told that Jesus' birthday is on
March 19—"according as we reckon time now"—and
in another reading we are told that we keep Christmas
about the right time—24th, 25th of December, "as ye
have your time now". (Still another mentions January
6th). Please explain the seeming contradiction.
A. All are correct according to the time from which
same were reckoned (in the akasha?). How many times
have there been the reckoning? Take these into consideration with the period of events being followed in
the information being indicated. Just as there was the
reckoning from the various groups for their individual
activities, so was the information given as to the records
from that source with which those seeking were concerned. (2067)

Q. What about the Innkeeper and his family? Did they
ever know who it was they turned away?
A. Much of that which has been recorded, as we find, is
not so correct, nor in keeping with what the keeper of
the Inn did then—as Apsafar, who was of the Essenes
though of Jewish descent (rather, a combination of

Jewish and Grecian). For the entity (Apsafar) then made a study of those people (the Essenes), knew of those things which had been foretold by the teachers of the Essenes; and made all preparations as nearly in keeping with what had been foretold as possible.

While among the entity's stables was indeed the place of rest, it was (chosen in preference to the Inn itself) because of the very rabble, the very act of those who were in authority both as to the Roman as well as the various groups that in their discussions were making for the very things which would hinder or prevent the experiences that had been foretold.

The Innkeeper did this rather for protection (of the Holy Family) than because—as had been said—there was "no room at the inn". By this it was meant to be implied or conveyed that they were "turned away". Yet in (respect to) the entity's activities it was really for the protection. For the entity too had seen a vision; the entity, too, had heard, had known of the voices that were in the air. The entity too had seen the star in the east. The entity too had known of the experiences which must befall those who were making all the preparations possible, under those existent conditions, for Him who should come as a teacher, as a shepherd, as a Saviour. (1196)

Closely associated with the Innkeeper and those activities there, was Sodaphe, the wife of the Innkeeper.

In the experience, she was pulled between confusing influences. Though the customs of the day called for the entity's position to be rather hidden, the entity in its purpose and in its very activity was quite outspoken. (2550)

The Wise Men

Q. Explain the relationship of the Wise men and Jesus' birth.

A.   As indicated by the travels of the Master during the periods of preparation, *the whole earth, the whole world looked for, sought the closer understanding.* Hence through the efforts of the students of the various phases of experiences of man in the earth, *as may be literally interpreted from the first chapters of Genesis, ye find that* those who subdued—not that were ruled by, but subdued the understandings of that in the earth —were considered, or were in the position of the wise, or the sages, or the ones that were holy, in body and mind in accord with high purposes.

Hence we find as the Wise Men those that were seekers for the truth, for this happening; and in and *through the application of those forces—as ye would term today psychic—we find them coming to the place "where the child was".* Or they were drawn as those that were giving the thanks for this Gift, this expression of a Soul seeking to show wayward man back to God.

So they represent in the metaphysical sense the three phases of man's experience in materiality: gold, the material; frankincense, the ether or ethereal; myrrh, the healing force as brought with same; or body, mind, soul.

These were the positions then of the Wise Men in their relationship; or to put into the parlance of the day—they were the encouragement needed for the Mother and those that had nourished, that had cherished this event in the experience of mankind.

They came during the days of purification, but, to be sure, only after she was purified were they presented to the Child.

Q.   What relation did they have with the later travels of Jesus?

A.   As has just been indicated, they represented then the three phases of man's experience as well as the three phases of the teacher from Egypt, from Persia, from India. (5749-7)

Q.   What were the names of the Wise Men, and what gift did each bring?

A.   Achlar was the Wise Man who brought incense to the child Jesus. For he lived in a period which has meant and does bring hope to the world.

Preceding the advent of the Prince of Peace in the earth, he was in Persia as a wise man, counselor, and sage; and he counseled with the people of that country. Using the mathematical methods which had been handed down through the ages, as well as the teachings of the Persians from the days of Zend, Og, and Uhjltd, he interpreted both the astrological and the natural laws.

Thus, he was associated often with individuals who looked for the place and hour when that Great Purpose or Event was to be in the earth a literal experience. And he was one of the fabled Wise Men who came from the East, seeking during that period. In the present, those often told tales are accepted by him, because of the conviction and purpose they have produced and do produce in the hearts and minds of individuals.

He gained in soul development. For he manifested his love for his fellow man by searching for helpful influences, mentally, spiritually, and materially. Although he often then lost sight of materiality. (1908)

Ashtucil was among those who were of the Wise Men coming into Jerusalem and Bethlehem when the Master came into the earth. And he came from the mountains of what is now known as Arabia and India. He gained in soul development in that period by teaching that when the various forces of man are added to the creative forces necessary to keep the balance in the universal forces, the earth must bring forth that which would make man's balance of force with the Creative Energy as One. And the Son of Man appeared. He brought the frankincense and gave it to the Master at that time. (256)

Puloaus was in the Holy Land when preparations were being made for the Prince of Peace, the Son of God, to come into the earth. He was an overseer for tax collectors. And he was the first to suggest that individuals should be chosen from the various faiths, so that the Romans, Jews, Grecians, Helvetians, and Egyptians should all have charge of collecting the taxes.

During the turmoils which occurred when the Jews rebelled, he was a commander in charge of the soldiers who put down such uprisings. In this manner, he had a clean record. And when the Wise Men came, he was given charge by the Romans that he should conduct these Wise Men to the place they sought. (1220)

Rebkah lived when they were looking for the coming of the Prince of Peace, the Master of masters. And she directed the Wise Men to the Inn, where His manifestation of light, hope, and joy was proclaimed by the sages of old. Likewise, she may in the present give light to both people of high estate and the common people.

For as you learned then, He, your Lord, your God, is not a respecter of persons, but of hopes, desires, and purposes in individual lives. Thus, make your purpose one with His, so that all men may know the glory of the Lord, and it may fill their lives also. (3297)

In that sojourn, she was a seeker after knowledge and the way of truth. And she was used as a channel, although it was not mentioned. (3297)

Eucuo lived during the periods of hardships and activities when the Master walked in the earth. And *he was among the shepherds* who heard the cry "Glory to God in the Highest. Peace on earth and good will to men."

He had the ability to play on the harp and the reeded instruments. And most of the songs that were played were created by intuition from the conditions surrounding them.

He beheld Him as a Babe. And this becomes an influence in Him. In the present, he has a greater need for that Creative Force, which arouses the latent feelings in minds and hearts, as such is set to music, to move people in their relationships to others and to their Creator. (1815)

Q. In one answer we are told that the Wise Men came from Egypt, India and Gobi. Now we are told the Wise Man who brought the incense came from Persia? Which is correct?

A. Both are correct. There was more than one visit of the Wise Men. One is a record of three Wise Men. There was the fourth, as well as the fifth. And then a second group. They came from Persia, India, Egypt, and also from Chaldea, Gobi, and what is now the Indo or Tao Land. (2067)

Mateal was one of those people to whom the Mother of the Master came for help when it was necessary to flee from the decree of Herod. And she physically fulfilled God's plans in the material world. Think on that; and live it also today. For it was through her that the beasts were obtained upon which the Infant and the Mother fled into Egypt.

This also explains your interest in the individuals who were bereft by the edict, for your own child became a part of that destruction. Later, you learned to comprehend and apply the teachings of Him in that experience. You gained in soul development. For who may be a channel, or have the full knowledge of being used as a messenger of the all-powerful, and not attain some development of the soul? All are in that position of being able to be used, if they will recognize their opportunities day by day in their choices of dealings with their fellow men. (1992)

The final reading in our chapter on the Master's Nativity is one which is somewhat typical, yet unusual because of its content and scope. Consider the emotional impact this must have had upon the individual who received it!

Jenife (Sarapha or Sara) (1152) was in the earth when great changes and opportunities were coming to man by the fulfilling of time and the prayers of many. At the time, there was much turmoil and strife; and the people were pulled between that which was being presented by the Romans, and the truths or lessons given by the people of the land.

When the Prince of Peace came to complete His own development in the earth, He overcame the flesh and temptation. So He became the first of those who overcame death in the body. This enabled Him to illuminate and revivify that body so as to take it up again, even when the fluids of the body had been drained away by the nail holes in His hands and by the spear piercing His side.

Yet this body, this entity, Jenife, too, may do these things, through those promises that were so new yet so old, as given by Him. "Not of myself do I these things," saith He, "But God, the Father that worketh in me; for I come from Him; I go to Him."

He came, the Master, in flesh and blood, even as thou didst come in flesh and blood. Yet as He then proclaimed to thee, there is a cleansing of the body, of the flesh, of the blood, in such measures that it may become illumined with power from on high. That is within thine own body to will. "Thy will, O God; not mine, but Thine, be done in me, through me."

This was the message which He gave when He, too, overcame. He surrendered all power unto Power itself, surrendering all will unto the will of the Father. Thus, He made of Himself a channel through which others, taking hope through the knowledge that He has perfected Himself, may find the grace and mercy which is eternity with Him and in Him.

Jenife was a daughter of the Innkeeper, and she stood by and was the second of those who took the Babe into her arms. What should this mean in thy experience? Is it any wonder that you have looked long into the faces of those who were newly born, and wondered what their purpose, hardships, joys, and sorrows would be in the earth?

In that time, she not only beheld the experiences of the shepherds, but also heard the words of the sages of the East who came bringing gifts to Him whom it had been proclaimed of old should come again. And He will come again and again in the hearts, minds, and experiences of those who love His coming. But those who, when they think about Him, and know what His Presence would mean, and become fearful, He passes by. This will be the same as it was in that sojourn, when many heard but harkened not to the simple words of Him who gave, "Know thyself; know that thy Father abideth in' thee. And if ye love Him, ye may know His ways, His experiences."

In connection with interpreting the records of this entity, it would be well to show how a soul's records are made and kept, and how they may be read. For the entity's study of the records will attune the consciousness with respect to the reality of life. And the entity may come to know that the expression of life in the material world is the expression of the force called God.

Upon the skein of time and space, the records are

made. For thoughts and deeds are things, and their currents run with time and space and make their impressions there. It is like in the mental, where, as a man thinketh in his heart, so is he. Then as ye turn within to meet your Maker, and as ye abide in Him and He in the Father, ye will have the influences within your inner self which will create that which He gave, "There will be brought to thy remembrance all things from the foundation of the world, that ye have need of in thine experience for the glorifying of the Father through the Son".

In that sojourn, Jenife (1152) was just a year younger than the little Mother who came to the Inn where the entity helped her parents. And she knew of the event through the meetings which were half forbidden by those in the Jewish law, and questioned by the authorities for the penal law. She was filled with wonder and desire to know about the occurrence, and she felt that some great thing in the experience of the world was about to come to pass.

The entity, named (Jenife) Sarapha, or Sara (1152), requested that she might aid in the preparation of the quarters for the Mother-to-be and father, who were revered by all. For the leaders had arranged with the Innkeeper for the care which must be provided for them when they came to register for their contribution to the Romans. Yet, as the entity waited, expectant, there was the general rabble, and there were the discussions of those who journeyed to Jerusalem for the meetings, as well as to the centers for their tax registration.

Sara was attractive, and was sought by one of the registrars as a companion; yet she rejected him. She has met him in the present sojourn, and the association has been both helpful and disturbing.

Then, Sara helped so that all was in readiness. And the late afternoon sun shone in all its glory on the Palestine hills, as if the voice of nature were proclaiming the heralding of a new hope, a new birth to the earth, and the glorifying of man's hope in God. The spectre of His Star in the evening sky brought awe and wonder to all who saw it. And Sara, being anxious, gazed with wondering awe at that unusual experience. And she wept with joy in expectancy of a glory surpassing what had been told of all the glories of her people in the days of old. There, she felt similar to the experience at present, that a new light, a new vision, and a new experience were being born in every atom of her being.

When she knew that the den, the cave, the stable had been occupied, she felt consumed with desire to rush off to see what was happening. And as soon as her work was finished about the home, she started for the stable. But as she walked into the open, the brightness of His Star came nearer and nearer. And she heard, even as the shepherds, "Peace on earth, Good Will to Men". Again, she felt the awe, and the feeling of a new creation and a new experience as she, with the closer attendant of the Mother, hastened. And all the rabble and all the jeers of a world were stopped.

She hastened to the quarters where the Mother lay, in all the awe of a new experience, and as the light as from His Star filled the place, she first beheld the Babe. That was the crowning experience until the plea that she, too, might hold the glorious Child in her arms. And as this became a reality, she had the feeling, oh that the world might know the beauty, joy, and glory of His Life in their own hearts, minds, and beings.

There, she saw the shepherds gather. And on the next day, she saw the Wise Men, with their ladened camels; and she heard their praise for those who had kept the faith in preserving, keeping, and helping those who were in need and alone, yet having God with them. She heard the strange tongues spoken by the Wise Men, and knew and felt the reverence and awe which were experienced by all.

Sara sought to keep in touch with the Mother and Child; and when the edict was declared, her heart was filled with fear. For her experience was something to be cherished; yet she feared the law, and the hatred which would naturally arise in the hearts of those who were persecuted. For often was her father questioned as to which way the Wise Men went, and as to the activities of these men who defied the authorities of Rome, as well as of Herod the king.

For days, weeks, and months, she wondered. And the necessity for menial labor at the Inn brought her mental and material distress. Yet often in the stillness of the evening, she reviewed the events, and wondered what had become of His Star, His Light.

After the receding of the Star, she learned of the flight into Egypt through the devious ways in which news came by word of mouth, and yet was kept secret. All of these experiences have become an innate part of her, so that when she sits alone in the twilight, she can almost again feel the music of the spheres, and the singing of the morning stars, as the earth is quieted. And there enters again that peace, which is only troubled by the cares of a workaday world.

In the years that followed, she became closer to those in Bethany and upon Mount Olive; for she took up her abode upon the edge of Olivet, on the road that led to the great city. And there, word was sought again of what had become of the participants in that marvelous event which had become a burning memory in her heart. Yet when persecutions came from the Romans, and from the Sadducees who persecuted especially the groups to which she had belonged and from which she had received so much help, doubts and fears arose within her.

From what she heard, the Child had apparently become only another child among the people. And not until the

days when He went again with His parents and a great
company to again register did she learn the truth of
what had happened. This was when it was commanded
that the Passover feast should be kept by all the children of Israel, and she sought again that glorious Child
who questioned the doctors. And she kept close that she
might hear. By this time, Sara had put away all
thoughts of association or union with men, although she
was often disturbed about it. Hence, she became what
might be called the first individual to dedicate mind,
body, and purpose to a child.

From time to time, she sought word of His progress,
following His life almost like a story. And she held to
the memories of that evening when she saw the light,
and the Child in the Mother's arms. Also, she relived
many times the glorious moment when the Child had
been placed in her own arms, and she had pressed her
lips to the brow of the Babe.

When the ministry of Jesus began, she learned every
word which could be gathered from those who heard
Him often. And when His visits brought Him near, and
yet her duties kept her close to home near the highways
over which throngs often passed, she became fearful because of the things that were said. The rejection of His
own people when He first began His ministry, brought
tears of scalding shame to her for the ones who seemed
to doubt when they should know.

At last came the triumphal entry from Bethany to the
Temple in Jerusalem, and Sara was among the great
throng which cried, "Hosanna to the Highest; the King
cometh". Again, she was disappointed when that
glorious man among men was not proclaimed king. And
He seemed to exert so little of His power to help those
who were sick, or in doubt or fear. For the entity knew
many who had been healed. And she was especially
close to Bartaemus who had often rested on the road
close to her home.

After the Crucifixion, she was with the Holy Women and others who sustained the household which was beginning to feel that possibly the Mother, Mary, had misjudged. Yet Sara knew from her own experience; for she had not forgotten that choir before the celestial throne which sang: "Glory, Glory in the highest. Peace, peace on earth to all men of good will."

She held to those experiences, and they are innate in the present. She was among the first to suffer martyrdom because of the roughness of the Romans as they attempted to disperse the crowds. As a result of her injuries, broken in body, she suffered in the flesh. But then, as now, she looked ever to Him who is life, light, and immortality to those who put their trust wholly in Him.

For those who have tasted, felt, and known within themselves that He is the Way, the Truth, and the Light—no other name is given under heaven whereby man may be made whole, or whereby man may know his true relationships to God.

Hold fast to that, O Daughter of the Innkeeper, O the Beholder of His Glory. O the joyous, gracious feelings that fill thy soul and being with the richness of the earth poured out at His feet. You were with the lowly shepherds who came to see that glorious sight; and they, too, were not hindered from beholding the face of their Savior.

And ye, too, O Daughter, may know His face; but turn within. For there ye may meet Him, as so often ye did in those days, weeks, months, and years, as ye recounted in your inner self the glorious events of that day when the Babe, the Child Jesus, lay in your arms.

For He is very near unto all who call on His Holy name. He has promised, and His promises are sure to

you, and in you may you know. Listen to those things
which you heard when wonder was so much a portion
of your experience. Embrace Him now, even as ye did
on the glorious day when the earth saw, heard, and felt
her King, her Maker. So may ye, too, take on God in
Him, and become a part of His dealings with man.

To become purified, if ye will but empty thyself, ye may
be filled with that glory, even as you were then. Count
not judgments as the judgments of man. For man
looketh on the outward appearance, but God seeth the
heart, and the purpose, will, and desire there.

You merited being the Innkeeper's daughter because, in
your previous experiences, you had been seeking and
willing to dedicate yourself. O that man would gain the
willingness to be a channel to be used, even as He gave,
"Not my will but Thine, O God, be done in and through
me". That has been the cry and the experience of all,
even as Sara, who may come to know His face.

As the Innkeeper's daughter, you helped to care for the
home and the Inn. Following the persecutions, and at
last the death of your father, you prepared and kept an
inn on the Mount of Olives near Bethany, on the road
from Jerusalem to Gizeh.

There were in that sojourn some doubts and fears with
respect to why the other members of His family could
not see in the Child and the Man, that which had been
experienced by the entity. After the Crucifixion and
Resurrection, there was greater knowledge, and even
many of the Romans admitted, "Indeed, this was the
Son of God". Then you were closely associated with
Ruth (1158), the sister of Jesus, but only for a short
time. For Ruth was among the people of another class
or group who were to be hated for their part in her own
father's death, and for the persecutions and questions
prior thereto.

(Then) give your Christmas Reading wherever there may be an audience. For from this day forth, this will have a new meaning, not only to you, but also to your listeners. In His name, then, may the blessings of the Father, in the Christ, be upon thee and thy efforts to point the Way to the Child, Jesus, who in His humbleness and glory made Himself as man, that men might know the love of God to the sons of men that seek to know His ways. Amen. (1152)

THE EARLY YEARS AND MINISTRY

Flight into Egypt

The earthly sojourn of Sophie or Josie (1010) would have a great deal of influence, and lay the foundation for giving much historical data. Not that it would be materially helpful, but it would add information with respect to those mysterious surroundings. For her sojourn was when the Master was born in the earth, in Bethlehem of Judea, and He was of the city of Nazareth. It was when the proclamations were made by Herod for the destruction of the young, and when Joseph was warned to flee into Egypt, that the prophecy might be fulfilled, "Lo, my son has been called from Egypt", as given by Jeremiah and Isaiah.

She was with the Holy Family in the capacity of hand-maid to the Mother and Child, and waited on Joseph. For she dwelt by the brooks or the portions where there were wells, in the upper portion of the Egyptian land to which they fled.

During the journey, she ministered to them; and it was no short distance for a very young Mother and Child. And the ministering in that sojourn, first to the Mother and Child, and (in later years) to the aging Joseph, has given her the ability which she now has to minister to the needs of those who are ill in body and mind. This

applies to both nursing and care. Josie was close to the
Innkeeper who made the preparations for the birth, owing to the close association of the Holy Family to the
Essenes and the holy ones who protected them. She
gained in soul development. After the return of the
family to Capernaum, and the other children came to
Mary, she still ministered to them. And the activities of
the growing child Jesus, His teachings and ministerings,
all became a portion of her experience. Yet she was
much disturbed by the manner in which the members of
the family deserted the teachings, owing to their
economic needs.

In applying yourself, study again and again that which
has been written. And you will gradually become conscious and aware that in Him is the Light that lightens
the world, and that only in living His way may we be
like Him. Such awareness may come only by being the
character of individual with the purpose and attitude
which He manifested ever. Though He came to His own
and His own received Him not, never did He rail at
them. Never did He manifest anything other than
gentleness, kindness, brotherly love, and patience with
those who were the most unkind.

The entity's activities then were directed toward keeping and preserving the family intact, following the death
of Joseph. For this, she saw; and she closed his eyes
and laid him to rest.

As the entity reads of those activities, there will come
more and more an awakening. Read especially the first
chapter of John, and the first, second, and third John.
For the second epistle of John *as a letter, was directed
to Josie by John the Beloved.* Read also the fourteenth,
fifteenth, sixteenth, and seventeenth chapters of John.
And as you read it, you will find that even He is speaking to thee.

Look not for discarnate (occult) influences. Instead,

know that the promise, "As ye abide in me and love me and keep my commandments", is to thee. This is from the Maker, the Giver of all good and perfect gifts, even Jesus who became the Christ, and gave Himself a ransom for thee and thy friends, and for the world in which ye labor. (1010)

Quienllo was among the rulers in Herod's court. And he was one of them who carried out the search under the decree for beheading or death of the male children in the land. This was when the cry went up to the powers on high for the weeping in Israel.

In service rendered, he gained in soul development. But in taking advantage of the oppressions to secure personal gain, he lost. (1629)

Jacobinus (daughter of Leveudus) was in Palestine, or the Promised Land, when many about Nazareth, Bethany, and Capernaum suffered from the edict of the ruler, Herod the Great, who only ruled with a reflected power. And she was one of the mothers whose young were taken from them by the edict, for the destruction of the children so that the Son of Mary might be destroyed also.

Her name was Jacobinus, and she came to know Elizabeth, the mother of John, the forerunner, as a real friend. Later, she was familiar with the works of many who followed the teachings of Him of Capernaum and Galilee.

You fear the darkness, because of the destruction by the soldiers. For the young were hidden in darkness, and they took the body unaware.

The eyes which you see during meditation have a meaning. For the soul which you lost in Nazareth may come again to you in this incarnation, if you will make yourself a channel for such an event.

You have a great love for children because of what He gave, "It is as Rachel weeping for her children, and is not comforted until she knows that which was lost there is in her arms materially again". This may bring to you an awakening which no other experience may, for in Him will be the blessing to many. (578)

Ruth (not the sister of Jesus, but another named Ruth) lived during the turmoils, and when the preparations were being made by individuals and groups who expected the coming of the Prince of Peace. She was one of the mothers who suffered under the edict of Herod; Hence, she was rebellious against the people who favored religious freedom or rote.

As a result, it was not until the latter portion of that sojourn, when she came under the influence of the teachings of Bartholomew and Titus, that she realized the real import of what had happened.

Then she knew how she, even as a mother, had been martyr to a cause. At that time, she became a personal aid to members of the church which was established in Jerusalem. And she suffered with the persecuted, yet strengthened the weak during the persecutions. She did not see the Crucifixion of the Lord. (308)

With the return of the Mother and Joseph to Nazareth there was the edict that all children up to two years of age, were to be destroyed. Indeed, did Rachel weep for her sons. (5749-16)

Q. Why do historians like Josephus ignore the massacre of the innocents, and the history of Christ, when they record minute details of all other historical events?

A. What was the purpose of Josephus' writing—for the Jews or for the Christian? This answers itself.

Q. What new light can you throw on this obscure portion of history?

A. Those very happenings of that land were written by
the entity Thesea . . . a queen of no mean estate who
took hold upon the words of the Master, though never
personally coming in contact with Him; for the entity
then was the companion, or wife, of Herod who sought
His destruction; yet Thesea sought a closer comprehension of the Wise Men. . . . For as she reasoned with the
Essenes, as well as conversed with the Wise Men who
came with new messages to the world, the entity proclaimed yea, that same announcement that He, Himself,
then being announced, had given (as Ioshua): "Others
may do as they may, but as for me and my house, we
will serve the living God".

Hence the entity wrote concerning those people,
through the periods of the Prophets to the periods when
the announcement had come to those groups who
sought for His coming. And these (writings) were a
part of the records as destroyed in the Alexandrian
Library, as well as in the city in the hills and the plains.

Thesea (wife of Herod) was not entirely Jewish, not
entirely Roman, but chosen because of her beauty, as
well as for political influence. For the entity's brother-
in-law was a priest, and he—Caiaphas (the Elder)—made overtures to Herod, in his proclaiming the
closer relationships to the Roman Rule. This—as well
as the early education of the entity—fitted the entity for
the social as well as political affiliations, for the
companion of one in such a position (as Herod). Yet
these were never very close as would be considered for
companions of that period. (2067)

Owing to the conditions which arose from the visit of
the Wise Men and their not returning to Herod to
report, the decrees were issued that there should be the
destruction of the children of that age from six months
to two years, especially in that region from Bethlehem
to Nazareth. (1010)

This (action by Herod) brought abhorrence, and a

turning-away from any close associations with the activitities of her companion at the period.

(Hers) was not an easy life through the sojourn, for the
entity was wedded when only fourteen . . . and lived until the experiences of that announcement of the Christian or Christ experience (i.e. the announcement of His
birth).

Q. What vital statistics can be given for Thesea, the
Roman Queen of Palestine?
A. Beginning 28 B.C. and extending to A.D. 6. As to
the children, there were only two and neither of these
became the ruler, but were associated with the ruler in a
portion of the divided district.

As to the appearance; five feet, six inches of height;
black of hair; almost blue of eyes; prominent cheeks but
a great deal of color in the general or whole figure or
make-up; weight 129 lb.

The death was brought about by the decrees issued
before the *carcinoma germs brought death to Herod*
himself—because of his aversion to her living beyond
the period of Herod, and the order issued by him before
his death. (2067)

Q. Getting back to the activities of the Holy Family,
please tell what happened next.
A. There was that journey into Egypt, which is recorded
in the varied manners in Matthew and in Luke. To
many there might be questionings as to whether Mary
was informed of the necessity for the flight, or merely
Joseph—as Matthew records. However, as we find,
they were of one mind, and the flight into Egypt—as is
recorded—was the fulfilling of the prophecy. For, it
had been said, "and my son shall be called from
Egypt", as given by Jeremiah as well as Isaiah. (5749-
16)

Q. That must have been a very perilous journey.

A. Do not understand that there were only Joseph, Mary, and the Child. For there were other groups which preceded and followed, so that there might be physical protection for that which had been considered by these groups of poeple as the fulfilling of the Promised One . . . (also) soon after the birth there was the issuing of orders—first by Judy—that there should be some-one selected to be with the parents during their period of sojourn in Egypt. . . .

Thus the entity, Josie, was selected or chosen by those of the Brotherhood—sometimes called White Brother-hood in the present—as the handmaid or companion of Mary, Jesus, and Joseph in their flight into Egypt. . . .

This began on an evening, and the journey through por-tions of Palestine, from Nazareth to the borders of Egypt, was made only during the night, dwelling by the brooks or the portions where there were wells, in the upper portion of the Egyptian land to which they fled . . . close to what was then Alexandria.

During those periods of the journey, the entity ministered; and it was no mean distance for a very young child and a very young mother. (1010)

In the journey to Egypt, little of great significance might be indicated, but the care and attention to the Child and the Mother was greatly in the hands of this entity, Josie, through that journey.

The period of sojourn in Egypt was in and about, or close to, what was then Alexandria.

Josie and Mary were not idle; during that period of so-journ, but those records—that had been a part of those activities preserved in portions of the libraries there—were a part of the work that had been

designated for this entity. And the interest in same was
reported to the Brotherhood in the Judean country.
(1010-17)

The sojourn there was a period of some four
years—four years, six months, three days.

When there were those beginnings of the journey back
to the Promised Land, there were naturally—from
some of the records that had been read by the entity Josie, as well as the parents—the desires to know whether
there were those unusual powers indicated in this child
now, that was in every manner a normal developed
body, ready for those activities of children of that particular period.

Hence much of the early education, the early activities,
were those prompted or directed by that leader in that
particular experience, but were administered by—or in
the closer associations by—Josie. Though from the idea
of the Brotherhood the activities of the entity were no
longer necessitated, the entity Josie preferred to remain—and did remain until those periods when there
was the sending or the administering of the teachings to
the young Master, first in Persia and later in India, and
then in Egypt again—where there were the comple-
tions.

But the entity, Josie, following the return, was active in
all the educational activities as well as in the care of the
body and the attending to those things pertaining to the
household duties with every developing child. And Josie
was among those who went with Mary and Joseph when
they went to the city, or to Jerusalem, at the time of the
age of twelve. It was thought by Joseph and Mary that
it was in the care of Josie that He had stayed, when He
was missed, in those periods when there was the returning to find Him in the temple.

Josie (1010) was with Mary throughout those activities. And is it any wonder that when there were those preparations of the body for burial that Josie was the one who brought the spices, the ointments, that were to consecrate the preparations of this body for whom it had cared through those early periods of its experience in the earth?

Q. What was the nature of the records studied by Josie in Egypt?

A. Those same records from which the men of the East said and gave, "By those records we have seen his star". These pertained, then, to what you would call to-day astrological forecasts, as well as those records which had been compiled and gathered by all of those of that period pertaining to the coming of the Messiah. These had been a part of the records from those in Carmel, in the early experiences, as of those given by Elijah, who was the forerunner, who was the cousin, who was the Baptist. All of these had been a part of the records—pertaining not only to the nature of work of the parents but as to their places of sojourn, and the very characteristics that would indicate these individuals; the nature and the character that would be a part of the experiences to those coming in contact with the young Child; as to how the garments worn by the Child would heal children. For the body being perfect radiated that which was health, life itself. Just as today, individuals may radiate, by their spiritual selves, health, life, that vibration which is destruction to disease in any form in bodies. These were the characters and natures of things studied by Josie.

For, is it not quoted oft, "All of these things she kept, and pondered them in her heart"? With what? With the records that Josie as well as herself (Mary) had seen. These records were destroyed, of course, in a much later period.

Q. Can any more details be given as to the training of the Child?

A. Only those that covered the period from six years to about sixteen which were in keeping with the tenets of the Brotherhood; as well as that training in the law—which was the Jewish or Mosaic law in that period. This was read, this was interpreted in accordance with those activities defined and outlined for the parents and the companions of the developing body. Remember and keep in mind, He was normal. He developed normally. Those about Him saw those characteristics that may be anyone's who wholly puts the trust in God! And to every parent might it not be said, daily, dedicate thy life that thy offspring may be called of God into service—to the glory of God and to the honor of thy name! (1010-17)

Much might be given as to how or why and when there were the purposes that brought about the materialization of Jesus in the flesh. In giving then the history:

. . . Then there was the return to Judea and to Capernaum, where dwelt many of those who were later the closer companions of the Master.

Here, after the period again of presentation at the Temple, when there were those questionings among the groups of the leaders, the entity then was sent again into Egypt for only a short period, and then into India, and then into what is now Persia.

Hence in all the ways of the teachers the entity was trained.

From Persia he was called to Judea at the death of Joseph, and then into Egypt for the completion of the preparation as a teacher.

He was with John, the Messenger, during the portion of the training there in Egypt.

Then to Capernaum, Cana, and those periods of the first preparation in the land of the nativity.

The rest ye have according to Mark, John, Matthew and Luke; these in their order record most of the material experiences of the Master.

Many of the details may be given in the varied fields of the preparation, but these were the experiences. (5749-7)

The Stay in Egypt

The period of stay in Egypt was something over two and one-half years—until another ruler was in authority or power. (5749-16)

Note: Reading 5749-6 states, "There (Egypt) five years were spent, as ye term time." This gives a period that is twice as long, to be sure, but both could be true if the longer time included the journeys from and back to Judea.

Q. Did the Holy Family return then to Nazareth?
A. The return was made to Capernaum, not Nazareth; not only for political reasons, because of the death of Herod, but (also because of) the division that had been made within the kingdom after the death of Herod, and (so that) there might be the ministry or teaching which was to be a role of the Brotherhood (supervised in that period by Judy, as one among the leaders of the Essenes in that particular period). (1010)

Q. Was Jesus as a child also able to perform miracles as the Catholic Church claims, and was He clairaudient, clairvoyant, and did He remember His past incarnations?

A. Read the first chapter of John and you will see. As to the activity of the child; the apparel brought more of

such influences as today would be called lucky charm
or lucky chance. Not as a consciousness. This began—
the consciousness—with the ministry. From that period
when He sought the activities from the entrance to the
Temple and disputing or conversing with the Rabbi at
the age of twelve. Thus His seeking for study, through
the associations with the teachers, at that period.
(2067)

Q. Were there any others besides Josie who were associated with the training or early education of Jesus?
A. [Yes, To regress slightly,] Sofa was one of the
women educated to service in the temple (of the
Essenes). . . . The entity was chosen by—what would
be, what is termed in the Kabala—the moving of the
symbols on the vesture of the priest . . . to be the attendant or the nurse to the babe when there was the
birth then of John—for remember he was not called the
Baptist until after his death. In the periods of training,
the entity Sofa also acted as the instructor, as one in the
position to look after or care for one in those periods.
[And too often there is not sufficient attention to the
care of the developing body through those first eighteen
months or two years.]

Then, Sofa was associated with Jesus: with the last year
of the experience (of the Child Jesus) in the household
of Mary and Joseph. While the offices had been fulfilled by that one, as we have indicated, the entity was
especially given this office to indicate the nature, the
character of the cousin (the forerunner, John). (2175)

Q. At what time after the birth of Jesus did Mary and
Joseph take up the normal life of a married couple, and
bring forth the issue called James?
A. Ten years. Then came in succession: James, the
daughter Ruth, and Jude. (5749-7)

This incarnation was Ruth's outstanding one. She had
glory, yet suffering; turmoil, yet joy; beautiful experiences, yet sorrow and shame. For she was in the

land where the Master walked, and she was (Ruth) the daughter of Mary—Mother of The Lord. (1158)

Jude lived in the days when the Master came into the Promised Land. *And he followed closely in the ways of the Teachings, as set by Him, being His brother in the flesh.* In the present, he has a leniency toward all laws concerning every mode of worship to Jehova, and a respect for every person's own belief. (137)

Q. Please give facts about Jesus' education in Palestine, the schools He attended, how long, what He studied and under what name He was registered.

A. The periods of study in Palestine were only at the time of His sojourn in the Temple or in Jerusalem during those periods when He was quoted by Luke as being among the Rabbi, or teachers. His studies in Persia, India, and Egypt covered much greater periods. He was always registered under the name Jeshua. (2067)

Q. How closely was Judy, the head of the Essenes, associated with Jesus in His Palestine sojourn?

A. For a portion of the experience the entity Judy was the Teacher. How close? So close that the very heart and purposes were proclaimed as to those things that were traditions! For the entity sent Him to Persia, to Egypt, yea to India, that there might be completed the more perfect knowledge of the material ways in the activities of Him who became the Way, the Truth! (1471)

Q. Tell about Judy teaching Jesus, where and what subjects she taught him, and what subjects she planned to have him study abroad.

A. The prophecies! Where? In her home. When? During those periods from his twelfth to his fifteenth-sixteenth year, when he went to Persia and then to India. In Persia, when his father died. In India when John first went to Egypt—where Jesus joined him and both became the initiates in the pyramid or temple there.

Q. What subjects did Judy plan to have him study abroad?
A. What you would today call astrology.

Q. At what major events in Jesus' life was Judy present—such as casting out of demons, healing, feeding five thousand, etc.?
A. At his teaching—for a period of some five years.

Q. Was she present at any of the healings or the feeding of the multitudes?
A. Those where she chose to, but, she was very old then. She lived to be sufficiently old to know, of course, of the feeding of the first five thousand. She was present, but rather as one that brought the crowds together, than as contributing to the activities at the time. For, there the divisions arose, to be sure.

Q. Was Judy present at the Crucifixion or the Resurrection?
A. No. In spirit—that is, in mind—present. For, remember, Judy's experience at that time was such that she might be present in many places without the physical body being there! (2067-11)

Q. Under whom did He study in India?
A. Kahjian.

Q. Under whom in Persia?
A. Junner.

Q. Egypt?
A. Zar.

Q. Please outline the teachings which were received in India, Persia, and Egypt.
A. (In India), those cleansings of the body as related to preparation for strength in the physical, as well as in the mental man. In the travels and in Persia, the unison of forces as related to those teachings of that given by Zu

and Ra. In Egypt, that which had been the basis of all the teachings in those of the Temple, and the after actions of the crucifying of self in relationship to ideals, and (which) made for the abilities of carrying on that called to be done. (5749-2)

Q. Please describe Jesus' education in Egypt—in the Essene schools of Alexandria and Hilleopolis—in more detail; naming some of His outstanding teachers and subjects studied?

A. Not in Alexandria; rather in Hilleopolis for the periods of attaining to the priesthood; in the taking of the examinations there, as did John. One was in one class, one in the other. Not (with) teachers, but being examined by them. Passing the tests there. These tests—as they have been since their establishment—were tests through which one attained to that place of being accepted or rejected by the influences of the mystics, as well as of the various groups or schools in other lands. .

For, as indicated oft through this channel (Cayce) the unification of the teachings of many lands were brought together in Egypt; for that was the center from which there was to be the radial activity of influence in the Earth—as indicated by the first establishing of those tests on the recording of time as it has been, was, and is to be until the new cycle is begun. (2067)

Q. Please describe Jesus' initiation in Egypt, telling if the Bible reference to three days and nights in the grave or tomb—possibly in the shape of a cross—indicates a special initiation.

A. This is a portion of the initiation. It is a part of the passage through which each soul is to attain its development, as has the world through each period, of its incarnation in the earth; just as the record of the earth through the passage through the tomb, or the pyramid, is supposed to be that through which each soul, each entity, as an initiate, must pass for the attaining to the releasing of same—as indicated by the empty tomb which has never been filled, see! Only Jesus was able to break same, which indicated His fulfillment. And there, as the initiate, He went out for the passing through the initiation by fulfilling—as indicated by the baptism in the Jordan. . . . He passed from that activity into the wilderness to meet that which had been His undoing in the beginning. (2067)

Q.   Did Jesus study under Greek philosophers? And was it through educational contacts that the Greeks later came to Him to beg Him to come to their country when the Jews cast Him out?
A.   We do not find such. Jesus, as Jesus, never appealed to the worldly wise.

Q.   Why does not the Bible tell of Jesus' education, or are there manuscripts now on earth that will give these missing details?
A.   There are some that have been forged manuscripts. All those that existed were destroyed—that is, the originals—with the activities in Alexandria. (2067)

Q.   Are there any written records which have not been found of His teachings?
A.   More (written records), rather, of those of His close associates; and those records that are yet to be found regarding the preparation of the Man, of the Christ, in those (records) of the tomb—or those yet to be uncovered in the pyramid.

Q.   When will this chance be given for these to be uncovered?
A.   When there has been sufficient of the reckoning through which the world is passing in the present. (364-3)

Q.   Before going further upon the ministry of Jesus we should like to get something straightened out; It has been given that Jesus lived and died a man; also, it has been given that "God so loved the world that He gave His only begotten Son". Please explain these things to us. How may we regard the truth of Jesus in relation to the Jewish and Christian religion, and to all other religions of the world?

A. In that the man, Jesus, manifested in the world the Oneness of His will with the Father, He becomes—from man's viewpoint—the only, the first begotten of the Father. Thus He is the example of the world, whether Jew, Gentile or any other religious force. (364-9)

Hast thou not found that the essence, the truth, the real truth is One? Mercy and justice; peace and harmony. For without Moses and his leader Joshua [that was bodily Jesus at another time in the earth] there *is* no Christ. Christ is not a man! Jesus was the man; Christ, the messenger; Christ in all ages: Jesus in one, Joshua in another, Melchizedek in another; these be those that led Judaism! These be they that came as that Child of Promise, as to the Children of Promise; And the promise is in thee, that ye lead as He has given thee, "Feed my sheep". (991-1)

Then, though He were the first of man (as Adam, as explained before), the first of the sons of God in spirit, in flesh, it became necessary that He fulfill all those associations, those connections that were to wipe away in the experience of man that which separates him from his Maker. (5749-6)

In this we find the True Advocate with the Father, in that He—as Man—manifested in the flesh the ability of flesh to make fleshly desires one with the will of the spirit—for God is spirit, and they who worship Him must worship in spirit and in truth; just as Jesus manifested in the flesh. He was able to partake of the Divine because He made all laws susceptible to His mandate by His will being one with the Father. Since He took on all law, He became a law unto himself.

(The compliance even with an earthly, or material law enables the person to *be* the law.) In that example, Jesus, who lived as a man, who died as a man, became the example of all who would approach the throne of God. (364-9)

Q. What is the significance and meaning of the words "Jesus" and "Christ" as they should be understood and applied?

A. Jesus is the man—the activity, the mind, the relationships that He bore to others. Yea, He was mindful of friends, He was sociable, He was loving, He was kind, He was gentle. He grew faint, He grew weak, and yet gained that strength which He had promised in becoming the Christ, by fulfilling and overcoming the world. Ye are made strong in body, in mind, in soul and purpose, by that power in Christ. The power, then, is in the Christ. The pattern is in Jesus. (2533)

Q. You have already mentioned that after Jesus' baptism by John in the River Jordan, He went into the wilderness "to meet that which had been His undoing in the beginning". Did He spend those 40 days alone, or did he have his disciples with Him?

A. When pointed out by John (the Baptist) as the "one that should be greater and increase as he decreased", Andrew (who was) first an adherent and a disciple of that teacher (John), and remained close as an aide, from first conviction until the appearance of Jesus . . . then followed the new leader into the wilderness, and was close with Him during the temptation [as is recorded by Matthew]. With the return to the seashore, (Andrew) sought out the brother (Peter), telling of those ideas, ideals, as were propounded by Him who had been pointed out, and became the close disciple then of the Teacher and Master. (341)

Q. Was this the time that James and John, the sons of Zebedee, also became disciples?

A. Not only the brothers but those employed by the

brothers joined in . . . (for) the (business) activities of
Zebedee required that the purposes and aims be rather
carried on through or by agents. Or, to put in the
parlance of the present, the entity was rather in the fishing business as a wholesaler, than being in active service himself. As indicated, or given, that "as He passed
by He saw James and John with their father Zebedee
mending their nets"; rather were the brothers and the
father supervising and reasoning with the employees as
to their activities. (540)

It is sometimes judged that most of the disciples were
poor, but this was not true. For Zebedee and his sons,
Matthew the Publican, all who were closely associated
were rather well-to-do! Peter and Andrew, of course,
were servants or laborers with the sons of Zebedee, but
Zebedee was among the wealthy—and among those
closely associated with those in authority.

John . . . was the wealthiest of the disciples of the
Christ. His estate would be counted in the present in
American money as being near to a quarter of a million
dollars . . . he was influential with those in Roman and
Jewish power at the period. (1151)

The Wedding in Cana

Q. The first recorded miracle is at the wedding in Cana
of Galilee when the Master changed water into wine.
Would you please give a complete word picture of the
event with such details as weather, names of people in
wedding, food and drink, games and dances, etc.?
A. That came about soon after the return of the Master
from the Jordan and His dwelling by the sea, His conversation with Peter—after Andrew had told Peter of
the happenings at the Jordan—(then) there was the
wedding in Cana of Galilee.

The girl was a relative of those close to the Mother of
Jesus, who prepared the wedding feast—as was the

custom in that period, and is yet among those of the Jewish faith who adhere to the traditions as well as custom of those people chosen as the channel because of their purpose with God.

The girl to be wed was a daughter of a cousin of Mary, a daughter of a younger sister of Elizabeth, whose name was also Mary. And she was the one spoken of as "The Other Mary", and not as some have supposed.

The customs required that there be a feast which was composed of the roasted lamb with the herbs; the breads that had been prepared in the special ways which were the custom and tradition of those who followed close to the faith of Moses' law, Moses' custom, Moses' ordinances.

The families of Mary were present as well as those of the groom

The groom, in the name of Roael, was among the sons of Zebedee; being an older brother of James and John who later became the close friends and closer followers of Jesus.

The Master, returning with those who were hangers-on, naturally sought to speak with His mother. Learning of this happening, He too—with the followers—were bid to remain at the feast.

Much wine was part of the custom. The day was what ye could call June third. There were plenty of flowers and things of the field, yet only a part of those things needed, for the custom called for more of the meats prepared with certain herbs and wines.

The day had been fine; the evening was fair; the moon was full. This then brought the activities with the imbibing more and more of wine, more hilarity, and the dance—which was in the form of the circles that were part of the customs, not only of that land then, but that are in your own land now and then being revived.

With those activities, as indicated, the wine ran low. Remember, the sons of Zebedee were among those of the upper class, as would be termed; not the poorer ones. Thus the reason why Mary served or prepared the feast for her relatives.

From those happenings that were a portion of her (Mary's) experience upon their return from Egypt—as to how the increase had come in the food when they had been turned aside as they journeyed back toward the Promised Land—Mary felt, knew, and was convinced within herself that here again there might be such an experience, with her son returning as a man starting upon His mission.

For what was the pronouncement to the mother when Gabriel spoke to her? What was the happening with Elizabeth when the mother spoke to her?

This might be called a first period of test. For had He not just ten days ago sent Satan away, and received ministry from the angels? This had come to be known as hearsay: Hence (there was) the natural questioning of the mother love for the purposes—this son, strange in many ways—had chosen, by the dwelling in the wilderness for the forty days, and then His returning to the lowly people, the fishermen, about this country. It brought on the questioning by the Mother. (5749-15)

Xaneres was in the land of Promise when the Master walked in the earth. And he was of the priesthood and closely associated with Zacharias. He announced by the blowing of the ram's horn, the various services in the Temple, such as the morning and evening sacrifice, the times when the offerings might be accepted by the priests, or the activities of the sacrificial priests at the altars.

Hence, he knew much of the activities and experiences of John, as well as the procedure in the Temple when the child Jesus was presented before the priests, which was required by Jewish law.

Thus, the entity's whole activities during that sojourn related to ritual, or to circumstances which were mental and spiritual. While his name was Grecian, he was of the children of Judah who had taken other names in order to preserve the interest of the Parthenians, Samaritans, and Essenes. Hence, while he was in good repute with the rest of the leaders, he had much knowledge of the mysterious influences pertaining to the reasons for the coming of the Wise Men, and of their teachings, in addition to the education of John and Jesus to become teachers and leaders. (1581)

Myra was in the earth when the Master came as a Babe, and she was in the household of Salone, a sister of Mary, the mother of the Lord. She was a babe that viewed the body and played as a child with the Holy Child. And yet she was taken, as if by the angels themselves, that she might know the realms of aid which come to those who would counsel in the flesh and in the spirit with our Lord.

(This reads as two sojourns or incarnations: The first when she played with Jesus as a Child, then passed on; the second when she was under the influence of Paul and Titus, then died at sixteen.)

After that, she was in the Roman land when individuals were subject to physical sufferings. This was because they had accepted the tenets and lessons which were being brought to the people, not only by the soldiers, but also by the teachers and ministers.

She came under the influence of Saul of Tarsus, or Paul, through the teaching of Titus, the beloved friend of Paul. (509)

Morao lived when the Master walked in the earth. She was a member of one of the families in Bethsaida, which provided a home for Him to rest. Hence, she was well acquainted with Him, and helped personally to look after the pleasure and comfort of a tired man, the Son of God. (1223)

Ponticales was in the time of the Roman activities when the Jews and the laity were being questioned. He was a Roman soldier in the service of Pontius, and under the supervision of Pilate, during the sojourn of the Son of Man, or Jesus of Nazareth, [so-called, should be Nazarite!] in Galilee, Judea, and thereabouts. (961)

She was in the land where the Master walked, and was well acquainted with the disciples, as well as with His teachings. And she knew the forerunner, John, and also Zacharias. Hence, the things that pertain to religious thought are very sacred to her. However, in such an environment or surroundings, she tends to be more tolerant with others than with herself regarding duties, obligations, or relationships through which she may attempt to express her purposes in the spiritual life.

But hold fast to that which you gained in the knowledge that He is your elder brother. He is the Way, the Truth, and the Light. He is the Law. And if we as individuals walk in that way, there will be no faltering. Condemn not, as He condemned not. For as He taught, so is it ever, "As ye do it unto the least of thy brethren, of thy acquaintances, yea thine enemies, ye do it unto Him". You were then in close association with the sons of Zebedee, and the people about the lake. Therefore, waters that are quiet, waters that are like the ripple in the brook, and the falls, have a great attraction for you at times. (1744)

Puella lived following the sojourn of the Prince of Peace. She was one of the children of the followers of the Master, who were closely associated with His household. *For she was a daughter of the sister of Joseph who was the husband of Mary, the Mother of Jesus.*

She was acquainted with the hardships of that time, the edicts of the Romans, and of the Jewish leader. And she knew of the hardships caused by priests. In the present, people who set themselves up as being an authority are as dirt to her. These she disliked. (1709)

The entity was among those who were students of the law, those who were interested in the activities having to do with questionings pertaining to the law that had been interpreted from the priests and rabbis of the day pertaining to the Mosaic law, and the interesting facts and fancies that had come from the eastern lands from which the Wise Men had come. These, as parts of the teachings, had become adopted by those groups of the Essenes of which John and Joseph and Mary had been a part before the entering of the Master, Jesus in the earth. (3344-2)

She lived when the Master walked in the earth, and was one of the children who were blessed by Him, when He taught His disciples humility on the last journey to Jerusalem. She resided in and about Bethany, and her acquaintances and kinspeople were Martha, Mary, Lazarus, and those of that city.

She was young in years then; yet she was a zealot, and was inclined to good works throughout that sojourn. She was a weaver of cloth. Hence, she will in the present always want something new to wear, with bright colors; and she will be fussy about clothes.

She was a daughter of Zelot, who was a nephew of Nicodemus, the one who went to the Master by night. Thus, she was familiar with the rulers during that period, and with the synagogue and its teachings. As a result, it will be easy to find an answering chord when you train her in spiritual things. But tell her the reason why. And remember; train one when it is young and when it is old, it will not depart from the Lord. (1775)

Smaleuen was in Palestine when the Master walked in the earth. And he was one of the scoffers in the San-hedrin. He represented the tribe of Reuben, and was of a household of that particular people. And he had represented them in the beginning of the separation of that house; *for he had himself been Reuben*. (693)

Eloise lived when the Master walked in the earth. And although she was only a child, she was among those who joined in pilgrimages to go up on the mountainside to listen to the words of the Master.

She was blessed by Him on that day when, "And He took a little child and sat it in the midst of them and said, 'lest ye become as a little child, ye shall in no wise enter in' ". And as she has heard this again and again, there has come a feeling even in her spine that, "It means me; it means me". Yet she has not held to that. For at other times, she has had the feeling instead that, "It couldn't be me; I am not worthy. It couldn't be me; I don't feel I am worthy."

He that the Lord has blessed shall never lose his hold upon that strength which His might gives to them who seek to know His way. *She was a kinsman then of Peter and Andrew*, and was close to the members of An-drew's household. Hold fast to the tenets which ye learned in those experiences. For although they caused material hardships, they brought and will bring ever in the experience of each soul the awareness that He, thy Lord, is in His holy temple, and you may meet Him there. (1129)

Before that we find the entity (Thaddeus) during that sojourn of the Prince of Peace in the earth, when men were called unto an activity in that land now known as the Promised Land, or Palestine; during those periods when there was the ministry in Galilee, even in the Holy City, even unto Tyre and Sidon.

The entity followed with the Master in these activities, in the name then Thaddeus, among those that were chosen as a light bearer to a people that had been shown a light as shining into the darkness of those periods.

Through that experience the entity gained, though oft was among those that were weighing well the material gains to be had; yet gaining throughout the sojourn, for it was among those who came under the sound of the Voice and heard, "Believe ye not for my words. For the very works' sake believe ye!" (361-4)

Patricia lived in Galilee just after the Prince or Peace came into the land. She was one of the Samaritans, which was a people misunderstood by the Jews, by their theological associates, and by the Romans. As a result, she now often finds herself disliking some things about the Jews, while at the same time favoring some of their spiritual ideals. (954)

Julia was among the Holy Women, not only when the actions of the Man of Galilee were being lauded, but also during the periods of dissension and railing, and during the sorrow because of separations.

She knew of and experienced that day upon the mount when the last benediction was given, and she is a believer in those promises. Although she has often been deceived in the promises of some of her friends, associates, or even members of her own household, this has never caused her to waver. For her belief in those promises is sure. Hold fast to that purpose which you understood then.

She was of the household of the doubter, Thomas. And she gave to many the hope and faith which had been and was a part of the experience. So may she in the present, under the very shadow of doubts and fears, create within the hearts and minds of others who seek to know His way, that hope which springs eternally anew within the human breast. And she will do this by those influences which He, the Man of Galilee, brought into the experiences of those gathered about Him there.

In her efforts, through her studies, or in organizations of one kind or another, she may bring hope to others. For it isn't those who do the great deed who are written the highest. For even as He gave, he that is the greatest among you is the servant of all. So as ye have found, and as ye may find in the present, doubt and fear are cast away when the thoughts are lifted to the hope that comes in the Cross, even the Cross of Jesus. (2272)

Matthew lived in the period when there were changes in the Land of Promise. He was called by the Master in the place of the collector of customs, and much has been given to the world about his attempt to explain the position of his people to the Master. He gained in soul development. He gained in his association, through his intent and purpose, and his desire to set others right. In the present, that which is truth to him is innate; and he desires to give to others in the manner received by himself. (417)

Zebedee lived when the Master walked in the earth. He was drawn to the Master, not only through the teachings, but also because of the material persecutions. This was when there were the interpretations of the material laws, as controlled by the proletariat, Romans, Jews, Parthenians, and Scythians.

He was one of the disciples who walked with Him, although he was not one of the chosen twelve. He labored with Peter, Andrew, John, and James; for he was the father and encouraged the young. He helped, yet kept himself partially aloof. However, when the disciples, the twelve and the seventy, were dispersed, many of them often came to him for counsel as to ways and means, and as to whether this was the true prophet and teacher.

For Zebedee was first a follower of John, and then of those who had separated themselves from the Jewish Sanhedrin and the Jewish law. And he also followed the Essenes to whom both John the Baptist and the Master came first as teachers and instructors.

He gained in soul development, although he often withheld himself when he might have attained a greater understanding. Yet he now has the ability to counsel them who seek knowledge of Him who became the Son of Man, the Son of Mary who became the Son of God. In this manner, he may now render the greatest service and thereby help his fellow man.

Remember the admonition which the Master gave, "Feed my sheep. Feed my lambs". Thus, you may attain joy, happiness, peace, and understanding; and you may know wherein you have been called. In order to prepare yourself, study to show yourself approved unto That Ideal, rightly divining the words of Truth, For He is the Word; He is that which may not be divided. But He may be divined in each word that helps you to understand the motivative force of your activities in the earth.

Meditate oft. Separate yourself for a season from the cares of the world. Get close to nature, and learn from the lowliest of that which manifests in nature. Learn from the birds, the trees, the grass, the flowers, and the bees that the life of each is manifesting and is a song of glory to its Maker. And you do likewise. Make your heart, mind, and body one with Him, then, by the laying on of hands, and by counseling with them who are weak in body and spirit. (1089)

Naomi, a sister of James and John, came under the influence of the Master in Galilee; for she was a daughter of Zebedee and a sister of those who were close to the Master.

She gained in soul development. While fears and doubts arose during the periods of persecution, she developed the ability then to be helpful to others both mentally and physically. Also, she developed within herself the purposefulness that may bring joy, peace, and harmony. Often, in her visions, she has walked closely again with the ones she knew in that sojourn.

In giving the interpretation here, do not let it become confusing because of the difference in customs or language in the present compared to your sojourn in Palestine.

The events described here are those which made impressions upon the skein of time and space. Hence, they may be often viewed by others who see them, from a different angle. Yet that is being given which may be more helpful to the entity when it reviews these events. And it may become a part of the mind which is the builder insofar as practical application is concerned.

Naomi was the daughter of Zebedee and "the other" Mary, and these individuals were not of the rabble or political elements, nor were they of great spiritual influence among the members of the group. While both Zebedee and Mary were of the Jewish or Hebraic faith, they were socially above ordinary individuals.

With respect to Mary and Zebedee, one was descended from the house of Judah, and the other from the lineage of Levi. Therefore, they were closely associated with the priesthood. Yet through Zebedee, they had contacts with the Essenes who were inclined to a more universal application of the tenets and teachings of that time.

In this environment, Naomi was born just after the birth of the Master to Joseph and Mary, who were descended from the household of Judah. And she was born between James and John, and during the period when the Master, Jesus, was in Egypt. Their home was outside of Jerusalem, near to Bethany. As a result of all of this, the influences upon Naomi during the early part of that experience were varied.

Owing to the circumstances or tradition of the group to which Zebedee belonged, it was customary to choose a vocation somewhat similar to that of the forefathers. Nevertheless, the location of their home was at variance to the general custom. This was owing to the political situations under the Roman rule, where the edicts were often contrary to those of Herod, who ruled over a part of Judea, which later became known as Galilee or Samaria, the residents of which became a questioned people.

Zebedee was not a fisherman himself, but rather was in the fishing business as a wholesaler, and carried on most of his business through agents. It was stated that, as He passed by, He saw James and John with their father Zebedee mending their net. Rather it was the brothers mending the nets, and their father was supervising the employees.

Remember the situation. Mary, the mother, was of the priesthood that was renounced by the cousin, John the Baptist. Also, the activities of the Essenes demanded that the meetings of their members should be kept secret during the conflicting edicts of the Roman ruler and of Herod. But after the death of Herod the Great, when Herod the Less came to political power, more consideration was given to these people when they called their meetings. This situation arose, then, when Naomi was nearly thirty years of age. And this was when she first became interested in these activities.

Naomi's home life, of course, was out of the ordinary, even for that time. For she was drawn between the training of her mother and the interests of her father and brother. In addition, she had associates among the Romans, as well as a position in the Jewish faith.

She was educated in schools which had teachers from Carmel, yet were connected with the activities of the people about the temple. These latter were dedicated to the service which was to bring that faith to the world today. In one section were the sisters of the orders known as Catholic, or the Church, at present. In another were the orthodox activities of the sisters of mercy among certain Jewish sects. These then, were the conditions in which Naomi, during her teen years, found herself. She was drawn between the holy activities of the Essenes, and the dedicating of herself to the faith of her fathers.

When John the Baptist first began his teaching, she joined with those of the Essene group. For John first taught that the women who desired might dedicate their lives to a specific service. Hence, not only the brothers, Peter, Andrew, and Judas (not Iscariot), but also the employees of the brothers, joined the Essenes. These employees were of the fisherfolk who aided in establishing the teachings among the people, and they held to both the old and new faith.

Naomi's complexion was fair, and she had gray eyes and dark hair, with a brownish tinge. She was a gentle person, and a good cook, a good housekeeper, a wonderful singer and interested in meditation. Not until after the teachings of the Master which resulted in the establishing of home altars, did she get married, being then thirty-four years of age. And it was when the wedding feast was held in Cana that she met the man who later became her husband. This also brought about a reconciliation with Mary and Martha and Lazarus, and a closer association with Elizabeth, the mother of John.

After Naomi's marriage, Elizabeth who was one of her own kinspeople came to live with her. This was during the time when the Holy Women dedicated their lives, bodies, purposes, and aims to the changed teachings between John the forerunner and the Master, Jesus. And the entity gained in soul development during those experiences.

The individual in this sojourn is similar to what she was in that one. She was often seen and not heard; yet she was like the women of that time; she pondered often in her heart that which she had seen and heard.

Hold fast to that purpose which you had then in your heart and soul. Some, He gave to you direct; and some you received from associates in your visits. "Abide in me and I in thee, and ye in me. Ask and it shall be given thee."

John the Beloved, Naomi's brother, may again come and be known among men (540)

Mihaieol was among the lepers healed by the Master at the gate, when the Master walked in Galilee. He was among those healed, and was "the leper at the gate". He gained in soul development, for with the cleansing came the desire to manifest that which he had found. He has the ability now to express well all of his knowledge, and to draw on his inner thoughts in both a spiritual and a physical manner, which is exemplified in a physical way. (2482)

To explain the statement, "Verily I say unto you, this generation shall not pass, till all these things be fulfilled". (it meant) The individuals who heard the things presented by the Master (eventually) would be in the earth when the prophecies described would be fulfilled. *It did not mean in that incarnation, but (that) they would return again at the time mentioned.*

To explain the Master's statement to Nicodemus, "Ye

must be born again": Nicodemus was one of the teachers and elders of the Sanhedrin. And he had access to all the information given from the time Moses received on the mount, the ordinances, and the relationships of individuals to individuals, and of the individual soul to its Maker. Much, however, had become like hearsay or omens, rather than ordinances of old.

And when Nicodemus asked, "How can such things be?" the rebuke came in His answer, "Art thou a teacher in Israel and knoweth not these things?" Ye must be born of water, of blood, or of the spirit and through the flesh. Or all must pass under the rod, even as Moses and the children of Israel passed through the sea; and they were baptized in the cloud and in the sea. This was an example or omen. It was a physical sign of a spiritual and physical separation from their sojourn in Egypt.

As the Master gave to Nicodemus, you must be born of the spirit where you may make manifest the fruits of the spirit. This would be in the earth. These (births) would not necessarily come in the order indicated in the question by Nicodemus. But the relative position would be according to the development, the necessity, the need for soul growth and for soul understanding.

The soul is a body; and the physical is the mere temple, or shell, or material manifestation of that which may not be touched by hands. For it appears that we must be born again, so that we may dwell in these mansions not made with hands, but prepared for those who have washed their robes, their bodies, their souls in the blood.

For you may know the truth, if you will manifest in your experiences that which you have learned in your meditations with your God. You must be born in flesh, and in spirit again, so that you may manifest that which you have experienced in your soul. (262-50)

He was *in the land of the Gadarenes,* where the Prince of Peace visited, and was in the company of the person that the works of Him were enacted through. (900)

Pleadila was in Gadara, in the land of Samaria, when the people of that city came to hear the Master teach by the well. He was chief counsel to the police and was one of the elders of that city.

He gained and lost in soul development. He gained throughout the time while he was occupied in his official capacity. After he accepted the teachings of the Master, dissensions arose; and he was falsely accused of using his position for his own selfish interest. These criticisms caused him a great deal of mental suffering. However, it gave him equal satisfaction and strength when he was able to prove through the records made that all was right. Is it any wonder then how tedious and accurate he is now in making marks, or how carefully he speaks of his ideals.

Later, he became a teacher, and aided in establishing and building a city, which was separate even from the people of that land. And he became an old patriarch, living to one hundred and nine years of age.

In the present, he is constantly drawn to people who counsel and interpret with regard to the teachings of the man of Galilee. (322)

Idailie was in the country of the Gardenians, when the Prince of Peace entered there. And she was a messenger for the Master, being in close contact to the one who received the influence of the Prince of Peace.

In the present, she has an innate desire towards everything pertaining to holiness to the Lord; and she accepts the belief of any that would serve Him, irrespective of their creed or ism. (2484)

Zioul lived when the Master came into the land of

Galilee. And he was one of the fishermen who heard and saw much of the teaching and ministering by the Master. And while he did not wholly accept the teachings, he never rejected them. (2480)

Selma was in and about the Holy Land where the Master walked. *She was a sister of the woman whom He met at the well,* and she followed His ministry from afar. Later, however, she spread the glad tidings to those in Mount Seir. She lost and gained in soul development. In the early portion, she lost because of aggrandizing of selfish interests; but in the latter part, she gained by changing her ideas to ideals.

At present, it fills her with awe to hear that particular portion of the Scripture, Gospel, or Message read of the journey through that land. From that experience, she now has ability with the needle, and to make things which adorn the body. (2112)

Josie lived when the Master traveled throughout the land. And she lived in the city where the residents came to the well to hear the truths propounded on that day. *She was a sister of the woman at the well.* (428)

Phoebe lived when the Master walked among men. In the latter portion of His sojourn, she journeyed from afar to live in that land. And she came as a result of the teachings of the Master given to the people about the well in the land of the Samaritans. She was not a member of the household of the woman spoken to at the well, but *she was a companion of one who joined in the message given by the woman at the well.*

She gained mentally and spiritually in that incarnation. She wandered from place to place. For she became a singer and dancer to pay her expenses, so that she might hear more of the messages and teachings of this Man who had taught at the well.

In the latter portion of that experience, she joined with

the followers who met in the upper chamber. And the particular activities recorded in the first chapters in Acts have a special significance to her. This also applies to the parts of the Bible which deal with the visits of the Man of Galilee, the Man who walked among His fellow man in order that others might be shown the way to a better understanding.

In the latter portion of her sojourn, when the persecutions began in Jerusalem, *she journeyed to the land of her birth in Galilee. There, she became associated with Andrew, Bartholomew, Jude, and others who became ministers.* And she helped to pass on what she had learned to people who were in despair in body and mind, and troubled in spirit. As a result, she has the ability to be a nurse, to tend the sick, and to help individuals in trouble. These abilities are innate in the present. (379)

(Jesus at the wedding of Cana) caused the wine to blush—water saw its Master, blushed and became wine even by activity. Remember, only when it was poured out would it become wine. Had it remained still, no wine would have filled those conditions where embarrassment was being brought even to the friend. (3681)

Q. Speaking of marriages and family relationships, would you please give us a quick review of the marital status and relationships of some of the other Apostles?
A. That physical body known as Andrew, we find (was) the second brother in a family of four, and, in the early childhood, one willful in many ways, taking up the physical vocation of the parents and brother. (341)

(The difference in the character of Andrew and Peter can be seen in the reaction of their mutual friend Elias, who) leaned more to the staid Andrew than to the boisterous Peter—for he argued with Peter and reasoned with Andrew. (4016)

Andrew . . . followed closely throughout the whole

physical career of the Master; not as (one of) the chosen three, yet one who was given often the greater physical conditions (tasks) to do and to carry out. One often spoken to for the reference to others, and this is particularly seen . . . in the feeding of the multitudes. (341)

. . . When there were those gatherings about the mount in the wilderness, and the call of the five thousand that they be sent not away in their weakness, but the supplying of physical needs to the material man.

(At that time, Ardocn)—as the son of Andrew —brought to his father . . . that companion, the lad with the loaves and the few fishes . . . that there might be supplied from what was in hand sufficient of the material needs to feed the multitude. (2549)

The mother of Peter's wife . . . Esdrela (was) once healed of a terrible fever by the Master himself. (1541) This brought about great changes in Nicodemus and (his wife) Martha—the younger sister of Esdrela. (3175)

(Extract from physical reading—Peter's mother-in-law.) In the physical at present are conditions that have had, and do have, an unusual effect. It is not that the healing was not entire at that time, and holy, in the touch of the Master; but the ailment has again become manifest because of the person's neglect of herself. A life reading would be most interesting to her.

Oh, so much may be said. There may be many ways or channels through which she may aid, whether associated with or working in accord with others. Many come to this source for aid, in which this individual would be better able to help than almost anyone who could be found.

Then, cooperate in such a way that the work of each is for the same purpose. So much may be said to her

respecting her abilities, for she has kept herself a channel. So few have the purity of purpose as this person.
Blessed may she be called among the women of the day.
(2358) (She never requested a Life Reading)

The entity Jose was closely associated with many of
these, becoming the wife even of one of the Apostles
. . . Thomas. (2037)

Q. Aside from the Apostles, what were the reactions of
people who were closely related to Jesus? For example,
you have mentioned that He had two brothers and a
sister. We know that James and Jude became Apostles,
and that James—later referred to as James the
Less—was appointed the head of the church. But what
of Ruth? Would you please fill in some details of her
life and her reaction to Jesus?
A. With the return of Joseph and Mary to Palestine
from the Egyptian sojourn, and with their return to active service among the peoples, there was created quite
a different environ for Joseph and Mary.

For soon after the return—that (return) recorded in
Holy Writ, from the journey to the city for the period of
the Passover—we find that James, the elder brother of
the entity Ruth, was born into that experience.

In the next year, after there had been the beginnings of
the teaching of Jesus by the Wise Men of the East and
His sojourn in Persia, India—and when those activities
brought about the change in the material or financial
status of the family—Ruth then was born in the city of
Capernaum; and (she was) surrounded by such activities as befitted the peoples of that period, that day.

There was awe in the minds of the people as to what
had   taken   place   at   the   birth   of   the   mother
—Mary's—first son. Hence, the entity, Ruth, was rather
in awe of the suggestions, the intimations which surrounded that experience and questioned the mother concerning same. As the entity grew into maidenhood, and

after the birth of Jude, then the death of Joseph brought that brother—Jesus—home! And there were those activities which surrounded the entity (Ruth) concerning that unknown, that strange kinsman—that kinsman whom the people held in awe, yet about whom some said many unkind things.

With the departure of this brother to Egypt for the final initiations or teachings, with John—another kinsman who had been spoken of and held in awe, since his (John's) mother had been a chosen vessel by the priests of the Essenes, and since he, John, was the lineal descendant of the high priests of the Jews—we find that in the entity's latter teens such ponderings brought a great many disturbing influences to the entity, Ruth. . . . Hence we find the entity was divided in thought and activity between the tenets held by the elder brother, James, those held by the mother, and the actual activities of the entity as one among a people who were being questioned, and doubted. Then with the return of John, the cousin, and the beginning of his ministry—one who had renounced his position as a priest, who might serve in the temple, in order to become an outcast and a teacher in the wilderness—there was brought consternation to the entity, Ruth.

And again there was a questioning of the mother as to those experiences of the mother preceding the birth of that (brother) Jesus.

Then (came) the return of Jesus to the Palestine Land, after those periods of the tests in the wilderness, after His meeting with John; and then the return to Capernaum and the teaching which He, Jesus, accorded there. The entity (Ruth) then, for the first time, heard His first utterances in the synagogue: as to the prophecies of Isaiah, Jeremiah, and the teachings of the lesser prophets, and as to how they applied to the experiences of that day.

Returning from this meeting, where a tumult was raised

owing to the utterances of that new teacher, the entity encountered the entity Philoas—a collector, not in the sense of the "taker in", but the supervisor (overseer or examiner) as to the abilities of various individuals in various positions to pay that tribute—a Roman. Because of her beauty, their mutual interest in helping the less fortunate, and the natural consequence of their ages, there was brought about a bond of sympathy between the two.

. . . In her haste to acquaint the mother with the sayings of that teacher, her brother, of whom so much had been asked, by whom so much had been said but so little understood by Ruth, the entity (Ruth) with those two companions (Philoas and a doctor friend) went to Mary, warning her of the possible entanglements with those new authorities—or the Roman activities. (1158)

(Thus, Philoas, the Roman) came in close contact with those of the household from which the Master had gone out, becoming associated with and later married to (and by the Master) the sister of the Master—the only sister, who had received education in Greece and Rome, because of the family's associations with the sects, and the Jews, and a portion that favoured the Romans. (1151) For it is not, as so oft considered, that the family of the Master lacked material opportunities, for from many sources there had come opportunities for those in the household of the Master to have greater training. (1179)

In the latter portion of the entity's (Ruth's) sojourn, while children were born in Rome, during those activities of the entity and the companion (Philoas), much aid was brought to those in the Roman experience who accepted the new teachings. Much that gave help and strength to bear the persecutions later was established in the hearts and the minds and the experiences of those peoples during the entity's sojourn. . . . For she did bring the heart of the people to Him as she did bring the younger brother (Jude)—though he faltered much—as she did give strength to the elder brother to head the church under all those vicissitudes of distress without, turmoils within. (1158)

Q. With the beginning of Jesus' ministry come the healings and miracles. Would you tell us of these?

A. As to the healings, the miracles performed by the Master, the first record begins with that miracle in Capernaum, or Cana, nigh unto Capernaum, when He had recently returned from the wilderness, when the water was turned into wine. It was one of the few instances where miracles were performed among His own people, among His own kindred. (5749-14)

Q. Some might easily ask the question: If He were the healer, why was it necessary that Joseph pass away?

A. Did the Master come to be about His work or His Father's work? As individuals, as representatives of the Master, as heirs with Him, do we go about our Father's work or (what we choose as) our work? There is a difference.

Respecting the miracles of healing, there were many instances where individual healings were of such nature as to be instantaneous—as that one when He said to him sick of the palsy, "Son, thy sins be forgiven thee". When the questions came (as He knew they would), He answered: "Which is easier to say, 'Thy sins be forgiven thee', or 'Take up thy bed and go into thine house?' ". Immediately the man arose, took up his bed and went unto his house! Here we find that it (the healing) was not the command (He issued), but by His own personage. *For the question was not as to whether He healed, but as to whether He had the power to forgive sin.* It was recognized that sin had caused the physical disturbance.

Then these are part of the experience of each and every soul in their search for, in their relationships with, their fellowmen. Ye may ask, does this apply in the present?

In Him ye live, ye move, ye have thy being. "If ye love me," saith the Master, "ye will keep my commandments. My commandments are not grievous; my commandment is that ye love one another, even as I have loved you. If ye love me, I and the Father will come and abide with thee."

Believe ye His words? (5749-14)

Q. Please explain further why the Master in many cases forgave sins in healing individuals.
A. Sins are of commission and omission. Sins of commission were forgiven, while sins of omission were called to mind, even by the Master. (281-2)

Q. What is the greatest sin?
A. What is ever the worst fault of each soul? Self—self!

What is the meaning of self? That the hurts, the hindrances are hurts to the self-consciousness. And these create what? Disturbing forces, and these bring confusions and faults of every nature. For the only sin of man is selfishness! (978-1)

Self-awareness, selfishness, is what makes men afraid. The awareness of the necessities of the carnal forces in a material world, seeking their gratification. Know ye not that, whether ye live or die, ye live or die in the Lord? As He gave, "If thine eye offend thee, pluck it out". (262-29)

Q. These ideas are not always so easy to understand.
A. Only in those answers that come to (reach) the inner self is there brought an understanding—[as with Adahr, daughter of Elizabeth and Zacharias, sister of John the Baptist]—for through the entity's own expression and seeking there came that answer, "Go tell John the things ye have seen and heard: the lame walk, the blind see, the sick are healed, the poor have the gospel preached unto them".

Then there came in the entity's experience the full meaning of the priesthood in Israel, and how the lowly Nazarene was the fulfillment of that priesthood, in His offering of Himself as the Lamb that was not to roll back, but to take away the sins of the people. Not as an escape, but as an atonement in which each soul does find, would find, the Lamb standing ever as such an offering in its relationships as an individual to its fellow man. (1000)

Q. Still we must strive to know, to understand and to do; yet all with patience. Is that correct?

A. That keep. Don't lose patience with thy children, or thy friends who become impatient. For He did not lose patience with His disciples when they said, "Should we go away to buy bread to feed this mob?" What have we here? (That is, what have we to do with, to offer?)

Did you ever hear this used to answer individuals? Try it! It is one of the most disturbing, yet one of the most quieting words which may be used, even to a mob. "What have we here?" Only a few loaves, a few fishes, yet in the hands of those who could realize "Of myself, I can do nothing, but through His power. . . ." it may be multiplied into blessings. And remember, it can be multiplied in curses also, if ye use not thy abilities aright. (5089)

Mary Magdalene

Mary Magdalene lived during the period when the Master walked among men. And it was to her that the Master said, "She hath chosen the better part". She ministered to Him through that experience, and was loved by Him; and as the sister of Martha and Lazarus, she gained in soul development. And it is little wonder that the desire of her soul is to help others; for it was only that others might be aided that she entered into another sojourn in the earth. As was said by Him, "Wherever my gospel is preached, her works will be spoken of". (Matthew 26:13) What a heritage. In the present, His tenets and truths are easily taught and understood by her. Only, be broader in vision and condemn none; as He condemned not, even those who persecuted Him. Condemnation is built with the entity. Blot this from your experience, through Him who makes all things possible. (295)

Q. Please give a detailed account of the conversion of Mary Magdalene.

A. In giving a detailed account of the experience of Mary, the sister of Martha and Lazarus, indeed much might be given respecting the activities of the entity in that experience. For, as given in the Gospel account, this entity was then the Mary of Magdalene; or the courtesan who was active in the experience of both of those who in the capacity of the Roman officers, Roman peoples, and those who were of her native land and country.

When the body first met the Master it was the woman brought before the council, who was taken in adultery; and the one whom the whole council or court at the time asked that, according to the law, the woman be stoned.

With the cleansing of the body-mind, through this experience, the entity then rejoined, in Bethany, those of the family from whom she had been separated, became again a member of the household of those who dwelt there. Hence the showing in the Gospel of the difference in attitude, in the manner of approach, with the various visits of the Master through the period.

As to the experiences before the meeting with the Master, these were of a worldly nature, wherein there was the giving of self in body in the indulgences of the period, such that there was brought for the body, and those associated with same, activities that brought condemnation, as well as the pomp, the power, the splendor—when considered from that angle. In activities, then, the activity after the cleansing in the temple should be—as we find—more dwelt upon. (295-8)

Q. Please describe the personal appearance of the body of Mary Magdalene.

A. This is well drawn by da Vinci, "The Magdalene". A body five feet four inches in height; weight, a hundred and twenty-one pounds—in the general. Hair almost red. The eyes were blue. The features were those impelled both from the Grecian and Jewish ancestry. (295-8)

Q. Please recall any scene or conversation which may be helpful and enlightening between this entity or her associates and the Master.

A. None greater than that given to the entity by the Master, that means whereby the entity had an awakening: "Neither do I condemn thee—neither do I condemn thee". That has awakened, will awaken, within the soul of the entity more of the love and the oneness of the force or power able to cleanse, when condemnation is not in self. Hence, as given then—and as had been given oft—do not condemn self!

Q. What did the Master write in the sand at the time of that experience?

A. That which condemned each individual, as each looked over His shoulder as He wrote.

Q. In relation to this information describing this incident of the woman taken in adultery (John 8:3-11) —consider the information given through this channel for (1436) which seems to describe the same incident. Please clarify this seeming duplication.

A. In the interpretations, all the conditions present should be taken into consideration. The incidents are apparently the same, yet the individuals are different in the two incidents.

Those were periods when there were those who questioned the Master, as was done by the Pharisees. There were those who questioned Him, impelled by the Sadducees; others who questioned, impelled by those of the Roman authority.

There were then, two separate experiences when He was questioned as to the law in relation to that given by Moses respecting those taken in adultery. The one incident about which the first information was given was (in connection with) the associate of John and James; while the last one was (in connection with) the associate of the Roman soldiery. And the questions in each instance were by the different sects of people. These are overlapping in the records that are given (or that you have), though in the original they are given as two different experiences. (295-8)

Q. Which one was 1436?
A. The one taken in the act with the Roman soldiery, and questioned by the Sadducee peoples; while the other was the sister of Martha, and hence the associate (or cohort) of those who were later the disciples or apostles.

Q. In which instance did Jesus stoop and write?
A. In each; in both of these. In one, (1436) that (which) was written was as given, "Medi, Medici, Cui", or the expression of mercy and not sacrifice which showed to those who looked upon the individual awakening of the entity. In the other (Mary Magdalene incident) that written was that which made the accusers recognize their own activities.

The entity (1436) was in Palestine when the Master walked in the earth, when he had trials and temptations, and when those in authority desired to trap Him.

She was the maid who was condemned as one that had been taken in adultery, and was brought before the Master in the temple. Because of the judgment which was passed upon her according to the law, the high

priest and the Sanhedrin declared that He must make a
statement. And He said, "Let him that is without sin
cast the first stone. Let him that has been faultless
make the first move to fulfill the letter of the law."

Is it any wonder that the entity was remoulded in the
days that followed. However, she kept to herself; and
not until after the persecutions began did she venture to
come near to those who were called of the household of
faith.

But to have had the words direct from the Master of
Masters, the Teacher of Teachers, "I do not condemn
thee", has meant and must mean more to her than
words can describe. It can only be shown by deeds, and
desire to bring hope and faith in the Lord and Master
who is able to save unto the utmost, and who has given
to all, "My peace I leave with you, my peace I give unto
you". (1436)

The Rising of Lazarus

Hence the entity Ulai withheld self from such associations, until there came the period in which Lazarus
was ill of fever—what today would be called the slow
fever, or typhoid—and there was the eventual death.
Then the entity was among those of the mourners—not
the hired mourners—and came in contact again with
Mary and Martha during those periods of the Master's
expressions regarding, and activities among, His disciples; not the apostles, but the (twelve) disciples.

And to the entity even today, the shortest (Bible) verse
recorded is that to which the entity responds the more
oft, deepest within self. For with the concept of how
He—the Friend—wept with those of His friends in the
face of criticism, in the company of the great and near
great—there came conviction to the entity that changed
the (entity's) whole concept of the purposes, of the
whys and wherefores of that which had taken place in

the mind and heart of Mary; also as to why and how
Martha and Lazarus had again accepted this sister into
their home, their company. (993)

Q. Please give us further information concerning that
experience at Bethany when Jesus called Lazarus from
the arms of death. What were the reactions of others
who witnessed this event?
A. There we find . . . those who were the acquaintances
of Martha and Mary, to whom the Master came oft.
Then the entity Thelda—as well as Larue (1290) were
among those who were the hired mourners at the time
of Lazarus' death, and became believers—(through)
seeking the activities, experiencing the influence, of the
Master's life on the friends, associates and acquaintances of that group. (1986)

During those periods . . . there were great understandings and great turmoils especially about those of the
city of Bethany, when Lazarus was raised from the
grave, when certain ones of the followers and the sisters, Martha, Mary, made preparation for the supper,
after the resurrection or the bringing to life of the
brother.

The entity Susane—then as a neighbor child, and as a
child of Cleopas—saw these activities and also saw the
fear created by those about the feast. Also the entity
heard the words of the Teacher, the Master, and these
especially . . . came to mean a great deal to the entity.
(1179)

The raising of Lazarus at Bethany was experienced (also) by the entity (Ruth, the sister of Jesus) as well as
the companion (the Roman, Philoas). That (event)
brought a change which made for a new life, a new understanding, a new conception of the manifestations of
the Creative Forces, or God, among the children of
men.

Then, just before the Crucifixion, there was the consummation of the wedding between Ruth and that friend. . . .

And Jesus attended that wedding also; blessed them. And with the recall of the companion (Philoas) to come, during those experiences in Rome, the Crucifixion came about. (1158)

Teleman lived when people were being influenced by the teachings of Him who had walked in Galilee, He that is your Lord. There, your environment brought you in close association with many of both sexes who were in authority. For you heard from Pilate's wife how He had healed her son who was a lunatic, or what would now be termed an epileptic. This kind of thing made impressions upon you. And you wavered as to what would be your choice, and to which group you would join. This was when Paul, Peter, Titus, and Philemon came. And you were in the household of the family in which Philemon was a servant. (1754)

Martha lived in Bethany when the Promised One walked in the land. She was close to the Master, being *a sister to the one that the Master raised from the dead.* Hence, those of that period are near and dear to her. She gained in soul development, and gave much to many. Although she was censured by some because of her attitude towards the secular things of life, from that experience she has gained practicability. While she was a dreamer, she believed that all practical thought must be in accord with the life lived, and with the circumstances and conditions in which people find themselves. (560)

Deul was in the Promised Land when the Christ, or Jesus, walked in the earth. She was aided by the ministry of this Teacher, the Master; and she was the woman who received back alive her son, as they walked from Nain during His Ministry there. (601)

Anilen lived when the Master of Men, the Son of Mary,

walked in the earth; and when many gathered who were helped by the Master. He was the one to whom the Master said, "Must I give to those not of this household?" After the healing of his body, he followed the Master closely, gained in soul development, and helped the weak during the persecutions caused by political and social strife. In the present, he often has to choose between that toward which he is inwardly guided, and the material or social life to which he would be otherwise attracted.

He blessed many people; for the Master put His hands upon him, and He loved him. In that sojourn, he used his hands to aid others, by making things with his hands and by attending to the weak and cripples. Innately, he has a deep sympathy for people who are afflicted in body, and has sought to help them.

You were a Syrophenician, and a companion of the woman of the same nationality, who sought healing for her daughter, as recorded in the Bible. (585)

Cleopas (mother of Bartaemus) lived when the Master of men walked in the earth. It was during the days of toil and strife for the common people who heard His messages and sought in His name. *She was the mother of Bartaemus, the blind man who was healed,* although at the same time he was a strong man. Nevertheless, in her seeking and faith, she held to the tenets of the law of the Jews. (688)

Bartamaeus lived in a land which was separate from the Promised Land when the Master walked in the earth. And he came in close contact with Him and received benefits in the flesh from the acts of the Master.

Hence, there is built in the warp and woof of his being the desire to lift up, to aid, and to succor people in distress. Yet he is mindful that those aided are not spongers upon the good graces of the individuals who aid them. He was strong of body, but was lacking in sight. And he was a worker in metals, and a power to strengthen the weak. (2124)

Marie lived when the people were persecuted who harkened to the Teachings of Him who had come and walked among men. She was one of the household of Chloe when the Master blessed the little children. She sat upon his knee and was blessed by Him. And she became a close follower of the lessons which were taught by Him. Although she was persecuted, she gloried in the fact that the blessings of Him who provided a way of understanding for all, had come in her experience in that sojourn. (403)

Jairus' Daughter

She was in Palestine when the teachings were heard and received during the walk of the Son of Man in the earth. And she was the one whom the Master called again from the deep sleep, Jairus' daughter.

Before and after that event, she gave much of herself to attain a closer relation with the mental attributes of the spirit as it related to material things, rather than to the material things themselves. Hence, is it any wonder that during her early years in the present, more of the same spiritual influence which held her in the earth then will be necessary, rather than that which pertains wholly to material things. *Yet, when one is any environ, one is subject to the laws of that plane. And unless material laws are spiritualized in the mental activity of souls, those who are healed physically often remain sick spiritually.* (559-7)

Fillipe was in the Promised Land when the Master walked in the earth, when the entity then was distressed—as the wife of Jairus, as the mother of Jairus' daughter had that awakening within of the powers that may bring life again to that which has fallen away. And there was established the seal, the bridge of the Cross, that led from sorrow to gladness, not only in the material experience, but also in the quickening within which came with the renewal of life within the presence of the entity (Fillipe).

And how often has she experienced in meditation, not the activities of the Man called a lowly one, but rather the Man of Might and Power through Galilee. (1246-2)

Talitha was the daughter of Jairus, and was of the household of the ruler. And she heard the Voice that called her back to service in that experience, "Talitha, Talitha, Arise!" She gained in soul development because of the service rendered to others in that life, for she gave hope and the understanding which she had received by that touch. All of the experiences of the Master raise her consciousness when she tells them. Hence, when she is proclaiming His teachings, she often feels that little sensation which seems to go from the base of the spine to her head and back again, tingling her whole physical being. His teachings, then, are the judgment that the acts of your life in any phase must be judged by.

As the call was then, so may it ever in the present be, if you will harken to His call. From that experience, you now have a feeling of humbleness, although of a lordly nature, and the ability to carry on under all adverse circumstances. Often, when you have decided to do something, changes come suddenly. Some people would attribute this to astrological aspects. However, it is a warning to change the deeds in the physical body. (421)

The Blessing of The Children

When the Master walked in the earth, Cleopatria was among those who gathered by the way when, "A little child shall lead them", was given, and when the children were called so that He, the Master, might bless them. This entity was among those who were blessed on the wayside from Bethsaida. While she was in the household of a soldier of Rome, when she grew up, her efforts were devoted to those who followed the Nazarene. And the healing ability which was manifested later was gained from that sojourn.

She gained in soul development; and she was instrumental in paving the way for the return of her own household to Rome in order to carry the gospel of the Nazarene into that land. Although she was persecuted by those who came into power, her family returning with the other soldiers remembered what she had received through the blessings given by Him on the wayside.

The experiences in that sojourn were constructive. And when consternation or distress of any nature arises in the present, whether mental or physical, the visions and dreams of those lessons given by Him as He spoke to the children in a manner so that a child could understand, and the lessons of the lamb and of the household pets that were given to the children there, have remained with her. Now, when she visions those things, she may express them to others. And the joy of doing so will bring much to her, if the visions are applied in the field of art. (665)

Durey was in the Holy Land when the Master walked in the earth. Although she was very young, she knew and knew of the acquaintances of the Master. For she was one of the children blessed by the Master at the time of the feeding of the five thousand on the mountain. (2468)

Marie lived when the Master walked in the earth, and when many people gathered to hear Him as He taught by the sea and in the mountain. She was one of the children blessed by Him, and was present when He fed the five thousand and when He fed the four thousand. Hence, the multiplying of things in the hand, will always be a part of her understanding. While she is not stingy, she is careful with the material goods which she possesses. And the desire to have possessions is a part of her.

Do not let this desire become a selfish thing. Let it be rather as He gave when He blessed you, "Except ye become as little children, ye shall in no wise enter in". Unless you are as forgiving, as generous, and as dependent as little children—these become in the deeper sense the meaning of this statement. She gained in soul development. And she was married to one of the followers who was dispersed during the first persecutions of the disciples and Christians in Jerusalem.

She was in close contact with the church in Laodicea, for her husband became a deacon in that church. In the present experience you may meet him. And if he is in the ministry, "cabbage on" to him, and hold tight. You will need him; he will need you. (1532)

Thurmel lived principally during the development of the church. He was very young when the Master was in the earth, although he was one of the children present at the feeding of the five thousand in the wilderness. He has now a certain dread sometimes of being in the wilds, yet he feels the need of individual searching within himself.

His occupation then was as a keeper of an inn, which catered to both Jews and Romans, and at which meetings of various groups were held. For that experience, he is a good listener. (1681)

This entity lived in the Promised Land in that portion about the sea which the Master loved so well. He was young in years, yet he was often too careful in his preparations. And this became something which he never got away from in that sojourn. *For he was the lad from whom Andrew obtained the loaves and fishes to feed the five thousand.* (1821)

Q. What part did Jesus play in any of His incarnations in the development of the basic teachings of the following religions and philosophies: Buddhism, Mohammedanism, Confucianism, Shintoism, Brahmanism, Platonism, Judaism?

A. As has been indicated, the entity (Jesus)—as an entity—influenced either directly or indirectly all those forms of philosophy or religious thought that taught God is One. In all these, then, there is that same impelling spirit. What individuals have done to the principles or the spirit of same—in turning this aside to meet their own immediate needs in material planes or places, has made for that as becomes an outstanding thing, as a moralist or the head of any independent religious force or power; for, as has been given, "Know O Israel, the Lord thy God is One!" whether this is directing one of the Confucius thought, Brahman thought, Buddha thought, Mohammedan thought, these are as teachers or representatives. "Paul may minister, Apollos may have watered, but it is God that gives the increase."

The spirit (is) of the Creative Force, and such the Son represented in the spirit in that as was made manifest in the earth. Not as only one, but *the* only one; for as He gave, "He that climbs up any other way is a thief and a robber". (364-9)

Martha—The Weaver of The Robe

Mrs. C.: You will have before you the life existence in the earth plane of (3175) born September 21, 1900, in Manor Township, Lancaster County, Penna., and the earthly existence of this entity in Palestine, as Martha, a sister of Peter's mother-in-law and one of the Holy Women. You will give a biographical life of the entity in that day and plane of earthly existence, from entrance—and how—into the earth's plane, and the entity's departure; giving the development or retarding points in such an existence. You will answer the questions, as I ask them, concerning the associations and urges from that period in the present.

Mr. C.:   (3175) Yes, the entity's experience in the earth
plane as Martha, the sister of Peter's wife's mother.
Yes, we are again given the records here of that entity
now known or called: (3175) . . . *A lovely body!*

In giving the experiences of the entity in the earth plane
as Martha, the sister of Peter's wife's mother, it would
be well that much of the happenings or history of the
times be included, that there may be the more perfect
understanding of the conditions and as to how and why
urges from that experience apply in the experience of
the entity in the present.

As is understood by many, there had been long a looking forward to or for the advent of the promised
Messiah into the earth and there had been those various
groups through one channel or another who had banded
together to study the material which was handed down
through the varied groups in that day and period.

Here we find there had been, for the mother of Martha,
an experience of coming in touch with Judy (1472)
who had been the first of women appointed as the head
of the Essenes group who had the experience of having
voices, as well as those which would be called in the
present experiences in communications with the
influences which had been a part of man's experience
from the beginning, such that (from) the Divine within
man heard the experiences of those forces outside of
man and communicated in voices, in dreams, in signs
and symbols which had become a portion of the experience.

When the children of Martha's mother, Sophia, were in
those periods of development these had become a part
of what would be called today a play-experience for the
entity, Martha.

For Peter's wife's mother was many years the senior of
Martha but the coming of John, and the birth of Jesus,

the dispensation of Jesus and John in Egypt, all had an impression or imprint upon the mind of the entity Martha, who builded in her own mind how the King and how the announcer of the King should be dressed (as this had been a part of the experiences of the entity in other periods and thus the choice of things in this direction).

Then there came those great changes in the life experience of Martha. For one among those of the rulers of the synagogue sought the entity in marriage and through the individuals who made these arrangements the entity was espoused to Nicodemus. Through his activities, and personality, Martha learned first of what had happened to the peoples in the homes of John the Baptist and of Mary and Joseph and Jesus.

Thus, when there were later the experiences of those entering into activities, and then when the message was given out that Martha's older sister had been healed from a terrible fever by this man, Jesus, this brought about great changes in Nicodemus and Martha, as they had to do with the Temple and the service of the high priest.

Martha began the weaving of the robe that became as a part of the equipment the Master had. Thus the robe was made especially for the Master. In color, it was not as the robe of the priest, but woven in the one piece with the hole in the top through which the head was to be placed, and then over the body, so that with the cords it was bound about the waist.

Then: As to the activities of the entity, the abilities are indicated in weaving, in color. The color of the robe was pearl-gray, as would be called now, with selvage woven around the neck, as well as that upon the edge, as over the shoulder and to the bottom portion of same; no belts, no pomegranates, but those which are woven in such a manner that into the selvage portion of the bottom was woven the Thummin and Urim. These were as the balance in which judgments were passed by the priest. But these were woven, not placed upon the top of same. Neither were there jewels set in same.

This robe Nicodemus presented then to the Master, Jesus, after the healing of the widow of Nain's son, who was a relative of Nicodemus.

In the activities, then, when Nicodemus went to the Master by night and there became those discussions in the home, for Nicodemus and Martha there began the communion as man and wife rather than man and his chattel or his servant. They were more on a basis of equality, not in the same proportions which were established a bit later by some of the rulers from the Roman land but more in keeping with the happenings which had brought about the activities in the Essenes group.

Though Martha was an Essene, Nicodemus never accepted completely the tenets or the teachings of the Essenes group. These were a part of the principles and applications of Martha. The acquaintanceships, the friendships which were established between Mary, Elizabeth and the other Mary, all were parts of the experience and because of the position of Martha throughout those activities she was considered rather one of the leaders, or one to whom others made appeal to have positions or conditions set in motion so that there was given more concessions to the Holy Women who followed Jesus from place to place when there were those periods of His Palestine ministry.

The only differences which arose were with Martha and Mary in the household of Lazarus, Martha and Mary. Because of conditions there from which Mary had returned, from the houses which were a portion of her activity in various cities, questions as to morality arose. And yet, after there were the healings, or as it was discovered how she out of whom seven devils were cast became changed, or how there were even changes then and there, we find there was a greater working together with the activities of Mary, Martha, Lazarus, and Mary the mother of Jesus, Elijah and many of these others, including John Mark's mother. These were parts of the experience of the entity.

The entity stood, as indicated by the accomplishments of the robe from Nicodemus, as one particularly honored even by the Master.

During the periods of activity, during the missions after the Crucifixion and Resurrection of the Master, the entity Martha gathered with those in the upper room looking for the promise of the coming of the outpouring of the Holy Spirit. This, too, became a part of the activities.

For the entity later was among those who aided Stephen and Philip, as well as others of the various lands. For it was with these that the entity first became acquainted with Luke and Lucius who later became the heads of various organizations in other portions. These acquaintances were then rather as counsel from those to whom Luke, Lucius, Mark as the younger of the Disciples (not Apostles, but younger of the Disciples) went for counsel.

For the entity was one acquainted with the law, the entity Martha, taught the law to the young once, the children who sought knowledge.

The entity had its own family, two sons and one daughter. These became ministers in the church in Antioch, aiding the peoples who worked with Barnabas, and it is mentioned that one, Theopolus learned from the entity Sylvanus, and those who labored in the church in Jerusalem with John, James, Peter and the other, as a child. As a child, this one was known as Thaddeus. The daughter was wed to one of the companions of Paul, Silas, who was engaged in a position of the activities with Paul.

With the persecution the entity withdrew more and more because of its associations with those in authority, and its home became more and more a place of refuge and help for all of the young of the church.

The entity lived to be an elderly person, something like seventy-nine years of age in the experience, and was not among those ever beaten or placed in jail, though persecuted by only the Romans, feared by those of her own peoples.

Ready for questions:

Q. What place did I occupy at the Crucifixion?
A. As one of those upon the right hand of Mary, the Mother of Jesus, and the other Mary upon the left hand.

Q. In the meeting on the day of Pentecost?
A. Among those who heard all of the various places announce their hearing Peter in their own tongue.

Q. In what way was I acquainted with Lucius?
A. As indicated, as a teacher, as a helper, an advisor, when he was destined by being joined in the church activities in his own home areas. The entity never visited there.

Q. Any other advice?
A. Keep close to those things which draw thee nearer to the Cross of Christ. For it is in Him, through Him, ye each have thy being. As He accepted the work of thine hands then, may He accept the work of thy hands in the present. (3175-3)

A Description of The Master

Few people are aware that there is in existence today, in the Archives in Rome, a description of Jesus. It is contained in a report written nearly two thousand years ago, by a Roman, Publius Lentulus, to his Emperor, Tiberias. It reads thus:

There has appeared in Palestine a man who is still living and whose power is extraordinary. He has the title given him of Great Prophet; his disciples call him the Son of God. He raises the dead and heals all sorts of diseases.

He is a tall, well-proportioned man, and there is an air of severity in his countenance which at once attracts the love and reverence of those who see him. His hair is the color of new wine from the roots to the ears, and thence to the shoulders it is curled and falls down to the lowest part of them. Upon the forehead, it parts in two after the manner of Nazarenes.

His forehead is flat and fair, his face without blemish or defect, and adorned with a graceful expression. His nose and mouth are very well proportioned, his beard is thick and the color of his hair. His eyes are gray and extremely lively.

In his reproofs, he is terrible, but in his exhortations and instructions, amiable and courteous. There is something wonderfully charming in this face with a mixture of gravity. He is never seen to laugh, but has been observed to weep. He is very straight in stature, his hands large and spreading, his arms are very beautiful.

He talks little, but with a great quality and is the handsomest man in the world.

Then, too, we have His description as given in the Readings—

Q. Please give a physical description of Jesus.
A. A picture (of Jesus) that might be put on canvas . . . would be entirely different from all those that have depicted the face, the body, the eyes, the cut of the chin, and the lack entirely of the Jewish or Aryan profile. For these were clear, clean, ruddy. Hair almost like

that of David, a golden brown, yellow red. (5354)

The Last Supper

This Psychic Reading was given spontaneously by Edgar
Cayce at the end of check-physical reading (1315-1)
6/14/32, 11.30 a.m., after the usual suggestion had been
given three times for him to wake up:

E.C.: The Lord's Supper—here with the Master—see
what they had for supper—boiled fish, rice with leeks,
wine, and loaf. One of the pitchers in which it was
served was broken—the handle was broken, as was the
lip to same.

The whole robe of the Master was not white, but pearl
gray—all combined into one—the gift of Nicodemus to
the Lord.

The better looking of the twelve, of course, was Judas,
while the younger was John—oval face, dark hair,
smooth face—only one with the short hair. Peter, the
rough and ready—always that of very short beard,
rough, and not altogether clean; while Andrew's is just
the opposite—very sparse, but inclined to be long more
on the side and under the chin—long on the upper
lip—his robe was always near gray or black, while his
clouts or breeches were striped; while those of Philip
and Bartholemew were red and brown.

The Master's hair is 'most red, inclined to be curly in
portions yet not feminine or weak—*strong*, with heavy
piercing eyes that are blue or steel-gray.

His weight would be at least a hundred and seventy
pounds. Long tapering fingers, nails well kept. Long
nail, though, on the left little finger.

Merry—even in the hour of trial. Joking—even in the
moment of betrayal.

The sack is empty. Judas departs.

The last is given of the wine and loaf, with which He gives the emblems that should be so dear to every follower of Him. Lays aside His robe, which is all of one piece—girds the towel about His waist, which is dressed with linen that is blue and white. Rolls back the folds, kneels first before John, James, then to Peter—who refuses.

Then the dissertation as to "He that would be the greatest would be servant of all".

The basin is taken as without handle, and is made of wood. The water is from the gherkins, that are in the wide-mouth shibboleths that stand in the house of John's father, Zebedee.

And now comes "It is finished".

They sing the ninety-first Psalm—"He that dwelleth in the secret place of the Most High shall abide under the shadow of the Almighty. I will say of the Lord, He is my refuge and my fortress; my God; in Him I trust."

He is the musician as well, for He uses the harp.

They leave for the garden. (5749-1)

The Lord's Prayer

On April 27, 1934 Edgar Cayce was asked:

Q. Is the Lord's Prayer as recorded in the Bible correct? If not, would appreciate it as was given by the Master to the disciples.
A. This may be given, but rather should the seeker use that which *is* given . . . as the Lord calls on all to do. Make its purpose and its intent a portion of thine self. For, there be many misinterpretations, poor translations, but to find fault with that thou hast and not use same is to make excuses that you haven't it as it was

given. Art *thou* on speaking terms with thy Lord? If
not, why not? *Have* that rather that *He* would give thee,
than from *any* other source!

When he gave, "As Ye seek in my name, that ye may
have if ye believe", then act that way. He will draw
near unto thee, if thou wilt draw near unto Him.

Let thy prayer be that He will ever show thee, direct
thee, lead thee. (281-20)

Then, less than a month later, Cayce gave a spontaneous
version of the Lord's Prayer during a reading for Mr. 378.
This individual had disappeared from his home in New
York leaving behind a suicide note. Cayce located him,
but would not reveal the man's whereabouts. In several
readings the sleeping Cayce suggested that the family pray
for him while the soul of Cayce reasoned with the soul of
378. The man eventually reversed his intention of suicide
and returned to his family.

Given 5/21/34 Va. Beach, Va.

E.C.:   Yes. The physical body lives. It is among things
green, and yet it is (in) the city of those that are called
dead. Let the light of truth and hope so inspire the inner
self as to do that which is right in the sight of thine
Maker, respecting self and those that have looked and
do look to thee for counsel, succor, aid and advice.

Let not the material things so blind thee that they
become a stumblingblock in thine experience. Give
praise to thy Maker in the name of Him that taught thee
to pray:

OUR FATHER WHO ART IN HEAVEN,
HALLOWED BE THY NAME
THY KINGDOM COME. THY WILL BE DONE:
AS IN HEAVEN, SO IN EARTH.
GIVE US FOR TOMORROW THE NEEDS OF THE
BODY.

FORGET THOSE TRESPASSES AS WE FORGIVE
THOSE THAT HAVE TRESPASSED AND DO
TRESPASS AGAINST US.
BE THOU THE GUIDE IN THE TIME OF TROUBLE,
TURMOIL AND TEMPTATION.
LEAD US IN PATHS OF RIGHTEOUSNESS
FOR THY NAME'S SAKE.

We are through.

(E.C. gasped and coughed at first part of waking suggestion—rather slow to wake—seemed in a daze for some
minutes after apparently waking.) (378-44)

The Role of The Disciples

In considering the Disciples we find occasional asides in
the Readings which came forth unannounced, yet say
much in their description of the twelve and their relationship with the Master. One such is included here:

> For this entity we find in Saturn the influences that to
> many, and oft to self, become stumblingstones or block-
> ings of ways in which all the beautiful thoughts, all the
> good intentions come tumbling because of material or
> social hindrances. These should be used as stepping-
> stones. For in patience ye become aware of thy own
> soul, and thy own abilities.

> Think not that He in the flesh found not stumbling in
> the mind and in the experience of each of those He
> chose, even as His representatives in the earth.

> As each of the twelve Apostles represented major cen-
> ters or regions or realms through which consciousness
> became aware in the body of the earth itself, so did He
> find—as in thine own self ye find—those twelve
> stumblingstones, those twelve things that oft not only
> disgust but disappoint thee—as to the reaction and way
> people and things react. These are the price of flesh, of
> material consciousness, and are only passing. Know

deep within self that these, too, must pass away, but the beauty, the love, the hope, the faith remains ever. (2823)

How interesting it is to contemplate upon the fact that shortly after that Last Supper the Master was deserted by His Disciples—denied three times over by Peter— and left alone, friendless before Pilate.

According to Scripture, and according to Cayce, only one of the twelve was present at the final trial upon Golgotha—The beloved John, to whom the Master gave charge of his blessed Mother Mary.

Yet the remaining ten later returned to testify of the Masters' works, and His Resurrection—each with a conviction and awareness of consequence which sealed his own fate and led to the eventual martyrdom of all.

Could each of these men consequently have embarked upon the lives they did—and suffered to their deaths as they did—if they had not actually seen the Master arisen in the flesh?

It is upon this single point of logic that the author often returns when his own faith wavers concerning the enormity of it all.

Chapter Ten

CRUCIFIXION AND RESURRECTION

In considering that which materially passed through the minds of the followers of the Master Jesus and those experiences leading to the way of the cross: The decisive point in Berea (?) was the more trying even than the trial; and then those periods of taking leave after the establishing of the emblems as His body and blood, as a ritual for those who would honor and bring to remembrance those experiences through which each soul passes in putting on the whole armor of the Christ.

In those days preceding the entry into Jerusalem, we find those periods of much disturbance among the disciples who were of Galilee and those who were of the Judean ministry. These were in disputations as to what was to take place when He, Jesus, was to go to Jerusalem. Yet He chose to go, entering through the period of rest at Bethany with Mary, Martha, Lazarus; and (then) the triumphal entry and the message that was given to those throngs gathered there.

The next period we find in the upper chamber with the disciples and the humbleness that was manifested. Though He was their leader, their prophet, their Lord, their Master. He signified through the humbleness of the act (washing of the feet), the attitude to which each would come if he would know that true relationship with his God, his fellow man.

Those periods in the garden—these become that in which the great trial is shown, and the seeming indifference and the feeling of the loss of one to whom trust and hope had been given; and the fulfilling of all that had been in the purpose and the desire in the entrance into the world.

The trial—this was not with the pangs of pain, as so oft indicated, but rather glorying in the opportunity of taking upon self that which would RIGHT man's relationship to the Father, in that man, through his free will, had brought sin into activities of the children of God. Here HIS SON was bringing redemption through the shedding of blood that they might be free.

Here the law of love, of causation, of mercy, of justice, of all that makes for self becoming in the at-onement relationship, of filling the purpose for which one is called in materiality, becomes the activity of Him that is free indeed.

Thus in the hour of sacrifice, material, mental and spiritual relationships are attained and considered in His every word.

Then in those periods of transition from "It is finished", comes that which is to each heart the determination that it too may know the blessed hope that comes in seeing, knowing, experiencing the cross in the heart, the body, the mind.

The period of Resurrection—here we find that in which ye ALL may glory. For without the fact of His overcoming death, the whole of the experience would have been as naught.

Then may ye as seekers of The Way, may ye that have come seeking to know, to experience, to feel that presence of the Christ Consciousness within thine own breast, within thine own experience, open the door of thy heart! For He stands ready to enter, to those who will bid Him enter. He comes not unbidden, but as ye seek ye find, as ye knock it is opened. As ye live The Life, is the awareness of His closeness, of His presence, thine.

Be ye glad—be ye joyous when those things come to be thy lot that should or would disturb the material-minded. Like Him, look up. Lift up thy heart, thy mind, unto the Giver of all good and perfect gifts, and cry aloud even as He, "My God, my God!" "Be Thou near unto me!"

In this, as ye raise then thy voice to Him, ye may be sure He will answer, "Here am I—be not afraid. For as the Father hath sent me, so come I into thy heart and life to bring gladness, that there may be life more abundant in thy experience!" Then, be glad in Him.

Q. Please explain John 19:34, "Forthwith came out blood and water".

A. The fulfilling of "Without the shedding of blood there is no remission of sins". Hence His blood was shed as the sacrifice of the just for the unjust, that ye all may stand in the same light with the Father.

Q. What changes had to take place in the physical body of Jesus to become a glorified spiritual body?

A. The passing of the material life into the spiritual life brought the GLORIFIED body; thus enabling the PERFECT body to be materialized in material life—a GLORIFIED body made perfect!

Q. Please explain: "He breathed on them, and saith unto them, Receive ye the Holy Ghost".

A. That change of doubt and fear which arose in the minds and hearts of those gathered in that room. For the fear of the interpreting of the phenomenon being experienced, He breathed. As the breath of life was breathed into the body of the man, see, so breathed He that of love and hope into the experience of those who were to become witnesses of Him in the material world.

Q.   John 21:25. Does this verse have reference to the beginning as Adam?

A.   In the same manner of beginning, yes.

Q.   Who were the women at the Cross?

A.   Many were there. Those of His own household, Mary Magdalene, the mother of John and James, and those who were of that whole group were among the women at the Cross.

Q.   Are any of the women here (in this room) who were at the Cross?

A.   Two.

Q.   Who is giving this discourse?

A.   Are ye curious? Are ye serious? Look within self.

We are through. (5749-10)

Dienna, or Deunna. She lived when the Master walked in the earth, and when He made his triumphal march into the city. For she was among the Parthians who came at that particular season, not only for the service and the reckonings, but also for the social activities during the feasts. But hearing and seeing the influences which aroused the people to such an extent that they cried, "Hosanna in the Highest. . . ." aroused in her that which is innate. Now, when there is singing in unison by many people, this raises her vibrations to a worshipfulness which little else can do.

Later, she heard the cries of the rabble, and wondered how and why those in authority could override the people in such a manner. As a result, disturbances arise within her even now, when she hears the cry, "Lo, He is here . . . Lo, He is there".

But know, as it was given by the Psalmist, "Though I take the wings of the morning and fly unto the ut-

termost parts, He is there! Though I make my bed in
hell, He is there! Though I fly unto the uttermost parts
of the heavens, He is there!" For the consciousness of
his abiding presence is within, even as He gave, "The
kingdom of heaven is within thee". (1456)

Q. Could you tell more about the entity Mariaerh, especially in conjunction with Jesus' Triumphal Entry into
Jerusalem on Palm Sunday?

A. (Mariaerh) was then among those peoples of the hill
country that came to the city during those periods of
the feast—at which time occurred the triumphal entry
into Jerusalem. The entity then for the first time saw
(though it had heard of) the activities of the man called
Jesu, or Jesus, in those experiences. . . .

We find the entity grew up in the hill country near Judea, near to those places where Elizabeth and Zacharias
had lived. Zacharias becoming as it were, the first of the
martyrs, Elizabeth remaining in the land of the hill
country. There the entity was brought up and taught.
. . . Hence we find the entity only came to Jerusalem,
at the age of accountability according to women, in
about its fourteenth year; to be recorded, or polled, as to
those that were of marriageable age, or taxable—or for
the whole consideration both from the Jewish and the
Roman associations or requirements for the poll or taxation.

Hence it was during the entity's first visit with its own
parentage and Elizabeth and the older people that the
entity Mariaerh was in Jerusalem, or came to
Jerusalem, when the Master—Jesus—made the triumphal entry from Bethany into Jerusalem.

And when there were the cries of "Hosanna!" and there
were the processions, these brought strange feelings to
the entity . . . and the wonder became rather that of a
worshipfulness. For even as He gave on that memorable
day, if the people had not cried "Hosanna!" the very
rocks, the very trees, the very nature about would cry

out against such opportunities lost by the children of men—to proclaim the great day of the Lord!

Can ye not see the place . . . the city of the many strange lights, the many unusual customs . . . and then this new experience—He who brought hope and cheer to those ill in body, those who had lost hope through a holding on to material things and to the old tenets of tradition? And can you not see the great throng as they spread their garments—yea, those of high and low estate or position . . . (1468).

Though man would have most believe that there were great throngs, they were mostly women and children. (3615)

Sarapha (or Sara, the Innkeeper's daughter whom we have mentioned before) was among that mighty throng that cried, "Hosanna to the Highest . . . the King cometh". And there the entity met those disappointments again, when that mighty force, that glorious creature, that mighty man among men was not proclaimed king. And He seemed to exert so little of that necessary material application of a glorious power and might. (1152)

(But, oh!) the humbleness, the graciousness, the glory, the dignity of the Man, who—with His disciples—waited among friends who sought from a material angle that He not expose the physical Man to danger. And yet as He preached, or as He counseled: indeed for that purpose came He into the world, and a man must stand forth for what had been the purpose of his entrance.

(It was then) the entity, Mariaerh (who later became the wife of Lucius) caught the concept of how each soul must in each experience live as the grain of wheat, as the grain of mustard, as the seed of every nature, fulfilling that purpose for which it enters into an experience in a sojourn—irrespective of self's individual or personal desires, letting the personality of self be lost in the individuality of the Christ-purpose—as He so magnificently gave on that way from Bethany to Jerusalem. (1468)

Q. Was Judas Iscariot's intention in betraying Jesus to force Him to assert Himself as a king and bring about His kingdom on earth then?

A. Rather the desire of the man to force same—and the fulfilling of that which Jesus spoke about at the Supper.

Pray ye, then, that ye be ready in the hour of trial or temptation, that ye may say, even as He, "Not my will, but Thine, O God, be done in and through me, that I may have that state with Thee that was before the worlds were, and be conscious of same". (3188)

Marya helped in the outer court when there was the cleansing of the temple. Although she helped in the Gentile court, she was of the Hebraic faith.

Her work in the Temple brought her contentment, although the outward appearances were often of turmoil and strife, because of the continual bickering about the Romans. At various times, she was rebuked by those in charge at the temple, because of her adherence to the sect which was questioned by those in authority. *For those in authority were sons of Belial.*

She gained in soul development, for she was in the hearing of Life itself. The symbols were the dorna and the staff. The dorna was the symbol BB, representing people of another race who adhered to the faiths in Palestine. The staff was the shepherd's crook. (537)

Pitmumus (among the Roman soldiery) lived during the days when the Romans held a protectorship over Palestine, and when the Master walked in the earth. He was a soldier and was stationed in the garrisons of the Roman soldiers about Bethany and Jerusalem, or the southernmost gate through which the Master passed.

He saw the Master during the persecutions, but comprehended little about Him, and merely followed the dictates of them who were in authority. (1650)

Phlons was one of the Roman soldiers under Pilate, that ruled in Judea and Jerusalem during the sojourn of the Prince of Peace in the earth. And he gained in soul development by casting his lot with those people. (And a whole history might be written here of this entity's presenting to Caesar the activities of Pilate at His trial, as well as those of the high priest in the condemning.) *For Phlons was one of the soldiers who stood guard at the time of the Crucifixion, and he saw the Prince of Peace die on the Cross.*

He gained in soul development, for the people who later went from Jerusalem to Rome were often aided by him. In the present, when there has arisen controversies between the authorities of the State and the spiritual influences in men's lives, he has trembled within, as if harking back to the day when the sun was darkened—and not by an eclipse alone—and when the earth shook and the temple veil was rent. *For the entity viewed these experiences in the affairs of men. This should be written.* (333)

Q. Were the Roman soldiers so unmoved by the crucifixion as popular history would have us believe?
A. Romual (was) among those of the Roman Guard who were struck by the sincerity of the Man and of the followers of the Man, as men, and with the breaking up of the generally accepted rule on the last day, became a follower of those of the despised sect. (470)

Zebra was a Roman soldier in Palestine following the Crucifixion when people were being questioned, and Pilate was recalled. And he knew much of these activities, since he was acquainted with many who accepted the teaching of Him as a principle. (2021)

Cercel was in the Roman land when various countries

paid tribute to that country. And he was in charge of
the collectors of the customs in the various ports, for
which he made an accounting to them who were in
authority. Hence, he made trips to Alexandria,
Jerusalem, Antioch, and such places where he heard the
messages and tenets of Him who was sacrificed by the
people.

He did not contact the Son of Man in person, but he
knew many of the household of faith, including John,
Luke and Pylemus who was the brother-in-law of
Pilate. For he went to Pilate for the customs after the
condemnation by Pilate and the Crucifixion.

Cercel gained mentally, but was not awakened spiritually until the latter part of that incarnation. For when
he saw the persecutions in his own city, this caused
changes in his thinking.

In the present, he has been particularly interested in the
libraries of Alexandria, the influence of Rome, and the
activities of the people in the Holy Land. And he has
had dreams about them, for he is psychic as a result of
that experience. (877)

Polyneius was in the Roman land when the teachings
were questioned, which had been given by Him who
had brought disturbance to Palestine. He was a Roman,
but was in a position of authority in Palestine. He
gathered data with relation to the activities of the tax
gatherers. Thus, he came into contact with the unrest
among the various sects and classes, while at the same
time being in close contact with those in authority.

He lost and gained in soul development. He gained
when he accepted the teaching, "As ye would that men
should do to you, do ye unto them". (1470)

Martha was in Palestine when there was great turmoil.
For she was born in the period when the earth trembled
because of the event upon Golgotha. She was a member

of a household which were relatives of Mary, Martha
and Lazarus, as well as of the mother of John the Baptist, and some of the other disciples.

Hence, she grew up in an atmosphere of awe; and she
became fearful when in her younger years, the persecutions began and her cousin James (The Disciple) was
beheaded. As a result, fear and doubt are innate within
her. She must become aware, like every other soul, of
that which was given to those of old, "I am the resurrection and the life. I told you to destroy the body, and
in three days I would raise it again." This must become
a fact in your mind. Then, it will be understood how
this emblem represents God, The Way, the Cross, self
and the world. (1747)

And again He said, as He led the way, as He fulfilled in
giving His life, "In the day ye eat thereof ye shall surely
die". Yet the tempter said, "Not surely die", for it may
be put off—and it was, 600 years! And yet death
came—the pangs of the loss of self. Yet in that day
when the voice was raised on the cross, He said
"Father, Why WHY the way of the cross?" This is indeed the pattern that is interpreted in "I perceive that
the heart of man is to do evil. The spirit is willing, the
flesh is weak." (3188)

Q. Was that, then, the significance of "My God! My
God, why hast Thou forsaken me?"
A. This came, as He promised, so that anguish, that
despair may not be in thy experience. It was a fulfillment; so that the trials, the temptations might be shortened in the days of expression, that the very elect
might not be disturbed in their search for Him.

These are the high points in assurance. Be patient and
see. (2072) . . . (for) He is faithful who has promised
and is able to keep that which is committed unto His
keeping against any circumstance, any trial, which may
come in the experience of His children. For He has
promised that we shall not be chastened beyond what we

are able to bear, and he who endureth unto the end shall wear the crown of eternal life! and, "Even though He were the Son, yet learned He obedience through the things which He suffered".

So, as the cry went from Him, "Why—why—hast Thou forsaken me?" The same may oft be wrung from our own beings; yet even as He stayed and raised Him to perfection, giving unto Him all power, so may we in that love, know that contentment, that joy, of serving—even with Him. (2466)

Her name was Marlan, although she was called Sardenia. And she lived when preparations were being made for the coming of the Teacher, the lowly one, yet the Great I Am, into the experience of flesh. This was in order that man might again have an advocate with the Divine which had grown so far away from the hearts of men who were lost in the toils of the day.

She lived near Bethany at the time when Martha, Mary, Lazarus, Jesus, the disciples, Peter, James, John, Andrew, Batholomew, Philip, Thomas, and the others made many pilgrimages to and from various parts of the land. And she was from the same section of the country as Bartholomew. She was associated with Mary, the Mother, and with the daughter and sons of Joseph and Mary, the association of the latter two having brought the beauties of the Divine into the experiences of man during that sojourn.

She was active in the sect of the Essenes. *For she was one of the Holy Women, even when they stood beneath the Cross.* (1463)

So let thy joy in Him break forth in song, even as when He had given, "It is finished", and sang the song that raised the purposes in the minds and hearts of those that were gathered about Him with that wonderment and awe that made them know not what was come to pass! (827-1)

Ardemetus was in the Holy Land when there were the religious changes, and the Roman forces were in the land. He was one of the seventy elders, or the Sanhedrin. He was one of those who were close to him who came to the Master by night, and close to him who begged that the physical body of Jesus should be given to him so that it might be cared for and protected. He was one of the number who were in heart and mind with Joseph of Arimathaea, and he helped him; but he did not openly proclaim his thoughts and activities. (1497)

Josie was in the Promised Land when the Master walked in the earth. She was of the ruling powers, but her associations were with the people of that land. When the persecutions began, and it was questioned whether that proclaimed by the fisherfolk, or that proclaimed by those in power or authority, was to become the rule of the people, she was drawn between two forces.

As a lesson, learn humbleness and patience. There, you were neither hot or cold. *He without an ideal is sorry indeed, but he with an ideal and lacking courage to live it is sorrier still.*

The entity was of the household of the one who questioned at the trial of the Master, of the household of one of the Sanhedrin who cared for the Body when the burial time came—Nicodemus. (1402)

Cleopias lived when the Master walked among men. It was when many people were enduring trials and tribulations, and when He gave, "I must go up that I may be offered as the Living sacrifice".

You followed afar off when there were the hosannas in the triumphal entry into the city. And again you were afar off when He was lifted between the earth and sky. This was so that they who looked might know that they, themselves, must pass along that road. And they must crucify in their bodies that which gratified desires and exalted self, rather in the tenet which He gave, "The new commandment I give, that ye love one another".

She was one of the people who came from Lycaonia, a Grecian settlement in the upper part of Samaria. And she embraced the tenets, and joined with the Holy Women who cared for the body during its hurried preparation for burial. For it was the end of the day when it was delivered to Joseph of Arimathaea and to them who took care of it. These were her friends at that time. (897)

Eloise, or Lois, was in the Promised Land when the Master walked in the earth. And she found that which brought a gain in the innate forces, as well as in the urges from the emotions. For she was healed by the Master, and she gave a greater understanding to her particular circle of friends from other lands. While she lived in Palestine, she was not a Jew, but was a combination of Roman and Grecian. At certain times, when it is indicated that people from every land gathered together, she was the interpreter, and aided in bringing better relationships between them and the Apostles. This followed soon after the organization of the church. *For this entity was the one who pressed in the crowd and said, "Can I but touch the hem of His garment I will be healed".*

She was with the Mother at the Tomb, and was close to the household of Joseph and Mary. Her work extended far and wide; for because of her Roman and Grecian descent, she associated with the people who ruled politically that portion of the world. (1353)

Larue was in the earth when the Son, the Savior, walked therein. And he was among the mourners at Bethany when Lazarus was of the beloved of Him, who is Life, Light, and Immortality to the world today— ever. For He changes not. The entity came under the influence of the household of Mary and Martha, of the Disciples, and then of the Master. He joined with those activities, and was among those who ministered at the burial of the Savior, Jesus, and thereafter. (1290)

Beatrice lived when questions were being asked by the Roman' soldiers, and when John (the Baptist) was being questioned. She was occupied in furnishing entertainment, being a danseuse for Herod. She was closely associated with the people under Herod, with the members of Pilate's court, with the Romans, and with the representatives of the Emperor. Those experiences were spectacular for her, although she often lost in soul development because of self-indulgences and self gratification. Later, she harkened to the people who joined in the Triumphal Entry of the man of Galilee, and a change came over her. And she joined with the Holy Women, and rendered a service to people of many lands.

When the people gathered from all the lands for that particular feast, this entity was overcome by the bodily abuses of various kinds. And the healing that was accomplished, not only by the words spoken, but also by the look and touch of the Holy One, brought joy, glory, understanding, knowledge, and wisdom to her.

She helped in preparing the linens about the head of the Master when He was entombed by Josephus and the friends.

And then she gained in soul development, for she gave of herself, and brought aid and help. (1081)

Before that the entity was in the Holy Land, among the Roman peoples that were in high places during the sojourn of the Master in the earth.

And especially was the entity present (as has oft and may oft be a part of the present experience of the entity) during some of those periods when there were the trial, the Crucifixion. And the entity joined with the Holy Women in those periods when He was seen again, in that period of manifestation.

The name then was Amorela, and she was associated with those that kept guard at the temple. There the entity, at the trial before Pilate, in the throng, saw the face of the Master. The entity heard those words, saw that tenderness with which He felt and experienced His aloneness when deserted by those who had been close to Him. The entity was spoken to by the Master when He gave, "Be not afraid, for me nor for thyself. All is WELL with thee."

Thus, (the entity was there) when there were those reports of His Resurrection, when there were the attempts of the Romans to put aside the questionings of the Jews. (2620)

Andra lived when there were people who looked and longed for, and expected, the coming of a promise to a people who sought relief from both material and spiritual bondage. The latter consisted of the practices of those who gormandized themselves and served their own interests by the sale of privilege in connection with those things which were of the letter of the law without the spirit thereof.

She was in the household of, and was one of the sisters that were in the Temple with, that individual who was chosen as a channel through which the Spirit would manifest as the Holy One. Thus, she was the daughter of Elois, the priestess who, with Simeon, blessed the Holy One in the Temple.

In the latter portion of that experience, she joined what would be termed a prayer band, or ladies' aid, and waited upon those who became His followers. And she worked with Simon Peter's mother, his wife, the children of Zebedee and their families, as well as *Thomas and Luke. The latter two were brothers.*

She gained in soul development. Later, she helped to prepare paintings for the walls, and drawings that could be carried about, and were used as banners. *And she also helped prepare the wrappings for the last annointing of the body of the Holy One. She prepared the wrappings rather than the spices; for Mary Magdalene, (the other) Mary, Josie and the Mother of the Lord prepared the latter. Andra, however, prepared the napkins That were about His head,* with the seals which were later made as raised figures.

In connection with your relationship with Mary, the Mother of Jesus, you grew up with the individuals affiliated in that religious order, which bound together that particular group of individuals who were all associated at that time.

To explain, in the preparation for the coming of the Son of Man, there were various individuals in that period who joined together in their efforts to consecrate their lives and bodies for a service. This was in order to perfect a material channel through which an expression of the Creative Forces might come into the earth. Thus, there were twelve maidens in the temple, or the Order of the Temple, who were dedicated for such preparation. And you were one of the twelve, and you were associated with Mary in the preparations.

With respect to your dream about the children on the double staircase, this was an experience and not a dream. If this is dreamed again, it will be more complete. For you saw the maidens, including yourself, on the staircase which led to the ordination or coronation room for the dedicating of the twelve. That was the time when Mary was indicated, while she walked up the steps with the other children on the other steps, as being the one who was chosen or led by the Spirit.

Pray that you may have this dream again. Let yourself

enter into deep meditation so that the I AM consciousness may make you more aware of how the purpose of this experience may be applicable in your life now. This is highly to be desired.

The figures on the seals which you prepared on the Head of the Master were, the seals of the Holy One as the seals of the Son of David—the pear with the ball, with the pomegranates on either side. (649)

As given in the gospel account, this entity, Mary (295), the sister of Martha and Lazarus, *was then the Mary of Magdalene.* For she was a courtesan, and was active in the experience of both the Roman officers or Roman people, and people of her native land.

When she first met the Master, she was the woman brought before the council who has been taken in adultery. And the whole council or court at the time asked, according to the law, that she should be stoned.

As a result of the cleansing of her body and mind through that experience, she returned to her family in Bethany from whom she had been separated, and became again a member of the household that dwelt there. Hence, this is the reason for the showing in the Gospel of the difference in attitude and manner of approach at the times of the various visits of the Master.

She was the individual to whom the Master appeared first upon the Resurrection Morn. And it was to her that many of the Apostles and leaders went for counsel, as it is spoken of in the various accounts. . . .

You did not repay any fraction of the debt which you owed to the Master while He was in the earth. That would be impossible. For as each soul learns, to condemn yourself is to condemn the abilities of the Master. As the Master gave, "God is God of the living, not of the dead". For the dead are separated from the living.

As it is in the earth, so is it in the spiritual. Dead, or death, is separation. Death in the spiritual, then, is separation from life. And Life is God.

The Master, the Christ, manifested life in the earth through, not only the material manifestations that were given in the ministry, but also in laying aside the life. As He gave, "I give my life; I give it of myself, and I take it of myself". So in any attempt to repay, there can be no repayment. But when one lives the life that manifests the Christ life, love, joy, peace, harmony, grace, and glory, the joy is in the life of the Master as He manifests and manifested life in the earth.

She was so affected by the death of the Master that, when she saw Him at the sepulcher, she thought He was the gardener. This indicates all the hopelessness and all the sorrow that is possible to be indicated in hopelessness. Yet the joy, rather than the separation, should be the condition to be thought about. This is going backward, even to be affected by the separation, when there is the joy as manifested in, "My Lord and my God".

She was present when the Ascension occurred. (295)

After the Master's death and resurrection, it would take volumes to give in detail what Mary, Martha, and Lazarus accomplished in the remaining years of their lives. Lazarus' life continued only until the first of the rebellions arose. For beginning with the time when he was raised from the dead, much of the dissension in the minds of both the people and the high priest was caused by his activity.

Following the death and separation of the Master from the disciples, the home of Mary and Martha became, for a time, the center for most of the activities of the disciples. This was especially true with respect to them who were not altogether Galileans. Their associations became the closest with John, James, Matthew, Levi, and Thaddeus. The other disciples, of course, remained closer to the activities of the Galileans.

Following the return from Galilee, and the activities which took place there preceding and at the time of the Ascension, which was fifty days after the Resurrection, Mary, the mother of Christ, became a dweller in the home of John. This was close to Bethany. Also, John was the wealthiest of the disciples of Christ. His estate, as it would be valued in the present in American money, was nearly a quarter of a million dollars. Hence, he was a power with both the Romans and Jews in that period. As a result of all of this, the association of Mary, the sister of Martha, and John became the closest after that time.

The rebellions and dissension arose with the coming of the soldiers. At this time, Martha was joined with the people who caused the rebellion of Saul. And it was the persecutions and banishments conducted under his direction which brought about the death of Martha.

In addition to the Mother of Christ, John's household was now composed of Mary Magdalene and Elois, the sister of Mary who was the mother of James and John. These people then journeyed to John's summer home on the lake of Gennesaret, where the activities of those who came and went were supervised by all the members of the household.

The remaining period of the life of Mary, the sister of Lazarus, was about twenty-two years. She was twenty-three years old when Christ cleansed her of the seven devils; avarice, hate, self-indulgence, and the kindred selfishnesses, in addition to hopelessness and blasphemy.

The lesson to be learned here is the need to subdue the same conditions which existed there. These are continuing influences in your experience. *For one should remember that even the cleansing power used in the raising of Lazarus, raised him only for the moment. He then had his own life to live. He was forgiven—yes, entirely—by and through the blood of the Master; but he still had his own life to live.*

As shown in the illustration that has been given often: nails may be driven into a post and then removed, but the holes cannot. Neither can the scars that remain, which touched the soul as the devils do in their activity, be wholly erased, until the individual has passed through the whole cleansing in Him. All those then who were cleansed by Him, have been and are called for special missions in each of their sojourns among men. This is in order that they, as souls and as portions of the whole Creative Force, may demonstrate and give blessings to many.

This may be done by the entity now, even as Mary did in that sojourn. She stood as a monument and a memorial to the effect of the Christ life upon the life of a soul which was active in the earth during the Galilean or Palestine experience. Likewise, this individual may now become a channel through which blessings may come to many. And this will bring the things into the hearts, minds and souls of men that will cause the recognition of the saving grace in the love of the Christ, the Savior of men. (295)

The entity (1981) was in the Promised Land when the Essenes were preparing and consecrating the young girls, one of whom might be chosen as a channel through which He, the Prince of Peace, might come. She was in the house of lodging of the temple where the maidens were brought for that consecrated service, and she was the third in line upon the stair when the choice was made of Mary.

Hence, this entity was closely associated throughout that experience not only with the close followers of the Master, but also *she was: the wife of James, the brother of John, the beloved.* As a result, she was the wife of the first of the Martyrs for the Christ, and the wife of him who brought many of the Romans to a greater understanding of these teachings. Also, she was closely associated with the wife of Cornelius, and was with the disciples on the walk to Emmaus. She was among the Holy Women who helped in the preparations of the Body for burial, and was with the disciples and the Mother on that first Easter morn.

It is no wonder, then that she has thought of Easter as being significant and a time to be observed, yet has not been observed entirely in a proper manner. At that time, she instructed many of all classes and stations in life, in the need for individual service in order to attain the greater understanding. (1981)

The entity (Juana) was among those who went on the first Lord's Day, to view the Place of the Skull; who saw and heard the expressions of that one (Mary Magdalene) who had first beheld the risen Lord. (2519)

Q. Following the Crucifixion and Resurrection, did Mary, the mother of Jesus, indeed go to live in the household of the youngest disciple, John, the beloved?

A. The entity (Ulai) had made that journey to notify the Mother of that (which was) taking place in Jerusalem, missing the triumphal entry, but among those who saw and heard and spoke with the Master on the way to Calvary. (993)

(Then, as indicated in Holy Writ, He gave:) "Behold the Woman . . . To you (John) she is given. Be to her a son in my stead." (1158)

The entity (Ulai) remained with or took the mother, not to John's home, but to her own. Later, when there were those periods of rejoicing over the knowledge of the Resurrection (and there were) the meetings of the disciples and apostles in the upper room, the entity then went with the Mother—Mary—to the home of John and saw her established there. (993)

Philoas (1151) lived when the Master walked in the earth, when there were the teachings in the temple, and the journeys in and about Jerusalem. He was a Roman, not as a soldier, lord, or king, but rather as one who represented the Roman people. He was not a tax gatherer, but judged the ability of the people to contribute, not only of their commodities, but also of their services.

During the time of the Triumphal Entry into Jerusalem, he became closely associated with, and obtained a better understanding of, that which was being presented to a stiff-necked people. However, it touched the hearts, minds, and lives of many people in that period.

And he was with the people who proclaimed the Resurrection, and heard the teachings then. Also, he was present in the inn when He walked to Emmaus, and when there was the call for them who would come after Him and learn of Him. As a result, in the present, He has come again into his presence, thereby making secure his inmost feelings. And he is sure of His thought for men, and of the fulfilling of the promises that have been and are a part of man's heritage, "If ye abide in me, and I in thee, ask and it shall be given thee; for through such may the Father be glorified in you through me".

Hold fast to that which you have gained, as you gained then when you followed with His disciples to that hill from which He ascended to the glories which had been prepared by and for Him in that land where He gave, "I go to prepare a place, that where I am there ye may be also. The place ye know; the way ye know".

He was from Rome, but he helped many in Palestine during that sojourn.

The experience of Philoas in the present may be shaped by him, as he did then. For it was through his activity that those in authority required Pilate to make a personal report of what took place when a prophet, and more than a prophet, was condemned. While at the same time, by the voice of many people, a man who was known to be of unsavory repute was set free. And he may again through his associations cause many of those to be called who gave voice for that event then.

As a representative of the government then, he judged the abilities of groups and individuals, not as a spy, but rather as an analyst of their relationship under a divided spiritual guidance. And he analyzed their patriotism to the Romans, and also whether they worked in the interests of the people.

For the Roman rule did not merely consider people who were in authority or high estate, but its real purpose was to know the relationships between individuals. And the work of Philoas was to see that he had an authority higher than the local government or protectorate, or any other influence. This, then, was the background for his report to Caesar. And the report related to the activities of Herod who was the local representative of the people with respect to their religious thought.

On the other hand, there was the authority delegated to the protectorate, or proletariat, which controlled the civil government involving law and order.

Hence, this condition existed between the two forms of government. Tribute was collected by the Romans. And they attempted to understand and control both the religious and political activities. However, this often created undesirable conditions, because of the differences in the powers, and the fact that they were altered in their operation.

These were the conditions when this prophet, the

Master, was presented to the authorities for civil consideration. And it was claimed that he had neglected to pay tribute, and that there had been an attempt on the part of his followers to prevent the tax, or levies, from being paid. *This was the accusation, rather than that which is recorded, even in Holy Writ.*

Under these circumstances, Philoas came under the influence of the Prince of Peace, and of the teachings of the Nazarene. Nor did he see Him serving the people, the nation, the world, in a passive manner. Instead, He had a positive and active influence on the people who came in contact with Him as a Man, a Teacher, and a Healer.

These are the conditions, or shadows of them that present themselves as conditions, in the affairs of man in this land in the present. And here, there is a form of religious freedom, and an application in part of moral duty and economic duty, which guide a nation and a people. These have been handed down from them who, in faith to their Maker and in belief in their fellow man, established a freedom of speech, a freedom of press, and a freedom of worship of the Maker according to the dictates of their conscience.

This entity upheld these and all of their kindred influences in his sojourn in Palestine as a representative of the Roman government. Likewise, he must as a soldier of the Cross and of the Lamb, represent his Master and his Lord in the present. For as given, has he not been called? Has he not seen Him entering there and giving that command, "Ye must stand in my and thy brother's stead; for as they do it unto thy brethren, they do it unto Me".

In that sojourn also, there came a time when a report was to be made by him relating to the events there upon the hill of shame, upon the cross, yet of glory. Later, there was the command that there should be a report by the civil ruler, Pilate, before the emperor, the physical king.

Thus, this entity may have been an influence, even greater than the apostle Paul, in bringing to the Roman conscience a correct report of what happened in Jerusalem, and in Galilee and Samaria. For they who caused an accounting for what happened, brought to the people who seek to know His ways, an appointment and a judgment of the Father.

In the same manner, this individual at this period in the history of his own land, stands as a balance for the influences that will bring to judgment the conditions that exist in his native land today.

Then, call again and again upon that promise which has prompted from within, that you should be guided right, and that you should be led by Him, even as the Prince of Peace. For the burdens of them who would again crucify the truths of Him that is the Prince of Peace have been delivered to the people. *And the people have again come under the tyranny of the money changers, and of them who have let position, fame, or fortune become their god, rather than Him that guided those who established the land.*

You traveled along the road to Emmaus with the Master, rather than meeting him at the end.

And you knew the Master; although you did not understand wholly, as the conversation would indicate: Hast thou heard the happenings of the day? Hast thou known the considerations upon or of this man, both from the religious and the economic standpoint, and also the civil experiences of same? Yet only in the breaking of bread did the consciousness come of what He had said. Then it cannot be said that you fully understood Him from either the material or physical angle. Yet your inner consciousness did understand; otherwise, how would there have been that call again and again.

You were not condemned in Rome for the report you made by them you knew. You were condemned rather by them who became fearful of a change in the social order of the day, and only in that. You were not condemned by the civil or religious authorities, but rather by the social.

You passed on naturally in that incarnation; although you lost much of your strength, because of privation of yourself so that help might be given to others who were condemned later.

Do not confuse the condemnation which came years later, with the condemning which occurred during your sojourn. For about sixty to ninety years afterward, your activities were spoken of in a very evil manner. And only about two hundred years later were they lauded and put in their proper place. (1151)

Ruth (1158) (daughter of Mary, the mother of Jesus) in her incarnation in Palestine, after she was told about her husband (Philoas') walk to Emmaus with Christ after the Resurrection, she was convinced that He was, indeed, the Son of a living God. Likewise, in the present, when other souls contact and associate with this entity, they reach a conviction, even as in Palestine, souls were convicted not of themselves, but by a closer walk with Life itself.

You also saw a similar intent and purpose when your elder brother James, became the head of the church. He was not what would now be considered an elder, teacher, or minister. But your brother, James, was exalted to the position of leader in order to Honor Jesus, the Christ, to whom all honor and glory are due. It was for Him to whom all patience, suffering, and humbleness became a portion of His demonstration in Life.

And he only asked that we should be a part of this so that He might be strengthened in the earth.

For to the people of the earth, He has given the message, "Lo, I am with thee always, always". To you and to all who have named and do name His name is given the charge, "Feed my sheep; care for my lambs".

Afterward, there were the activities in defiance of the authorities. There were the changing viewpoints in Rome. And His death made possible a closer association of His representatives with the political and religious authorities in your own land. Then with the changes, there was a checking up on the people who followed the spirit of the new teachings.

For your light was not hid under a bushel. Your quietness, gentleness, and patience were shown, even in the courts of Bacchus. And the revelries that were to satisfy and gratify the material appetites of men and women during those periods were to you merely debaucheries.

As you saw the influences of wine and strong drink that excited the passions of men, you considered not the vileness. Rather, you saw the blood of your brother spilled in a wanton manner, so that the earth might know that He did not live in vain. For those who honor and love Him, even as He loved the world, give their own heart's blood so that the world may know that He lives, and He is at the right hand of the Father. This is in order that you and your brethren, friends, and enemies may have an advocate before the Throne of mercy.

There, He pleads the cause of the wayward, hears the cry of them that are persecuted, and says, "Be patient, be patient, my child. For know, thou daughter of Mary, the mother of Jesus, in patience you possess your soul."

And He said, "Become aware that I am able to sustain these, even though ye walk through the valleys, and in the shadows, of death". For death has no sting. It has no power over those who know the Resurrection, even as you have seen, known, and heard. For the Resurrection brought to the consciousness of man that power which God has given to man. This is the power that enables man to reconstruct and resuscitate every atom of a physically sick body. He may resurrect even every atom of a sin-sick soul. And He may resurrect the soul so that it will live on in the glory of a resurrected, regenerate Christ in the souls and hearts of men.

You saw the lasciviousness in Rome. And in Athens, you saw the unwarranted flow of blood of your own people, because they held to that saying, "Whether it is right that I should listen to the voice of God, or harken to the voices of men".

Then, you grow farther and farther away from the voices of men. And you come closer to the voice of Christ, in the lives of those who are weary with the toils of the physical, and that are sick with the doubts of the spiritual, because of their contacts with the worldly wise.

And you give a gentle smile of assurance and understanding, even as He looked upon your mother and friends and said, "Behold the Woman". And to your cousin and friend, (John) He said, "To you, she is given. Be to her a son in my stead".

Then as you, a mother, find in these about you in your daily life, the soft word turns away wrath, even of the worldly wise.

It lessens the fear of them that are in doubt because of their bodily needs. And you thereby bring to yourself more of the consciousness of your experiences in that sojourn as Ruth.

For as your name implies hope and new life, you may and do bring that into the lives of many in this sojourn. And as the little leaven leavens the whole lump, so may your gentleness, kindness, longsuffering, and patience bring into the world, that for which He gave His life and hope. Into yours and your friends' hands, and those who have named His Name, the power is given to bring to the consciousness of others an awakening to the glories of a Risen Lord.

In that incarnation, you had varied experiences. In Sicily, you came upon a people that was so bound by tradition, they believed that only members of the Household of Promise, through lineal descendants that had not been crossed by the blood of the heathen, might be saved. And they even pointed to you that you, as a blood sister of His, had mingled your blood with the Romans. (1158)

Thelda was an acquaintance of Martha and Mary, to whom the Master came often. And she was one of the hired mourners at the time of Lazarus' death. She became a believer after seeing the activities there, and seeing the influence of the Master's life on her friends, associates, and acquaintances.

Thereafter, she was known as one of the Holy Women. And she gained in soul development. While she was late in life when she became acquainted with the activities of the Disciples and the Apostles, she lived until after the Crucifixion.

And she saw the Crucifixion, the darkening of the day, and the rending of the veil of the temple; and she heard the noises. Later, she was in the upper room with the followers of the Master when they were made aware of His Resurrection. For those things which happened to the people, to her acquaintances and their children, to the heathen, and especially to the Romans, were witnessed by her.

*She was the aunt of Mariaerh who was the companion
of Lucius when he was bishop in Laodicea.* She gained
in soul development. For those tenets, as well as her
own desires, purposes, and intents became deep-seated
within her soul. The things which affected the lives of
individuals in that period become more and more important to her now. For she learned well the lesson
which she heard given to Martha and Mary by the
Master, "These things are not to be left undone; but
she, my daughter, hath chosen the greater part". Listen
to the voice which may come within, for it will not only
direct your activities in association with individuals
here and now, but also it will prompt your heart in your
relationships with others. (1986)

Q. Did the Essenes—or their leaders, such as
Judy—continue their activities in association with the
apostles and disciples of Jesus?
A. The entity Judy was held in reverence by all of the
followers of Jesus, though persecuted oft by the
Jews—or certain sects of the Jews—under various circumstances. (1151)

Hence we find the entity (Judy) in those periods soon
after the Crucifixion giving not only comfort but a better interpretation to the twelve, and to the Holy
Women; and understanding as to how woman was redeemed from a place of obscurity (and restored) to her
place in the activities of the affairs of the race, of the
world, of the empire—yea, of the home itself. (1472)

Q. Were there any of the more orthodox Jews con-
verted, as it were, by the Resurrection of our Lord?
A. Artemas lived when the Master walked in the earth.
He was one of the elders of the Sanhedrin, and was a
doubter and a questioner. And he often sought to give
an interpretation to the rulers about the activities of the
multitudes. He continued a doubter during the period of
Christ's material manifestation. However, as a result of
the events following the Crucifixion and the Resurrec-

tion Morn, and that which was related to him by Joseph of Arimathaea and Nicodemus, he became a staunch defender of the Apostles and disciples during the days of persecution.

And not until his demise was there any great amount of physical persecution to the first church. In the present, he has been a stickler for details. Also, visions and a closer association with the unseen forces have been a part of this experience. (1378)

The road to Gethsemane, to the minds of those who look upon their own Gethsemane, was a road of thorns; the perspiration, the sweat of blood, and all, appear anything but happiness. Yet the kind words spoken, even on the Way to Calvary, were indeed those which brought happiness. And as there were the words from the Cross—though spoken amid all the horrors of spite and fear caused by the activities of others—these words were such as to bring happiness into the hearts and minds of those who seek to know His Way. (262-111)

Think ye that Jesus went happily to the Cross, or that He went happily from the garden where there had been apparently so little consideration by His followers as to what the moment meant, when they slept as He wrestled with self?

Think yet then on thine own disturbances, which are of the moment . . . and thy worry as to this and that, or the shortcomings of those ye love. How was He with those He loved? Yea, He gave them His blessings. So in wisdom, in happiness, bless them that despitefully use thee or speak unkindly. Bless if ye would be wise, be happy—have happiness in thine own life. (262-108)

As He looked upon Peter in the hour of trial and of denial by him who had been declared . . . the foundation of that which He was to leave in the earth: did He frown or did He smile? What broke the heart of the man—the frown or the smile? (262-33)

And then as He hung upon the cross, He called to those He loved, and He remembered not only their spiritual purposes but their material lives. . . . For He committed unto those of His brethren not only the care of the spiritual life of the world, but the material life of those who were of His own flesh, His own blood. Yea, as He gave His physical blood that doubt and fear might be banished; so He overcame death—not only in the physical body but in the spirit body.

Not only was He dead in the body, but the soul was separated from that body. For when all phases of man are made manifest in the earth, the physical body, mental body and soul body become dependent upon their own experience. Is it any wonder, then, that the man cried out, "My God, my God, why hast thou forsaken me?"

Each man comes to stand, as He, before that throne of the Maker; presenting the deeds done in the body, in the mind, in the body—spiritual before the throne of the Maker, the Creator, God.

Yet, He the Father hath given to each of you: "I have given my angels charge concerning thee, and they shall bear thee up, and thou shalt not know corruption".

. . . Hence when those loved ones and His brethren came, on that glad morning when the tidings had come to them; those who stood guard heard a fearful voice and saw a light. "The stone has been rolled away". . . . Then they entered into the garden, and there Mary first saw her *risen* Lord. Then came those of His brethren with the faithful women, those who loved His mother, who were her companions in sorrow, and those who were making preparations that the law be kept and there be no desecration even of the ground about His Tomb. His friends, too, His loved ones and His brethren saw the angels. . . .

Open thine eyes and behold the Glory, even of the

Christ present here, now, in thy midst! Even as He appeared to them on that day. . . .

Ye, too, often doubt; ye, too, often fear. Yet He is surely with thee. And at this glad season when ye rededicate thy life, thy body and mind to His service, ye, too, *may know,* as did they, that He lives . . . and is at the right hand of God, to make intercession for you. If ye will believe that He is, ye may experience it. (5749-6)

But when the Prince of Peace came into the earth for the completion of His OWN development in the earth, He overcame the flesh AND temptation. So He became the first of those who overcame death in the body, (and this) enabled Him to illuminate, to so revivify that body that he could take it up again, even when those fluids of the body had been drained away by the nail holes in His hands and the spear piercing His side. . . .

He came, the Master, in flesh and blood, even as thou didst come in flesh and blood. Yet as He then proclaimed . . . there is a cleansing of the body, of the flesh, of the blood, in such measure that it may become illuminated with power from On High; that is within thine own body to WILL "Thy Will O God; not mine, but Thine, be done in me, through me". This was the message which He gave when He too overcame, surrendering all power unto the Will of the Father (1152) . . . (and thus) is an example for Man, and only as a man, for He lived only as a man. He died only as a man.

The soul was made perfect in the beginning; it passes through the Earth plane where it may obtain its body to present before the Creator. (900-17)

Q. Explain the transmutation of human flesh to flesh divine the real mystery of the Crucifixion and Resurrection.

A. There is no mystery to the transmutation of the body of the Christ. For having attained in the physical con-

sciousness the at-one-ment with The Father-Mother
God, the completeness was such that with the disin-
tegration of the body—as indicated in the manner in
which the shroud, the robe, the napkin lay—there was
then the taking of the body-physical form. This was the
manner. It was not a transmutation as of changing from
one to another.

Just as indicated in the manner in which the body-
physical entered the Upper Room with the door closed,
not by being a part of the wood through which the body
passed, but by forming from the ether waves that were
within the room, because of a meeting prepared by
faith. For as had been given, "Tarry ye in Jerusalem—in the upper chamber—until ye be embued with
power from on high". (2533-8)

As indicated in the spoken word to Mary in the garden,
"Touch me not, for I have not yet ascended to my
Father". The body (flesh) that formed that (which
was) seen by the normal or carnal eye of Mary was
such that it could not be handled until there had been
the conscious union with the sources of all power, or all
force.

But afterward—when there had been the first, second,
third, fourth and even the sixth meeting—He then said,
"Put forth thy hand and touch the nail prints in my
hands, in my feet. Thrust thy hand into my side and
believe." This indicated the transformation.

For, as indicated when the soul departs from the body
(this is not being spoken of the Christ, you see), it has
all of the form of the body from which it has passed, yet
it is not visible to the carnal mind unless that mind has
been, and is, attuned to the infinite. Then it appears, in
the infinite, as that which may be handled, with all the
attributes of the physical being, with the appetites, until
these have been accorded to a unit of activity with
universal consciousness.

Just as it was with the Christ body, "Children, have ye anything here to eat?" This indicated to the disciples and the apostles present that this was not transmutation but regeneration, re-creation of the atoms and cells of body that might, through desire; masticate material things; fish and honey (in the honeycomb) were given.

As also indicated later, when He stood by the sea and the disciples and apostles who saw Him from the distance could not, in the early morning light, discern, *but when He spoke the voice made the impression upon the mind of the beloved disciple (John) such that he spoke: "It is the Lord!" The body had prepared fire upon the earth*—fire, water, the elements that make for creation, for as the spirit is the beginning, water combined of elements is the mother of creation.*

Just as when there are those various realms about the solar system (represented by the planets around our sun) in which each entity may find itself when absent from the body, it takes on in those other realms not an earthly form, but a pattern conforming to the same dimensional elements of that individual planet or space. (2533-8)

Then, as the body of Christ in the flesh became perfect in the world, as it was laid aside on the Cross and in the tomb, the physical body moved away—through what man comes to know as dimensions—and the Spirit was then able to take hold on that Being in the way in which it entered again into the body. Thus it presented itself to the world, as it did to individuals at the time and as it does to man (in general) at present. (900-227)

---

* See ch. IV re. The Four Baptisms.

Chapter Eleven

PENTECOST—THE EARLY CHURCH

Q. It has been given through the Readings that the entity
now known as Edgar Cayce was active in the early
years of the Christian Church at Laodicea as Lucius
Ceptulus. Please summarize the history of the early
Church as seen through the activities of Lucius.

A. In those activities then that followed the Crucifixion,
and the days of the Pentecost, and the sermon or
teaching—when the outpouring of the Holy Spirit was
beheld by Lucius, when Peter spoke in tongues—or as
he spoke in his OWN tongue, the message was HEARD
by those of EVERY nation in their OWN tongue—this
so impressed Lucius that there came a re-dedicating,
and the determination within self to become closer
associated, closer affiliated with the Disciples or Apostles.

But when the persecutions arose, and there was the
choice of those who were to act as . . . the deacons—as
Philip and Stephen and the others—again he was rejected because of his close associations with one, Saul,
later called Paul; he (Lucius) being also of Tarsus or of
the country, and a Roman, and questioned as to his
Jewish ancestry—though claimed by Paul (or Saul)
that he was a Jew. His mother was indeed of the tribe
of Benjamin, though his father was not. Hence we find
the questions arose as to the advisability of putting into
positions either as teachers, ministers or those in active
service those who were questioned as to their lineal descent. And again the old question as to whether ANY
were to receive the word but those of the household of
faith, or the Jews.

During the sojourn in Jerusalem, though, before the greater persecution—that is, before the beheading of James, the brother of John, and the stoning of Stephen—here again we had a great question arise. For Lucius, through the associations with (Mariaerh) the one who became his companion or wife as ye would call, was entertained and kept by Mary and Martha and Lazarus—thus we find these again raised questions. And there is often the confusing of Lucius and Luke, for these were kinsmen (Merceden (2574), the mother of Lucius, being the sister of Luke)—and Lucius and Luke were drawn or thrown together; and with the conversion of Saul (or Paul, as he became) they followed closer and closer with the activities of Paul.

With the acceptance of Lucius by Paul, and part of those in the Caesarean church, Lucius determined —with his companion—to return to the portion of his own land, owing to the persecutions, and there to attempt to establish a church; to be the minister, to be the active force in that portion of the land.

Thus we find in those latter portions of the experience he became the bishop or director or the president of the Presbytery; or what ye would call the priest or the father or the high counselor as given to those in the early periods of the church; that is, the one to whom all questions were taken respecting what ye would term in the present as theology, or questions pertaining to the laws. In such, the entity—as the bishop—was the last word, except that there might be an appeal from his verdict to the church in Jerusalem—or the Apostles themselves. Such disputes brought disturbances at times, when there were questionings, especially as Paul brought into that region, as to whether it was well for those in such positions to be married or not.

And the declarations as made through the Corinthian and the Ephesian leaders indicate what disturbances there were; because differences arose between Lucius and Paul as between Silas and Paul and Barnabas and those who had become the leaders or the real ministers or the missionaries for the Church. Hence this brought into the experience of the entity, Lucius, disturbances between himself and his companion, because—in the first (place) the companion was younger in years than Lucius, and to them there had been no offspring, no child.

This confusion made for periods when there was the withdrawing of the companion, and the closer association of the companion with the teacher that had been the proclaimer and the director in the early experience of the Master's life Himself—or with Judy; and with Elizabeth and with Mary, the mother of the Lord.

With those experiences, and with Paul's going on his second and even his third missionary journey; and with many of the things propounded by him (Paul) that Lucius had declared as things that were unstable, there again—with Judy's teachings to the companion, by the mother of the Lord and Elizabeth, in their years of maturity, teaching this younger person there was brought to Lucius that which later John proclaimed; *that there is in this church of Laodicea no fault, yet it is neither hot nor cold—and that for the lack of its very stand (or staunchness), it would find condemning.* (294-192)

Q. Explain how all heard in their various tongues the message that was given by Peter in the one tongue.
A. This was the activity of the spirit, and what the spirit indeed meant and means in the experiences of the individuals during that period. For the one that was of Cyrene (Lucius) heard a mixture of the Greek and Aryan tongues, while—though Peter spoke in Aramaic—those that were of the Hebrews heard in the Hebrew language, those in Greek heard in Greek, see? (294-192)

Q. On the day of the Ascension of Jesus, was there a great crowd or only His disciples present?

A. Five hundred beheld Him as He entered into glory, and saw the angels, heard their announcement of the event that must one day come to pass, and will only be to those who believe, and have faith, who look for and expect to see Him as He is. (3615)

You (Philos) had personal contact with Jesus, the Master, especially when Jesus the Child reasoned with the rulers in the temple. Later, he was associated with the Roman and Jewish leaders, and he heard the Master teach just before the time of the Crucifixion. These two definite periods are a part of his inner consciousness. And you were one of them who watched from the mount when He took His way toward the Heavenly Hosts. (1486)

With the establishing of the church at Jerusalem, the entity was present when James . . . the brother of the Lord . . . was raised to that position or place as the head of the church, through the direct influence of James and John the sons of Zebedee. This brought about that first of the authorities putting forth their hand and laying James by the sword. This happened not by that of trial, but by that as would today be called a riot; and not incorrectly were James and John called the Sons of Thunder. (2390-3)

Barsaboi was in the Promised Land when the Master walked in the earth, and choices were being made by members of the brotherhood to whom he had belonged, and followers were gathering about the Teacher. For he was one of them who were given authority to become representatives and teachers during the first part of the ministry of the Teacher.

And he remained a teacher until questioning was begun by the authorities, such as the Pharisees, Sadducees, and Romans, who had become disturbed because of the advances made by the Essenes. He did not withdraw as an active teacher until the latter part of Christ's ministry.

When the rebellions began after the death of James, he again became an active figure in the work which had been presented by the Teacher. And he gained, lost, and gained in soul development. In the present, he often becomes confused in the stands he takes with respect to his companions and to spiritual matters. (1211)

The entity (Josie) passed on through those periods of riots following the beheading of James, the brother of John. (1010-17)

Josida was in the Promised Land when the church was established as a permanent institution. Many have not often considered, as this entity has, as to how the church took the place of the synagogues of the temple worship.

She was among the young in the group that heard Peter on the day of Pentecost. Later, Peter established the church in Antioch. And she was present during the activities in Laodicea; and she saw the members scattered by the early persecutions of the Romans who were sent to replace the Centurion in Antioch.

Thus, she became a follower of Paul and Barnabas in Laodicea, and was active there. For she was the Lady Superior or Mother of that church, which grew during the various disputes that arose with the Bishops, as well as with the members of what later was called the Presbytery of that particular group of individuals.

She gained in soul development, although she suffered at times during the turmoils among the leaders. These included the disputes between Lucius and Paul, and of Paul, Barnabas, and Mark. All of these became a portion of the records kept by her. Thus, she was kept between the fires of disputation. (1688)

Alphus was in the Promised Land when the Master walked in the earth, and when the men were chosen who were to carry on the work of the Master. He had a knowledge of, and was a friend of, all of the Twelve. For he was among the Seventy, who were set apart and sent for that contemporary service with Him. (2031)

Suphor was in the Promised Land when the Master walked in the earth, and she was one of the children in the land where the Master dwelt. And she came directly under His influence when the children gathered for His blessings, as He walked by the wayside.

She was closely acquainted with some, and casually with the others, of the Twelve who followed with Him; but she was blessed by all of them because of the care which she took of the Master's household after the Crucifixion. She gained in soul development then. And she aided James, the brother of the Lord, in the work of the first church. (2346)

Telka was in Palestine when the Master walked in the earth. She heard the tenets and saw the words of His disciples, and that which was practiced by Him in interpreting the letter and spirit of the law. And she gained in soul development, although *she suffered martyrdom. For she was carried to the Roman arena,* a practice which was used in connection with individuals of the groups that had embraced or listened to those tenets in the land. This was after many of the Romans had accepted the beliefs.

She renounced the tenets when martyrdom was presented. Yet she suffered death because of exposure and confinement when the groups were brought there. However, she gained, for she had determined to study and know the truths and tenets of the various groups which had religious experiences.

She became a mother while she was active in studying the truths which she learned there. And in the present, there will be opportunities for wedded life. However, if she would gain the most development, she should have a career before marriage. And she should be a teacher or educator of psychological subjects prepared for the young regarding their relationships with other teen-age children.

This ability comes from her incarnation as Telka, as well as the one as *Sister Teresa* (in nineteenth-century U.S.A.). And it is assisted by her determination to warn individuals as to how they may prepare themselves so that they may be a better generation in man's activity in the earth. (2444)

Marcia was in the Promised Land when the Master walked in the earth. And she was one of the people in Bethsaida with whom the Lord walked, talked, and worked. She was associated with those known as the keepers of the faith, and aided especially the teacher, Barnabas, who helped Paul in his ministrations. Hence, she worked closely with them who were teachers and writers at that time.

She was beautiful in body and mind, but she caused a good deal of disturbance during the early activities of the church in Antioch. However, as an associate and companion of Barnabas, and with the persecution of Paul, she helped in all of the work of the early church. *And she lost her life only when she was carried to Rome as an example for the people of that era.* (2283)

Sylvia lived in the Holy Land, or Promised Land, when turmoils arose because of the teachings of the Master. This was when the people came for the holy days from all the lands near to Galilee, such as Phoenicia, or Syro-Phoenicia, Tyre, and Sidon.

She learned of the visit of that Teacher to Tyre and Sidon. Then, she contacted those who had been companions with Him in Bethany, Bethsaida, Bethlehem, and Capernaum, and questioned them. The varied reports confused her. Later she saw the eyes of the Master as He passed by on the way to the city, on the day when He gave that, if it were not for the cry of the people, the very hills and mountains would cry out, "Hosanna, Glory in the Highest. For the Prince of Peace comes to make those decisions whereunto man again has his closer association with his Maker."

Then, she understood and realized that man as man may be far from God; but man as a god and acting godly may be close to The Divine.

Sylvia was stoned with Stephen, who was one of the first of the martyrs for a holy cause. Thus, the words in the declaration by Stephen, "Until I see my Lord standing I fear; then I know His presence is near", ring in her experience in her attempts to aid. (1301)

Gamaliel was in a position when the Master walked in the earth, where much was given and much was required of him. For he was a teacher in Jerusalem, and many went to him for counsel. To him was given the teaching of men who became great in the land, in the name of Him who came as the lamb to the world. He counseled that there should be justice to all, and this he has held innate, and lost in soul development only when he was persecuted by them in power when the rulers were changed by the Romans.

He lost because he became weak so that suffering might not come to him and to those who were near and dear to him. Hence in the present, the ones who were his relatives and children then, seem to him far away and like a dream, where he felt lonely in the night, then awoke and could remember only turmoil which was not understood. (933)

Lieoth lived in that period from which she has so often found a consciousness of rhythm and a song from without. *It was when Stephen was stoned for his beliefs* and because of his vision. And she heard the voices of the mob. And she also saw the brethren who listened with that awe which brought to the hearts and minds of the people the awareness that man, without his own power, had the ability to refuse, to reject even, the presence of God among men. He had the power to so raise his own ego that he could defy even God in His dealings with, and in His seeking to be a Loving Father to, the children of men.

She gained, lost, and gained in soul development. For there were periods when she felt resentment and hate because they mistreated that source through which she today often hears the voice as of the brethren. Awake to the awareness of the indwelling of the spirit of peace and harmony, which alone comes from the Prince of Peace, the Son of Light, the Way of Hope, the Voice of God in the earth. (2402)

Lydia was in the Promised Land when the teachings were spread by the disciples of the Master. She was young during the periods when many gathered following the death of Christ on the Cross and Pentecost. Although she was from the land about Thessalonica and spoke a different tongue from the Galileans, she came under the teachings of the Holy Women, as well as John and Philip, and the one who first became a martyr for a cause, Stephen who was from the same land. (1825)

Simeon was a follower of the Essenes whose preparations at that time made possible the entering of the Master. You were crippled in one limb then. However, if you will continue your activities of that sojourn now, you may bring to the hearts of many a greater concept of the love, mercy, strength, power, and might of the Master during His sojourn in the earth.

With respect to your ability as an artist, the pastoral scenes should be painted with religious subjects. And they should show the life of Christ with the disciples, and especially the ones chosen as special messengers or servants. Your greatest portrait should be of the Master and Stephen. And the latter should be shown, not as the martyr, but as the speaker to the people before his martyrdom.

In that picture, Stephen should be making the address to the people who would take his life. And this may be painted so that it will show every one what that address meant. Make it so that those who see it will consider the scene a personal experience.

In the portrait of the Master, show Him leaving the upper chamber; and there should not be seen in the faces of the eleven the fear which was created by the leaving of Judas. Rather, show the feeling in the hearts and minds of all when He gave, "My peace I leave with you. In my Father's house are many mansions; if it were not so, I would have told you. I go to prepare a place that where I am there ye may be also."

The canvas may show to the beholders, by color and position, the expression of that hour. And this will carry the message of hope, and of the eternal oneness of the Christlife, into the hearts of men. *You were Simeon, the one-legged man.* (1424)

Constantine Tupela was in the Grecian land, close to the time when the Master walked in the Promised Land. And he came under the influence of those who had been close followers of the Nazarene. And he became filled with the desire to depict for others the characters and characterizations, the love and the lovelight, as it was told by the teachers of that day.

Hence, he came under the influence of the followers of Paul, Silas, Philip, and the early fathers of the church. And he was among the first to attempt to depict upon the meeting place of the Grecians in Athens the raising of Lazarus, as well as painting upon the walls of meeting places, pictures of those who accepted or heard the calls of the teachers then.

He gained in soul development through the experience, although he became rather secular, and withdrew from the activities of the people unless they thought as he did. As a result, he now becomes easily depressed because of conditions or circumstances which may arise through disagreements with others. (2310)

Philose was a Roman soldier who was sent to Palestine to help keep the peace and to collect customs. He was one of the Soldiers of the Master, the Savior of men. He knew a great deal about that which occurred, and it brought conviction to him. Yet fear of what would be said about him embracing a cause which apparently was lost with the crucifixion of its leader, caused him to keep his conviction to himself. Only with the persecutions which took place after he returned to Rome did he take any active part, and this brought him much trouble. For when he befriended the ones who embraced the cause, he lost both physically and materially because of his kindness.

Because of those experiences, he does not now like to talk about such matters. However he has formed opinions which he keeps to himself. He lost physically, but gained in soul development. For that sojourn brought turmoil materially, but inner satisfaction. (670)

Pondus lived when the Romans were influenced by the people who journeyed from the land where the Nazarene taught, and these teachings caused many changes in her surroundings. For she came under the influence of Paul and Titus, and had a knowledge of Timothy. These people taught that which produced strength in the lowly, and gave them in high estate, authority, or social prestige the love of all who were of one purpose before the Creative Force.

She was among those in the Roman rule who first induced the rulers to consider that these teachings were becoming a part of the Empire. As a result, she is now often affected by great speakers, and by conditions which arise as problems in the lives of nations, cities, households, and individuals. Such things are of interest to her. (1230)

Apoloir was in Palestine when the Master walked in the earth, being among the Romans who were garrisoned there previous to, during, and after the activities of the Master and His disciples and the Apostles. He knew of their activities, but kept himself in such a position that he was never required to apply direct punishment to any of them.

He gained and lost, and gained and lost, in soul development. For convictions arose within him, but owing to the circumstances, he never took active part in that which he believed. Hence, we find similar experiences arising in the present. For a soul is ever meeting itself—in its shortcomings, and when it has chosen in the improper direction . . . the good lives on, and is magnified. The errors become as stumbling-stones which may be kept, or which may be turned into stepping-stones that lead to a more excellent way. (843)

This entity, Anneuel, was in the Roman land when they first began to oppress those who followed the teachings of the Nazarene. This was when the disciples started to preach the gospel, as understood by them, in the various lands.

He was among the soldiers who had returned from Palestine, or Judea as called then. At first, he was indifferent, or somewhat in awe; but as the activities became more generally known, his interest increased. And when the time came when it was necessary for individuals to take a stand, he joined the outcasts. Yet many of those in power were influenced by the life and teachings of this entity, Anneuel, not only among his friends, but also among his acquaintances and associates. He gained in soul development.

Often, he suffered in material things, as well as in both the mental and physical body; yet this brought joy and happiness in the latter portion of that experience. And there may still be found among the ruins where the meetings were held, something of Anneuel's teachings. For he was among the first in the Roman land to record the events, and the teachings of the ministers and Apostles. The activities then that were so guarded, are still guarded, and bring soul development. (851)

Cyprus was in the Parthenian-Grecian land following the Crucifixion. And he heard about it when the story was told in his own land of Him who had given, "Come unto me, all ye that are weak and heavy laden, and ye shall find rest unto your souls". This, for many who were oppressed, was a message of hope; and it brought hope to Cyprus, and a new experience.

He became a healing messenger as a result of the awakening which came to him from the teachings of Paul and Barnabas. And he gained in soul development throughout that incarnation. Hold fast to those visions of old; for as ye measure to thy fellow man, so measure ye to thy Maker. For ye must stand before Him, thy Maker, with the deeds done in the body as a witness of thy purpose and thy desires. (1613)

Sylvanus lived when the Master walked in the earth, when people gathered about the Disciples and His followers, and when the Master blessed the Seventy who were to go abroad and teach and minister to others and preach repentance, and that the day of the Lord was at hand. *You were among the Seventy, and again on the Day of Pentecost you rededicated yourself.*

As a teacher and minister in the churches of lower Asia and the upper portions of Palestine, you ministered to your fellow man. You gained in soul development. And you brought encouragement, hope, and faith into the hearts and minds of those who, because of the political, social, and economic forces, became weak and stumbling. *Furthermore, it was to your credit that in Caesarea the followers were first called Christ-like, or Christians.* In your associations with the Twelve, the Bishops, and the Deacons, you gave counsel and strength.

And so you may in the present, as it was bidden to thy neighbor, thy brother in the Lord, "Feed my lambs; feed my sheep". This is your work now. This should be directed, not by the eye-service of man, but to the oneness of purpose and desire to bring into the hearts of men hope and encouragement. And; you should sow again and again the seed that bear the fruits of the Spirit—patience, gentleness, kindness, brotherly love, and long-suffering. For against such, there is no law.

For it is the law that as ye sow, so shall ye reap. And ye are the sower; but leave what may be the results to thy Father. For He alone may increase. For unless the souls are quickened by precept and example, and the Father calls, how can they know Him? (1529)

Pilos was close to the disciples, the Apostles, when the Master walked in the earth. And he was among the Seventy who were sent to minister to the needs of the people during the Galilean and Judean ministry.

His work during the latter portion of that sojourn was of greatest importance. For he joined with Barnabas, Paul, Silas, Mark, Luke, and Lucius in their ministering. Also, he was endowed with a voice which enabled him to create a song service in connection with the ministry and teaching of the disciples, the Apostles. For he worked with various churches. (622)

Salome lived when the Master walked in the earth. And she came under the influence of the Master Himself. Later, following the Crucifixion, the Resurrection, and the days of Pentecost, she aided in establishing the ways of ministering to the people. For she was one of the women described as the Holy Women. First, she came into contact with those activities at the death and the raising of Lazarus. And afterwards, she worked with Mary, Martha, and Mary of Magda, otherwise known as Mary Magdalene. (1874)

Patience, or as termed then, Ullen (Patience)—Jhenge. She lived when changes were being made in the practices of the social, political, and religious world. This occurred especially as a result of the disciples and Apostles being scattered abroad. She lived in the Arab land, and it was to her household that Andrew and James came during the beginning of their preaching. This was James the less, not the brother of John but the brother of the Lord; and she learned much from them.

However, confusion resulted to some extent because of the differences in the practices of the Arabs, and that which was taught by the Apostles. This was particularly so when visions, dreams, and the use of quiet moments became a part of their teachings. Nevertheless, she gained in soul development. And this was in spite of the disturbances caused by the variations in the teachings of her own people, and the instructions of her visitors, which she embraced.

After the departure of the Apostles, she attempted to follow in their way. Later, when she was between twenty-five and thirty years of age, she journeyed to the city where the disciples' teachings were followed. There she also saw the persecutions involved. But in addition, she saw the dedication of individuals, instead of the scorn which had been a part of her own home surroundings.

In her new environment, she came to be looked upon as one who had embraced and manifested the teachings. And her life among the people in Jerusalem was considered an example to be followed in dealing with one's fellow man.

Her abilities in the culinary arts, in the household, with the needle, and as a home builder arise from that incarnation. However, she only enjoyed these occasionally; for there were many changes in her place of dwelling. Yet much may be gained from the lessons learned then, which manifest as urges. This particularly refers to the innate urges for meditation on spiritual and inspirational matters. (1431)

John Louis, or Louie, was a nephew of Peter the Apostle. While he was a leader, he was by occupation a weaver of nets, and a wholesale dealer in supplies for fishermen. He was a follower of the disciples; and during a part of that experience, he suffered privations because of being driven from place to place.

He gained, lost and gained in soul development. For material destruction and persecution brought distraughtness. However, the saying, "Those that are strong, strengthen the weak", applied to him there; for he became a minister and teacher. As a result of that, he gained much in soul development, and became a leader and a strong support to many who were troubled in those days. (1346)

Gieved was a follower of the Nazarene, under the tutelage of one who was close to the Master. He became a missionary, and suffered martyrdom with the individual with whom he had been associated in his labors. In the present, he is gifted in the study of religion, that was deep seated in his soul then, and remains a part of him, adding an ennobling influence to his life. Also, he has abilities as a teacher, lecturer, or writer for those seeking knowledge of the spiritual indwelling in man of the principles of Christ. (78)

Jessica was in Macedonia when turmoils were created by the Romans, as well as by the thought in the spiritual life from the teachings of the disciples and Apostles of the Master. She was in the church in Laodicea when that church came near to being divided. And she aided the sister of the minister there to bring order in the church's ministry. (1661)

Idoddxo—herdsman, was in the land now known as
Arabia. And he was in his thirtieth year when he came
under the influence of the teachings through a disciple
of the Master, Andrew. And he gained much. That was
in the year forty-four, according to our present calendar. (2483)

Petros was in Palestine following the period when the
Master was in the earth. He was very young then, but
he was closely associated with many who gave their all
in body, purse, and service to bring to others the hope
created by the tenets of that Teacher. He was with the
people who were close to Mark, John, and the other
John. (John Mark).

When the persecutions began, he went with others to
the desert lands, along with Andrew and Thomas. And
he helped to build up in the oases and other places in
the lands in that particular area, a great hope and light
in the experience of many. (1637)

Lectus was in the Promised Land when the Master
walked in the earth. He was aware of the activities, and
he questioned himself throughout the sojourn, as to
whether it was more expedient for him to accept or reject them. Moreover, he was convinced that there was
something worth while in them, because of their effect
upon his associates and friends.

There, he lost a great opportunity to embrace, comprehend, and know the meaning of what is truth in the
experience of an individual in its relationships to its
fellow man. For he was a tax gatherer, but of the people
who were of the faith in that land. And *he was especially well acquainted with Levi and Matthew.* (2478)

Lydia was in the uppermost portions of the Promised
Land, when the Greek church was established following
the dispersal of the followers of the Nazarene. She was
of the Greek faith, and thus tended to worship beauty

more than other things. Hence, as a result of that experience, she is inclined to be material minded. However, when she came in contact with the church at Thessalonica, *she became an ardent supporter of those teachings; although the disputes which arose caused her some concern.*

As a result of that sojourn, she is constantly attracted to rote and routine with respect to spiritual matters, and yet is never quite satisfied with the manner in which many such are conducted. She needs self-analysis with relation to her ideals. She gained in soul development, physically, mentally, and spiritually, although there were temporary disturbances and discouraging thoughts. (958)

Following the Crucifixion, Salone was among the children of those who were called of the household of faith. She was closely associated with the household of Peter, including many of the younger ones such as Mark, Silas, and John, in her Jerusalem experience.

Those were periods of turmoil, wonder, and bodily suffering in many ways. However, she gained in soul development. And that gives her at present the desire to help the less fortunate, and to assist those who have erred or wandered to find their way home. Thus, she has ability in welfare work, or as a nurse, or in missionary activity, including commercial work of these types. (1531)

Garcia was a Roman in Rome when entertainers provided entertainment for people in authority. This was during the latter part of the reign of the Roman ruler, Tiberius, when some people were in great fear because of the expressions of individuals from Palestine.

She was a member of the royalty, and was in a household which was closely associated with the households of both Claudius and Tiberius, when changes came. Thus, her very position resulted in disturbing conditions. For circumstances produced changes in the affairs of her acquaintances. Yet when she first heard of the tenets and truths from Palestine, this was a strange experience to her.

And as occurred to her, too deep a relationship in a religious life without purpose may cause disturbance in the peace of mind of an individual. However, when she became associated with Ruth, who had been so close to the activities in Palestine, she came to be a power among the groups that even gave their bodies for sacrifices for a Cause, a Purpose, and an Ideal.

She knew her present parents in the Roman incarnation. And they meant a great deal to her there. She was in the household of the Caesars, one of the stepchildren of Claudius. (1206)

Puburus was a Roman when that country expanded into various lands, and when there was supervision of Palestine, - or the Promised Land, while the Master walked in the earth. He was in a part of the government which supervised the resources of the land for use in the Roman land, such as corn, wheat, and other products of the soil, as well as the manufacture of wood for ships.

As a result of that experience, he now has a coldness or aloofness in his expression. While business must be done in a business way, you should find love, hope, patience, and joy in your dealings with your fellow man.

He was close to those in authority who levied the taxes, and made arrangements for the levying. One would discover an individual's ability to pay, while another would find where the individual had resources which could be taxed for development of the land or for the benefit of the Romans.

The entity believes that he was Judas Iscariot, because he is a sensitive at present; and the associations during that sojourn were of such a nature as to cause this "throw-back", as it were.

(According to the Readings he was not Judas.)

In his activities as a representative of those who were in power, he often came into contact with various of the disciples of the Master.

And among those who were most closely associated of the Romans and the disciples were this entity and Judas.

Stories of Judas had been told to him by members of a cult, and these stories were of interest, but he scoffed at them. These stories indicated that Judas would become one who would betray his Lord and commit murder, and would commit incest and the like with members of his own household. That such a person would be accepted by one who was proclaimed as a teacher and a master was of special interest to Puburus. And he followed these activities and reports of Judas in such a manner that, later, he berated himself, after he had become joined with the Master's family and kinsman.

Hence, in the present, through his own visions, according to his interpretation, he has been told that he was Judas. As a result, those urges, as it were, overshadow the entity at times.

But as has been indicated, never belittle yourself. For the Master, the Lord thy God, overlooks that which thou hast done, and has given, "Whosoever will may take the cup". Each soul is willing, but the flesh is weak. The Lord has not willed that any soul should perish; because of berating itself, for any activity of an individual among his fellows may cause such berating. He has willed that each soul should know the way, and has prepared a way. Then, look not back upon these associations, environmental conditions, or your own curiosity; but rather look up to Him who may call thee that you may know and see His face. (1265)

Here are the records of Susane (1179), *daughter of Cleopas who walked on the road to Emmaus*. Something should be understood of the history or background of her environs and surroundings.

At that time, there had been appointed by the Romans, collectors of the various forms of taxes which were imposed upon and collected from the people. Cleopas, like Matthew, was one of those who were of the faith of the people. He was in the position of being one who professed faith in the teachings of the Scribes and Pharisees, yet he collected tribute for a power which was over the people.

This brought condemnation to him and his household from those who adhered more to the orthodox manner of living.

Susane grew up during the early life of the Master in the earth, and she was acquainted with the members of the household of Joseph and Mary. For she lived in Capernaum at that time. She was near the age of the sister of the Master, and they were close friends; although there were varied degrees of association, owing to the questions which arose in the various groups that were in the synagogue activities. They were close companions, however, until they were separated because of the difference in their manner of education.

Hence, she knew a great deal about the events which occurred in the Master's household. She was acquainted with Jude and James; although the entity, more than most of the Holy Women as they were eventually called years afterward, followed the teachings of the Master. She was in the area around Bethsaida when there was the feeding of the five thousand, and when the people were rebuked who were especially close to (about was the word used) Judas at that time.

In the beginning, Susane rather favored the manner in

which the groups about Judas sought to proclaim Jesus as the deliverer of the people from bondage and taxation. This brought condemnation to her from her own group of people. Then when the ministry of the Master was shifted to the area closer to Jerusalem, she joined with those activities at Bethany.

Thus, in the latter portion of His ministry, she was near to, and present at, the demonstrations of His power over death. And the activities of the entity with Mary and Martha, and the closer association with the Mother of the Master, which came later after the Crucifixion and Resurrection, were the periods of her greatest soul development.

After the Pentecost, when the needs of the peoples were ministered to far and near, Susane sought, felt, and realized the real purposes of the tenets and expressions of the Master through His periods of ministry in the earth. Throughout the days of the teachings of those who followed, that is, of Stephen, Philip, Barnabas, and Paul, she was associated with all of these.

She was most active in the ministry to the physical, mental, and spiritual needs of the people following the Crucifixion, and during the periods of construction and application of the early church. Susane was not what would be in this day called a nun. But she was a nurse; she worked with her hands; she gave counsel; and she collected and distributed material aid. When there were the persecutions, and the individuals who had gathered at Jerusalem were dispersed, she went to the church in Laodicea, associating with Lucius, Mark, Luke, and Paul. There, she was established as one of the first deaconesses of that church. And she remained there throughout the rest of that sojourn, giving a great deal of herself in establishing and carrying on the ministry of the Holy One. (1179)

She gained in soul development, except during the period when she desired material gain from the political persecutions. For when she became aware of the full concept of the purposes, hopes, desires, and wishes expressed by Him, she devoted her life as a minister to the needs of those who sought to know the truth which makes men free, although they may be under the shadow of a service to a higher power, materially.

A great deal of her services were rendered in ministering to people who were without the faith. In like manner in the present, she may be a nurse. She may so live that others may take hope and find the way. Or she may encourage others to a greater search for that attuning of the self with the creative forces manifested in Him.

With respect to conversations which she had with Jesus, during the time at the sea when the five thousand were fed, she was somewhat rebuked. She was reminded of her association in the household of the Master, and the purpose for which He had entered into the earth. For He gave, not for himself, not for material gain, but that all should know the truth which would make all men free under every circumstance in a material plane.

She knew her present father (1151) in Palestine; for he accompanied Cleopas, her father at that time, on the walk to Emmaus.

She was born into her present family because of the attraction for her in her search for the way back to the full consciousness gained there. For each of her parents have been associated with the truths which live in the hearts of those who seek to know the Peace which passes understanding, as found in Him alone.

With respect to her present mother, she was acquainted with her then, she was often in her household, and they were separated only during the time of their education. For it was not as so often considered that the family of the Master lacked material opportunities. From many sources, there had come the opportunities for those in the household of the Master to have greater training. For the entity who is now your mother was educated then, not only in the best schools of that land, but also in other lands. Nevertheless, she was a companion of Susane in that experience.

When Susane saw the raising of Lazarus, it so inspired her that she determined to give herself in service to the ideal and principle set forth by Him.

She can help her present physical condition by deep meditation, as she learned in that experience, and as it was given by Him to all. Each should turn within and trust wholly in the power of God. Susane had many close contacts with Jesus. She not only saw Him when she was close to those in His household, but also when she ministered, for she followed closely with Him. Often, she was in the throngs who heard His ministry and His teachings to the people along the way. (1179)

Q. Considering reincarnation and the karmic ties that bring whole groups of individuals into the earth at certain times, does the story of Jesus, the Christ, have particular significance for us in the present?

A. Not only the material associations, but it may be seen as to how and why the teachings of the Master must become the factor in the experience ever . . . as well as in the present. (1158)

(Also,) as was shown by the Son of Man, Jesus . . . each and every soul must become, must be, the savior of some (other) soul, must comprehend the purpose of the entrance of the Son into the earth: that man might have the closer walk with, yea the open door to, the very heart of the Living God! (1472)

It is not knowledge that is so important, but the wisdom in application of that knowledge. It is not what or how much one knows that counts, but what one does about what one knows or experiences; or as to whether self, and its attitudes are to be exalted, or whether self-exaltation is to be renounced. (993)

So consider first things first. What is the first thing? *Self!* But a willingness to give self, a willingness to suffer in self, in the physical surroundings, for an ideal—not merely idealistic, but an ideal that requires, first, courage, to dare to do the impossible—for with God nothing is impossible. And the individual that may give himself as a channel through which the influences of good may come to others, may indeed be guided or shown the way.

Then it is necessary for the reliance upon Him who is the Truth and the Light—who, from the beginning, was that expressed in "And God said, 'Let there be light,' and there was light". Not of the s-u-n, but as of the S-o-n, born of the Father, God. Thus, the continuity of Life itself . . . for without Him, without Light, was not anything made that was made.

This applied, this fact conceived, this truth lived in the daily life, will put away fear and doubt of every nature. For the earth is the Lord's and the fullness thereof; the silver and the gold are His, and the cattle on a thousand hills. Then why worry when ye may pray? For He has promised, "Though ye are afar off, when ye call I will hear, and will answer speedily". (3188)

For He IS thy guardian here and now. Put thy whole trust in those things indicated by Him that ye have studied in this present experience; "As ye would that others should do to you do ye even so to them".

Is this become trite? Too oft such is the reaction. . . . In Him there is no fear. Of Himself little might have been accomplished in the earth, but being willing to be used He became the perfect channel. Be thou willing to be used as may be expressed in the very "trite" manner, to love the Lord with all thy might, to encourage those who are weak, to assist those who seek to admonish and to warn those who are of themselves self-sufficient in this material relationship. (2072-4)

(Oh) there is a form of religious freedom, yea, there is an application—in part—of that moral duty, of that economic duty to those influences and forces that are to guide a nation, a people; by that which has been handed down from those that in faith to their Maker, in their belief in their fellowman, established a freedom of speech, a freedom of press, a freedom of worship of the Maker according to the dictates of their conscience. . . .

(But remember) in these experiences oft—the more oft, yea, again and again—(to) call yet upon that promise, upon that influence which has prompted from within, that ye be guided aright, that ye be led by Him, even as the Prince of Peace. (1151)

We find all religions of the world approaching those conditions where man may become as the law in his connection with the Divine, the Supreme, the Oneness of the world's manifestation. In Jesus we find the answer. (364-9)

(Such) IS the understanding of those who have seen and known and become aware of His abiding presence. . . . "Lo, I am with you always, even unto the end of the world". (1602)

Q. Is Jesus Christ on any particular sphere, or is He manifesting on the earth plane in another body?
A. All power in heaven, in earth is given to Him who overcame the world. Hence He is of Himself in space, in the force that impels through faith, through belief, in the individual entity. As a spirit entity. Hence, not in a body in the earth, but may come at will to him who wills to be one with the acts in love to make same possible.

For He shall come as ye have seen Him go, in the body

He occupied in Galilee. The body that He formed, that was crucified on the cross, that appeared to Philip, that appeared to John. (5749-4)

Q. He said He would come again. What about His second coming, when shall that be?

A. The time no one knows. Even as He gave, not even the Son Himself, only the Father. Not until his enemies—and the earth—are wholly in subjection to His will, His powers. (5749-3)

Q. Are we entering the period of preparation for His coming?

A. Entering the test period, rather. (5749-3)

Q. When Jesus the Christ comes the second time will He set up His kingdom on earth, and will it be an everlasting kingdom?

A. Read His promises in that ye have written of His words, as John gave. He shall rule for a thousand years. Then shall Satan be loosed again for a season. (5749-4)

Then, as to that Second Coming into the world—He will come again and receive His own, those who have prepared themselves through belief in Him and acting in that manner; for the Spirit is abroad, and the time draws near, and there will be the reckoning of those even as at the first, so in the last, and the last shall be first; for there is that Spirit abroad—He standeth near

He that hath eyes to see, let him see. He that hath ears to hear, let him hear that music of the coming of the Lord of this vineyard. And art thou ready to give account of what thou hast done with thine opportunity in the earth as the Sons of God, as the heirs and joint heirs of glory with the Son? Then make thy paths straight, for there must come an answering for what thou hast done with thy Lord! He will not tarry; for having overcome He will appear even as the Lord and Master. Not as one born, but as one that returneth to his own, for He will walk and talk with men of every clime, and those who are faithful and just in their reckoning shall be caught up with Him to rule and to do judgment for a thousand years! (364-7)

Q. Explain what is meant by "He will walk and talk with men of every clime". Does this mean He will appear to many at once or appear to various peoples during a long period?

A. As given, for a thousand years He will walk and talk with men of every clime. Then in groups, in masses, and then they of the first resurrection shall reign for a thousand years; for this will be when changes —materially—come. (See other references about coming changes in the earth.)

In the manner in which He sat at the Peace Conference in Geneva, in the heart and soul of a man not reckoned by many as an even unusually godly man, yet raised for a purpose, and He chose him to be a channel of His thought for the world. (Woodrow Wilson) So, as there has been, so will it be—until the time is set. As was given of Him: "not given to man to know the time or the period of the end," nor to man other than by constituting himself a channel through which He may speak. (364-8)

And he comes again in the hearts and souls and minds of those who seek to know His ways. These are hard to be understood by those in the flesh. Yet those that call on Him will not go empty-handed. . . . What must be obliterated? Hate, prejudice, selfishness, backbiting, unkindness, anger, passion, and those things of the mire that are created in the activities of the sons of men. Then again, He may come in body to claim His own. (5749-5)

Q. When He comes again in the flesh, will that be the time of what is commonly called "Judgment Day"?

A. What was the judgment? What is the judgment? What will even be the judgment? *Those who deny that He came in the flesh are not worthy of acceptance. Those who give thee that which is not helpful, hopeful, and patient and humble, and not condemning any, are not worthy.* This is thy judgment. What, then, will you do with Jesus? For He is the Way, He is the Light, He is the Hope . . . He is ready.

Will you let Him into your heart? Or will you keep Him afar, or apart? Will you not eat of His Body, of the bread of Life? Drink from the fountain He builds in the minds, the hearts, the souls of those who seek to know Him and His purposes with men, with the world? For having overcome the world, He indeed has it—as it were in the palm of His hand, and has entrusted it to you, because of His faith in His Love for you. What will you do about Jesus? And His trust in you?

As these are things, that ye have oft heard in one manner or another, they have become to some passé, they have become to others as "How can it be?", they are to others still just a question . . . BUT try YE the spirits, know (that) those who know Him are in accord with that which He is, His purpose, His desire with men. Then, how may you as individuals, in your various spheres of activities, in your walks of life among men, think not of Him?

Carry on, by showing forth that which He has given: though others may be unjust, rail not, *for it indeed must be* that these things come, but woe to them *by* whom they come. Rather know that the meek, the patient, those that are of one mind in Him, shall— shall—inherit the earth, the possessions thereof. Learn ye what to do with them. You are only fooling yourselves by not giving, doing, being even thy little. For as He has given, it is the little leaven that leaveneth the whole lump; be gentle, be kind, be patient, for the earth is thy Lord's.

Do ye claim Him as brother, as friend, as neighbor? Do that—for thine own sake, for His sake—for much has

He given. What hast thou done? For as ye do it unto the
least of thy brethren ye do it unto Him. That is the
Law. (254-95)

Then may ye as Seekers of the Way, may ye who have
come seeking to know, to experience, to feel that
presence of the Christ-Consciousness within thine own
breast, within thine own experience, open the door of
thy heart! For He stands ready to enter, to those who
will bid Him enter. He comes not unbidden, but as ye
seek ye find, as ye knock it is opened.

As ye live the life, is the awareness of His closeness, of
His presence, thine? (5749-10)

Q. What association with the entity who is now Edgar
Cayce did I have in the Palestine experience?

A. The teacher of the Master (Josie) knew only of Lucius through those activities in Laodicea, for he (Lucius) came at the time of Pentecost, see? (1010)

Chapter Twelve

THE CHURCH OF LAODICEA—LUCIUS

This concluding chapter consists of Readings pertaining to Edgar Cayce as Lucius, Bishop of the Church at Laodicea,* along with many of the historical events and personalities closely associated with him at that time.

Herein, we will attempt to point out some of the more significant incidents in Edgar Cayce's 1st century existence as they relate to our overall theme.

Note the relationships—complicated and inter-involved as they are with biblical history and each other—and how they are consistently recalled, unwoven, scanned, and again threaded together by the unconscious mind of Edgar Cayce.

Yes, we have the records of that entity now called Edgar Cayce, and of those experiences in the earth's plane when he was known as Lucius of Cyrene, or in the early portion of the experience as Lucius of Ceptulus. He was of Grecian and Roman parentage, and from the city of Cyrene.

As a youth and young man, Lucius was rather a ne'er-do-well, or one that wandered from pillow to post, and

* The mention of Cayce as Lucius was not made until 1937, some fourteen years after Cayce's own first Life Reading, because—as later explained—the knowledge might have made him "puffed up."

became a soldier of fortune. And during the ministry of Jesus in and about Jerusalem and Galilee, Lucius came to those environs. As a result of his experiences with the followers of Jesus, and the great lessons given by that Teacher, he became what would be termed a "hanger-on", with the idea that this was to be the time when there would be a rebellion against the Roman legions, the Romans being in authority. And Lucius looked forward to it, and kept in touch with the edicts by the political forces, both in Rome and among the Jews.

The entity was disregarded and looked upon with questions by the Jews who were close followers of the Master, yet he was among the Seventy who were sent to be teachers. When the necessity arose for a closer association with the Teacher, Lucius being one of the foreign group was rejected as one of the Apostles. Yet he was questioned mostly by John, Peter, Andrew, James, and those of the closer followers such as Matthew and Bartholomew, and was more closely associated with Thomas.

When the loyalty of Lucius was questioned, Peter was the speaker, and Andrew the listener; and there were disputes as to the advisability of him being put into power. However, in the latter portion, Andrew and Lucius were closely associated, and Andrew defended him after he had become reunited with his companion. (294-192)

Mariaerh—Companion of Lucius

The growing up of the entity (Mariaerh, companion of Lucius) (1468) was during the life and ministry of the Master in the earth. Her birth was before time was recorded by the calendar first established in Carmel, and then in Caesarea and Jerusalem. The eras of the first, second, third and fourth centuries were gradually accepted by various nations; and now they are the records in the earth.

Mariaerh grew up in the hill country of Judea, near to the places where Elizabeth and Zacharias had lived. The latter became the first of the martyrs, Elizabeth remaining in the hill country. There, this entity was brought up and taught. And she was acquainted in her very early years with the visiting of John by the young man called Jesus, just before His ministry began.

Her parents were Jewish, and were from Galilee. Hence, she was not taught a great deal of the strictly orthodox Jewish views; nor was she instructed in the strictly orthodox teaching of that separate people, the Samaritans.

She came to Jerusalem in about her fourteenth year, which was the age of accountability for women. And she came to be recorded, or polled, as being of marriageable age and taxable. This poll was because of requirements of both the Jews and the Romans. Hence, her first visit to Jerusalem was with her own parents, and Elizabeth, and other older people. This was when the Master, Jesus made his triumphal entry from Bethany into Jerusalem. This was also the time when she first became fully aware of the raising of Lazarus in Bethany, and of the events connected with it. As a result of all of this, she became acquainted early in life with many of the women who were later called the Holy Women. It was they who stood about the Cross, and about the sepulcher, and who made preparations for the burial.

If this entity will apply herself and meditate deeply, she can see many of these events by vision. And she may write a description of them, including the road from Bethany to the temple in Jerusalem. For in that sojourn, there was first the hearing by her, then the experiencing of the events, then her conversion and her own activity. These, therefore, have become innate within her.

If you will attempt to apply in this incarnation that

which you applied in the latter part of that one, you may raise your vibrations to where you can picture and write in words of, not merely the triumphal entry, but also the humbleness, graciousness, glory, and dignity of the Man. He and His disciples waited among friends who tried to persuade Him not to expose Himself to physical danger. However, when He preached and counseled, He stated it was for that purpose that He came into the world; and as a man, He must continue with that which had been the purpose for His entrance. Mariaerh learned the concept of how each soul must in each incarnation live as a grain of wheat, a grain of mustard, or a seed of any nature. It thereby fulfills the purpose for which it enters into a sojourn, irrespective of personal desires. And it lets the personality of self be lost in the individuality of the Christ-purpose, as He so magnificently gave on the way from Bethany to Jerusalem.

After the triumphal entry, there soon followed the historical events of the arrest, the trial, and the Crucifixion. And in the days that followed, she remained in and around Bethany.
Fifty days later, there was the Pentecost, where many were gathered in Jerusalem. And people of many lands and tongues were brought to conviction by the teaching of the disciples, or Apostles. Following that memorial statement of Peter's on the day of Pentecost, this entity was one of the first ten who were baptized on that day.

After this, there was the selection of the ministers, or deacons, who were to minister to the people. That was when all of their material belongings had been turned over to the disciples, or Apostles; and they were all with one accord together. Mariaerh heard much about the activities of Philip and Peter; but she became more closely associated with Lucius, a kinsman of Luke. *And Lucius is the entity* (294) *through whom this information is being given.*

She and Lucius were closely associated with the founding of the ministry and the various missionary activities. They also had a part in the establishment of many portions of the Church during the early ministry of, not only the disciples, or Apostles, but also the early ministers of the Church. Among these were Mark, Luke, Lucius, Thaddeus, Saul or Paul, Barnabas, and others in Laodicea.

It was in the latter place that the entity went with Lucius when the Church was established there, and when Paul preached in Laodicea. Some of the people there were kinsmen of the Romans. And as the helpmeet or wife of Lucius, she spent the rest of her days in that place, ministering to the early members of the Church. (1468)

Mariaerh's story is here picked up and continued in a second reading. This is typical of how Cayce so often threaded one reading onto another.

Mariaerh (continued in undertone) "Mariaerh of the Samaritans, Judean hill country, triumphal entry, associations with the Women, affiliation with those during the Pentecost, companion or wedded to Lucius of Cyrene, the Bishop of the church in Laodicea".

She was with her companion, Lucius, in Laodicea, when Lucius was made head of the church by Paul and Barnabas. She suffered some hardships because of the teachings of Paul relating to the leaders or heads of the churches. As a result of such teaching, some people demanded celibacy as a prerequisite to appointment as a Bishop or leader.

Owing to the fact that she and Lucius had no children, this caused Mariaerh to feel that most of the teachings of Paul were directed at her. In addition, because of the close friendships which existed between John, Mark, and Mariaerh, questions arose in the minds of many, especially in view of the difference in the ages of Lucius and Mariaerh. This situation caused her much disturbance in that experience. And only after she had, through Luke and Barnabas, come to a better understanding, did she assume a marked activity in Laodicea.

In the latter portion of her sojourn, there was a son born to her and Lucius. This son grew in grace and favor, not only with all of those in the first church, but also with them who had been active with the Essenes, and preceding the coming of the Master. This aided her in her relationships. This, of course, was before the persecutions of the church began as a result of the enmity aroused here against Paul because of his disputes with the mother church. These disputes related to the first Church in Antioch and the first church in Jerusalem which was headed by James, the brother of the Lord, and Peter and Andrew and the others who visited there from time to time.

She lived to the age of sixty-nine, and saw her son, Sylvius, recognized by the leaders, and chosen for service in the name of the Master.

While she suffered many material disturbances, she gained mentally and spiritually. From that sojourn, she now has the ability to write, especially with regard to the triumphal entry from Bethany to the Temple. She could also write about herself and Lucius and their love story, or about the cry of the multitude at the triumphal entry and the words and messages of the Master on the way.

Her father and mother in that incarnation were, respectively, Jochim and Marh. They were Samaritans from the northern part of Judea, close to Galilee. She had two brothers and a sister. Her present brother and sister were her father and mother then.

Mariaerh was acquainted, especially in the latter years of that sojourn, with Judy, the leader, teacher, and prophetess of the Essenes. This was when there was a revival by Sylvius of Judys' teachings and prophecies. Later in her life, Judy was her advisor and counselor. Sylvius was her only child.

Judy

The entity Judy (1472) has been mentioned before in preliminary fashion as being integral to the Edgar Cayce story. The incident of her first Reading is quite interesting.

On 11/6/37 Cayce gave a reading for Mrs. (1472). To the surprise of those present, upon awakening he immediately went to the woman and kneeled before her as to humble himself. His explanation was that in returning to consciousness he had been met by the Master—who had walked along the way with him and placed an arm about his shoulder as they returned from the Hall of Records. Surely, Cayce felt, this woman must be someone important to the Master. But in looking at her reading they could find no clue as to why the appearance had occurred.

A check reading revealed her identity as Judy, the Essene Teacher of Jesus, but noted that in her present lifetime the entity was working on other matters than those associated with the Palestine period; consequently, that incarnation had not been included in her first reading.

All of this points out an interesting facet concerning the Life Readings—in that individuals apparently are only working on small segments from numerous past lives during any current incarnation. Another reason can best be exampled by an A.R.E. member who was perturbed about not being included during the Persian period. She felt somewhat "left out" as a result. Cayce's reply was that indeed she had been in Persia then, but the details of her existence would be "more than she could bear".

E.C.: Here are portions of the records, as scribed by the entity called Judy, the teacher, healer, and prophetess. About twenty-four years before the birth of Jesus, we find Phinehas and Elkatma active among the depleted group of the prophets in Mt. Carmel. This was the school for prophets begun by Samuel, Elisha, Elijah, and Saul during those early times.

Because of the divisions of the people into sects, such as the Pharisees and Sadducees, there had arisen the Essenes which had cherished not merely the stories and history which had come by word of mouth, but also had kept records of the periods when individuals had been visited with supernatural or out of the ordinary experiences. These related to dreams, visions, voices, and such that had been experienced by various individuals of this peculiar people.

Hence, we find that Phinehas and the Companion had received an experience similar to that received by Hannah and Elkanah. And then in answer to the promise, the child, Judy, was born. That the child was a daughter, rather than a son, caused disturbance and confusion in the minds of many. Yet the life and experiences of the parents had been such that, fulfilling their promise, they dedicated the life of their child, Judy, to the study of things which had been handed down by those who had received visitations from the unseen or unknown. And they believed that the Divine Spirit moved in the activities of men.

Hence, Judy was brought up in an environment, not of dispute and argument, but rather of rote and writ. This was considered necessary in order to develop her life so as to induce experiences with the Divine. The fact that her people had depended upon tradition rather than record made a great impression on Judy. Hence, she began to preserve by means of records the history, stories, and tradition which had been handed down by word of mouth.

Eventually, the manner of keeping the records was chosen from the methods used in Egypt, rather than in Persia; although much of that to be recorded originated in Persia because of the Jewish people dwelling in that land during the captivity. Hence, the traditions from Egypt, Persia, India, and from many of the Persian lands and the borders about them, became a part of the studies of Judy in her attempts to make and preserve such records.

Because communication was restricted, owing to the political situations as a result of the Romans in the land, Judy was somewhat of a recluse. Then, there was the visitations from the Wise Men of the East, one from Persia, one from India, and one from Egypt. These Wise Men talked with the brethren, but more was sought from the studies of Judy. Then, there was the report of the Wise Men to the king.

Why did the Wise Men go to Herod, who was only second or third in authority, rather than to the Romans who were the highest authority in the land? It was because of Judy. She knew that this would arouse in the heart and mind of this debased ruler, who only sought for the aggrandizement of himself such reactions as would bring to him, this despot, turmoils with those who were in authority. Why? Because this new king, Herod, was not to replace Rome. He was to replace the Jewish authority in the land!

Hence, attention was called to the activity of the Essenes, so that a little later, during the sojourn of the Child in Egypt, and because of Him, Herod issued the edict for the destruction. This brought experiences to many which were best described by Judy, in the cry of Rachel for her children that were being born into a period of opportunity, yet the destruction by the edict of this tyrant made them as naught.

During the ministry of John and Jesus, Judy was questioned more and more by the Roman authorities, the Roman spies, and the directors of those who collected and registered taxes for the Romans. Consequently, Judy came in contact with the Medes, Persians and Indians as a result of the commerce with those countries, as well as the influence of Saneid, Brahma, and Buddha.

In her work, she compared the traditions of the Egyptians with that of the Jews. Hence, after the Crucifixion, she was able to give a better understanding to the Twelve and to the Holy Women, how woman had been redeemed from a place of obscurity to her place in the affairs of the race, the world, the empire, and the home itself. As a result, many are the contacts which she must make in the present sojourn.

For, as then . . . the evolution of man's experiences is for the purpose of becoming more and more acquainted with the relationships with his fellow man, as a manifestation of Divine Love, as was shown by the Son of Man, Jesus. Each and every soul must be the Savior of some other soul, to even comprehend the purpose of the entrance of the Son into the earth. It was that man might have a closer walk with, yea the open door to, the very heart of the Living God.

Judy's activities during the persecutions aroused much antagonism in the minds of those who made war upon the followers of the Nazarene, of Jesus, and the Apostles. And she was hounded and persecuted more and more. Yet she lived until the sixty-seventh year after the birth of Jesus, or until Time itself began to be counted from same. For her records were begun during a period sixty years after. And they were reckoned first by the people at Carmel, then by the brethren in Antioch, then a portion of Jerusalem, and then to Smyrna, Philadelphia, and those places which were becoming more active.

Although she received many rebuffs, and even stripes on the body, she died a natural death in that experience at the age of ninety-one.

Condemn not, even as He did not condemn. For there is only one spirit, the Spirit of Truth, which has growth within it. If there is the spirit of strife, contention, or turmoils, it takes hold upon the fires which ye have so well put away. Yet these fires keep giving urges, even as the prince of this world (Satan) who goes about like a raging lion seeking whom he may destroy.

What, then, is this spirit of unrest, except that very cry as He gave in the triumphal entry, "If ye did not cry Hosanna, glory to the Lord, the king of kings, the very stones would cry out!" Is it, therefore, any wonder to you, after knowing and feeling that you have had these experiences, that you have heard many a voice crying, 'Lo, here am I; Lo, here is the way; Lo, listen".

As ye have pronounced, "It is the still small voice within that finds communion with that spirit that bareth witness that thy interpretation is true". For all the prophets pronounced Him as that star spoken of, as that voice raised in the wilderness, as the star of Jacob, of the household of Jacob, and as of Judah, that love that will bring that which He declared unto the world, "My peace I leave with thee". That ye declared; that hold to. For there is no other way than that each soul should be awakened to that which ye proclaimed in the earth, "Behold He cometh with power and might, and ye shall know Him as He is, for He convicts thee of thy purpose among thy fellow men".

During a portion of her experience in Palestine, Judy was the teacher of Jesus. And she taught Him those things which were traditions. Then, she sent Him to Persia, Egypt, and India so that the education might be completed of Him that became the Way and the Truth.

Put first into your own experience and activity those teachings of Him, not as tenets but as living experiences. *Learn that lesson which He so well manifested; That it was not in the separation, as John; not in the running away, as Elijah; not in sitting in high places, as Isaiah; not in mourning, as Jeremiah; not in*

*lording it over others, as Moses; but in being all things
to all men. Reach them in their own plane of experience, and not with a long face.*

For as He did; He wined; He dined with the rich; He
consorted with the poor; He entered the temple on state
occasions; He slept in the field with the shepherds; He
walked by the seashore with the throngs; He preached
to those in the mount—all things. Yet, He was ever
ready to present the tenets and truths in the form of
tales and parables, and in activities that took hold upon
the lives of men and women in every walk of human experience.

So ye will find that the lessons which ye gave then may
be used today. Why? Because Truth is Truth, ever, in
whatever stage of evolution or realm you find it. It is as
He gave, the little leaven. Think not, even as He, to do
some great deed that would make thy word ring
throughout the earth. Rather, know that it is the little
line, the little precept, and the little lessons given which
bring the awareness into the hearts and souls of men
and women. For, as proclaimed of old, it is not in the
thunder or lightning, it is not in the storm, it is not in
the loudness, but in the still small voice within.

So as ye write, as ye talk, as ye live, let it be in
meekness of spirit, in purposefulness of service, in an
activity and an eye single to the Glory of the Father
through those that are His children. For "Who is my
mother, my brother, my sister? They that do the will of
the Father, the same is my mother, my brother, my
sister."

Be patient even as He. This is the manner in which ye
may reach the whole world, even as ye did, Judy, in thy
counsel then, as given thee by thy father in the flesh.
For ye learned as ye gathered information from the
counsel and lessons of the Patriarchs of old. They were
the lessons of tradition that ye first, even as He, set in
order.

Ye have heard as of old "an eye for an eye and a tooth
for a tooth". Ye have heard, "He that does the good, do
the good to him". But, *"I say,* he that would smite thee
on the right cheek, turn thou the other also He that
would sue thee and take away thy cloak, give him thy
coat also." *Did ye (Judy) not set these as the very
words given by Him who is the Lord of Lords and the
King of Kings?* (1472)

Q. Please describe Judy's home life as well as her
Essene activities.

A. That as might be the description of an individual who
had set self aside as a channel for such activities. These
are very hard to be understood from the material mind,
or from the material understanding or concept, especially in this period of consciousness. For, then man
walked close with God. When there were those preparations—it is possible in the present, but not AC-
CEPTABLE. Consequently, to describe the home life
as to say they sat in the sun, ate three square meals a
day and wore little or nothing, or that they dressed in
the best—it must be that as from the spirit. May best be
described as given by Luke, in his description of those
things that disturbed Mary. "She kept these things and
pondered them in her heart." *This did not prevent her
from being, then, a material person, nor one with the
faculties and desires for material associations—as indicated in the lack of celibacy. Is this indicated in any
condition in the book, or man's relationship to God?
Nowhere is this indicated!* (2067-11)

The Holy Women—Ulai

In giving the associations of Ulai with the Master, the
following may be given, if it will be accepted in accord
with the desire and purpose with which it is given. For
in that sojourn, all was not good; neither was it all bad.
*Because of associations and activities in the present,
this information has previously been withheld. This was*

*because of the need for growth, and for determination
as to the purposes in this incarnation.*

You were a cousin of Martha, the sister of Lazarus, and
closely associated with her after his death.

John as a disciple, or even a forerunner, had been rejected by her. And when the teachings of the Nazarene
were first presented to her, they appeared like
mysteries. For with both the social and the more strict
religious groups, she was sometimes cold, and at other
times very enthusiastic regarding various forms.

In the days of the Master's teachings when he journeyed
often to Bethany, and with the return of Mary
(Magdalene) sister of Martha and Lazarus, after
her conversion and the casting out of the demons, Ulai was
even greater confused. For to her, how could anyone
who had been such a person, or who had so disregarded
persons except for material gains, become an honored
member and associate with a household such as
Lazarus and Martha.

As a result of that experience, and the raising of (her
cousin) Lazarus, she sought to know something of the
heart and experience of the Mother of Christ. And she
journeyed to notify the Mother about what was taking
place in Jerusalem. She missed the Triumphal entry; but
she was among those who saw, heard, and spoke with
the Master on the way to Calvary. This brought her into
close association with the group which was later
designated as the Apostles.

She remained with and took the Mother, not to John's
home but to her own home. Later, when there were the
periods of rejoicing over the knowledge of the Resurrection, and the meeting of the disciples and Apostles in
the upper room, she went with the Mother, Mary, to the
home of John, and saw her established there. Afterward, she became very active in the various meetings

which took place until the completion of the days when Pentecost came. And she was one of the group which listened to Peter upon that day.

Then, she became acquainted with the young converts of the Grecians as well as in Laodicea. Following the separation of the members of the group when persecutions began and Stephen was stoned, she developed an aversion to the activities of Paul, or Saul, at that particular time, which necessitated her withdrawing alone. For Stephen was a close friend of Lucius, Luke, and the younger group that became the companions of the teachers.

However, with the spread of the teachings, as brought about by the breaking up of the Holy Women—of which Ulai was classed, although she was one of the younger of that group—she joined in the church work in Laodicea. Because of what was termed by some the faithlessness of Lucius, and preached so even by Paul, she almost renounced all. And she brought about what might be called the first separation in the church of Laodicea.

Because of her activities, differences spread to many of the churches, not only locally around Laodicea, but also in Antioch, Pygarga, Jerusalem, and Patmos. Later, there came the report of Peter as to how the Gentiles had been granted the outpouring of the Holy Spirit. And it was not until then that she became united wholly with the members of the original of the group churches.

Throughout the rest of that sojourn, she developed continually. She was the companion of one named Pathaos, who became a leader in the Antioch church, and eventually the head of the deacons of the church. And she never tired of instructing the young, her own as well as those of the church, and the groups of the various faiths, concerning the events at Bethany and the speech of Stephen.

There were the great spiritual centers from which she drew during that sojourn. And she may draw from these now, if she will go deep within herself. That is the safest course; and that is the source of assurance in times of distress, disappointments, and aggravation. But know, as you understood then, that He is the Resurrection, He is mindful of the sorrows as well as the joys of mankind.

She lived to a good old age, being eighty-seven. And she lived through the period of the Apostles, as well as many of the teachers, ministers, and interpreters. She saw the various phases of differences which arose between Paul and Peter, Paul and Barnabas, Mark and Matthew, Thomas and all the rest. And she knew where there were differences and questions as to manner and form, and as to who was acceptable, and who might be trusted.

In the present, then, let not faults or failures raise questions. *It is not what one once did that counts, but what one will do about that which it knows to do today.* Let that mind be in your activities which you found in yourself in His presence when He wept with Mary, Martha, and that household. And let the mind be in you as it was when you listened to Stephen, as he explained the various influences which had caused the different beliefs in the groups of which you were a part in your early sojourn in that land.

Be in that mind you had as you listened and saw the people of all tongues and faiths hear the words of Peter, as he asked all to put away thoughts of themselves, and to accept, believe and be baptized. (993)

Holy Women—Eunice

During those periods when John and Jesus were receiving their training in other lands, Eunice kept in close touch with the household of Elizabeth. At this time, she was also affected by the edict of the king. Then, there came the death of the king, and the occurrence when the Romans robbed Elizabeth of her mate through his death at the altar. All of this began to bring changes in the outlook of Eunice. And her attempt to understand why those who were supposed to be endowed with powers and purposes divine should have such things happen to them. brought still greater resentment and wonder.

Afterwards, while Mary and Elizabeth were interested in the activities in their home land, and the journey from the upper part of Galilee to Capernaum, Eunice entered more into social activity. This was brought about through the ability of her mate to make friendships with those who were in power.

Subsequent to the rebuking by Jesus in the house of worship, and the imprisonment of John, she was expecting motherhood. And she sought counsel at this time with Mary, Martha, and others who, not only had renounced their relationships with the priests, but also were keeping alive the order of the Essenes.

In the latter days of Jesus' sojourn, she saw her child blessed by Him, and heard Him set forth the ideal manner in which all individuals were to accept their relationships with others, and with the pronouncement, "Unless ye become as little children, ye shall in no wise enter in". This brought closer adherence to the tenets which she had learned there. Yet with the knowledge that such a person as Magdala had become a close companion of those of the household, she again began to question, "How can such things be?" Such questionings, however, were blotted out when she, with Mary, Josie, and the other Mary, learned of the events at Jerusalem and what had brought them about.

And as she journeyed to Jerusalem, and became aware of the turmoils there, she leaned closer to those of her own land. For, remember, of the Twelve, seven of them came from that land, and were her own acquaintances.

As the days passed, she turned more and more to the tenets relating to the activities in Jerusalem. Then, the Pentecost came, and she heard her own kinsmen speak in tongues, and saw the tumult.

Thus, she determined to bring a greater awareness of the spirit of truth to those around her. This was the truth which was manifested by Him, and was spread abroad through the teaching of His disciples and Apostles to bring a new light to men. It was to void hate and those things which make one afraid, and to provide that position, power, wealth, or fame should be set at naught compared to the peace and understanding which comes to those who have seen, known, and become aware of His presence—even as the entity heard promised, "Lo, I am with you always, even unto the end of the world".

Through the latter portion of that sojourn, the entity ministered to the needs of the saints, as they were called, who dedicated their lives wholly to these activities. She gained in soul development by giving of herself, by just being kind to those who were heavily burdened by the cares of life, whether in illness, in the vicissitudes of relationships, in wants of the body, or in needs that brought desperate circumstances. These should be analyzed, and the petty jealousies and hates made less and less a part of the attitudes of mind and body in the present.

In the latter portion of that experience, Eunice was among the elderly mothers of the church in the southernmost part of Palestine. At one time, she was associated with those who were in authority among the Romans, including the wife of Cornelius. (1602)

Lucia

Before that the entity Lucia was in the Promised Land, especially in those periods of the early church in Laodicea; for the founders and teachers there were a part of the entity's experience, as well as the disputations that arose between Paul and Lucius, and the associates there.

The entity then was a sister, or *the elder sister of Lucius,* the head of the church there during a part of those experiences. This brought about periods of turmoils for the entity. Yet with the stand taken by a part of that same group or family, there came the greater experiences for all.

There the entity was the home builder, the weaver, or one who taught the young—or groups—to weave, and to make for such activities in the home and in the church.

Then in the name Lucia, or Lucy (as would be called in the present), the entity gained; though there were hardships of great numbers in the entity's own family, for there were eleven children in that experience. (2823)

Vesta

Vesta (cousin of the Caesars) lived in the Roman and Grecian lands when the church was being established in the land of the Romans. She was of the royalty; for although she was not of the Caesars who were in power and authority, she was in a household whose numbers were their cousins. And she was in a position to draw upon the influences of the court as well as of the established places of the empire in Macedonia, Greece, Palestine, and North Africa. However, her most valuable experiences came through her contacts with the missionaries who were in authority over the churches.

Although because of her secular training she was opposed to such affairs of the church, she was in the diplomatic service and reported with respect to their activities. She was of the same sex as at present. And she became associated especially with Lucius, who had knowledge of church matters in Macedonia, Mesopotamia, and Northern Palestine.

She was greatly influenced by her association with *Lucius*. However, when she became aware of the teachings of Paul, which caused the separation of Lucius and his companion, this caused her to withdraw into her activities in connections with the Roman rule. As a result, she now often becomes confused materially or mentally, and withdraws within herself and becomes moody. Yet she is able to put her "best foot foremost" when the occasion arises. However, this subjugating of her feelings causes people at times to question her motives relating to her associations with others.

She was of the royal families. Hence, in the present, she can bedeck herself in royal robes, or in the garments of the ash girl or goose girl, and still be queenly in either. (1523)

Celicene—Daughter of Cornelius

Celicene was in the Promised Land during the Roman rule, and she had friends in the household of Cornelius. She was a Roman, and in the same sex as at present. And she was familiar with both the intrigue and the religious trends.

These matters confused her; yet she followed the things in which she became very much interested, especially in the secret organizations. Hence, she has a tendency now to search out groups which organize themselves for certain activities.

She gained and lost in soul development. She gained when her interest turned to matters which brought individuals' minds towards universal peace. But she lost when she turned to self-aggrandizement or self-indulgence.

In the present, she will be in varied environments, activities, and groups. And at time, she will get along much better with men than with women. Although she is not disliked by women, for she is affable and makes friends where she chooses. But often, she hasn't chosen.

And in whatever field of service she chooses, she may accomplish a great deal, especially if she follows writing.

In giving a biographical sketch of her life in Palestine, something should be stated relating to the customs and conditions, in order that a better understanding may be had. For she was the elder daughter of the ruler, or judge, or proconsul connected with the Roman soldiers, since Cornelius was in the office of all of these in Caesarea.

Although she was not born in Rome, she came into that environ early in life. And the surroundings were such as to make her understand that differences existed in the lives of individuals about her. Consequently, the conditions of her early life caused her to feel somewhat above most of them about her, and that they were inferior. This is not given in the nature of criticism, for the environment which existed caused such a feeling.

Then, with the changes which occurred because of the conversion of Cornelius, and the association of his household with the disciples, the change in her was not so quick. Neither did she absorb wholly the ideas presented by those teachers, who to her appeared rather uncouth, and men who were not of the same class as herself. Yet she desired, because of the sincerity of the members of her household, to be in accord with that which was being practiced by them.

Hence, it is no wonder that there were turmoils in her inner feelings and emotions. For there were social and economic changes which naturally resulted from the household becoming so absorbed as to make the home a meeting place for the various groups.

And, of course, the followers, disciples, teachers, and ministers did not always hold the same tenets as the ones who were Roman citizens or Jews. Remember, there was a vast difference in the teachings, even of the leaders.

It is no wonder, then, that *in the present she finds the writings of some of them hard to correlate, who attempted to present their understanding. For example, there is the variation as to just what Peter meant—as expressed in Mark, compared to what is said in Luke, or in the writings by Paul.*

Luke and Lucius were very good friends of hers. On the other hand, Paul was one who, in her opinion, caused turmoils because of his manner of presentation to the various groups. *And she had great difficulty in that sojourn in unifying the teachings of Paul and the teachings of Peter. The latter was to her parents, the confessor.*

And there was a great variation in the teachings of Paul and Peter. One held that the body must be kept under surveillance at all times. And the other held that the use of the body, whether physical, social, or material, were not to be considered so much, just so the mind was kept in accord.

And again she has similar turmoils arising within her in the present. Yet these may be met in the manner which has been indicated. Each phase of the entity's personality has its own questions and problems. Yet they are all answered by having a oneness of purpose and desire that the body, mind, and soul should be in accord and attune with what He would have you be.

He (the Master) never condemned any one. Peter, Paul, Luke, Mark, and Lucius were all of them men. And they had appetites and desires which they indulged often. And this indulgence produced turmoils within the various groups. However, later in that sojourn, when she rejoined her own people in Rome, she found the answer which has been indicated above. And this resulted in constructive experiences throughout her sojourn there of many years, and she brought great blessings to those with whom she came in contact.

You saw phenomena in the household of Cornelius, in the servants and in your own parents, which you sought but never fully experienced. *Nevertheless, you learned later that it was not necessary that you should speak with tongues, except with the tongue of love, which is the language of all who seek His face.* (2205)

John Mark

John Mark (son of Josie, the sister of Mary) lived when there were many turmoils among the people of which he was a part. While he was young in years then, he saw much of the oppression of people for the thought which they held. *And the first account which was written by anyone—that remains as an account—was written by him under the direction of the person (Peter) to whom was given the Keys of the Kingdom.*

It would be well for him to call himself John in this incarnation. In that sojourn, he suffered in many ways; since he was afflicted in body, and was questioned often by his superiors as one not well grounded in faith. Yet he gained in soul development throughout, because of the service which he rendered to many. Later, he became a missionary.

He should ever seek to give the principles which are innate in him with respect to material, physical, and spiritual life. In the present, he seeks life, and seeks to expend himself in many directions. To some people, this will appear unreasonable, considering his physical abilities; and they will think that he does not outwardly appear capable of fulfilling or developing the best within himself. However, he will go steadily onward in giving the truths, lessons, and understandings which he received in that period.

He was a son of Josie who was the sister of Mary, mother of Christ.

John Mark was born in the sixteenth year of our Lord; and his parents were Josie Mary and Marcus, and his sisters Rhoda and Mary. He was close to, and a relative of, Chloe, Lois, and Josie; and they were all relatives of Mary, the mother of the Lord, of the tribe of Judah. He was of the household of Marcus; hence, he was sometimes referred to as Marcus, or son of Marcus.

In his twelfth year, he was healed of an infirmity by his associations with John, the cousin of the Lord, and the Lord. He was one at whose house Peter, the Apostle, came when he was released from prison; and he was a companion of Peter in their travels.

Later, he was an associate and companion with Paul, the Apostle, and Barnabas; and he returned from the first missionary journey with those two, having acted as secretary to Barnabas. And he was the first compiler of a letter which later became the gospel known as Mark, in the writing of which he collaborated with Peter and Barnabas.

He helped many of the early martyrs, and suffered martyrdom himself in the latter portion of that sojourn. However, his martyrdom consisted of expulsion and traveling. It was in the latter part of that period, after the writings in Rome. And he went to the eastern lands with Andrew, the brother of Peter, who had escaped from the same character of martyrdom suffered by those who had been sent to Rome. John Mark was sent by Peter and Paul as an emissary to carry their messages to the people whom Andrew was ministering to in Persia. And he aided often in strengthening the brethren in the various centers where churches or organizations had been established by the efforts of Paul, Barnabas, Silas, and the other ministers.

Often, he was a companion of Luke, who was an associate and companion of Paul in some of his travels. Luke was one of the people who were free, since he was not of Jewish descent. This aided John Mark in his ability to go and come. Hence, after becoming more stable—for he was then a young man—he was of much aid to the people during that period.

As yet, there are little of the writings or letters of John Mark, son of Marcus, other than that which is contained in the gospel known as Mark. This was written in the year fifty-nine, when he was 34 years old. (Since he was born in the year 16, this should be 43 years old. Possibly the numbers were transposed in the original transcription?)

He assisted Barnabas in establishing the church in nothern Africa, in Alexandria, where so much persecution took place later. Much that was compiled by him in that land was destroyed in the second century. This had been placed in the great library in Alexandria. There are still intact some writing which may yet be reclaimed, in some of the ruins about the place, as well as in some of the cities of Chaldea and Persia where he went, during his last days, in company with Andrew.

He wrote little poetry, except the reconstruction of some of the psalms, which were used to dedicate the places of meeting and in the services at times in the various places.

Much of the stability of purpose and intent of the entity was gained in that sojourn. And much of that which rings true to the gospels was stated to him by the companions, disciples, and Apostles of the Lord, the Master.

*The whole gospel of Mark was written by him in col-
laboration with Peter and Barnabas.* This was the first
of the written words respecting the acts, life, and deeds
of the Master. While it is shorter in words, it contains
more of the acts of the Master than most of the other
writings. It is nearer in accord with Matthew than with
any other, but it is not an abridged writing to that
gospel. For Matthew was written from the churches in
Pamphylia, while Mark wrote from Rome. There had
been some distribution of writings, which had been carried to the various groups, before Mark's was accepted.
This was also before Matthew's was given, for it was
written about ten to eighteen years later. (452)

Andrew—Brother of Peter

Andrew was a fisherman on the Sea of Galilee, and
became a follower of the Nazarene, the Gift to the
World. He sought out the Teacher, and brought many
to hear the Living Words which were given to the people. And he was one of those who studied the lessons
and learned the purpose for which the soul came into
the earth plane. In the present, his desire is to hold only
that which is acceptable to the Prince of Peace; and he
has the ability to give much knowledge to others
through such lessons and illustrations as were given by
the Master.

As Andrew, he was the second brother in a family of
four; and in early childhood, he was willful in many
ways. He followed the vocation of his parents and
brother, that of a fisherman. Then, in the days when
John began to teach in the wilderness, he became first
an adherent and disciple of that teacher, and remained
as an aide, until the appearance of Jesus to become a
disciple of John. When Jesus was pointed out by John
as the one who should be greater, and should increase as
he, himself, decreased, Andrew then followed the new
Leader into the wilderness.

He was close to Him during the temptation, as recorded by Matthew. And upon the return to the seashore, he sought out his brother, and told him of the ideas and ideals which were propounded by Him. He then became the close disciple of the Teacher and Master, following closely throughout the whole physical career of the Master.

He was not one of the chosen three, but was often given greater physical conditions to carry out than them. He was often spoken to with reference to others, and especially on the following occasions: In the feeding of the multitude; in the entrance to the city for the evening lodging to keep the Passover; and in the entering into the Garden on the last evening.

He was among those who held the higher attitude toward the spiritual teaching of the Master. And he has chosen often in the earth plane to manifest lessons gained. Also, he has sought often to know, or studied the physical action, and the spiritual insight which impels it.

After the followers were dispersed by the persecutions, Andrew went into Mesopotamia and the other countries where the Master had studied and traveled during His early education, and where he felt that the Master had obtained His learning. And Andrew remained true to His teaching, and brought many to the knowledge of God, or of that which is within every human being who seeks to know how God manifests through Him.

The urge, then, is to compare every measure of truth with the Master's teaching. It is to weigh present experiences in connection with that standard. For that standard is as high above all others as the heavens is above the earth; it is as superior as the sun's light is to the Moon's dull rays; it is great as the winds compared to the stench that arises from foul forces exhumed from the low places, or it is as high as the mountains are above the plains. And as the entity keeps these ideals and principles and applies them to his teaching, writing, and labors, this experience may give him that which is necessary to draw nigh unto that Creative Force which impelled the Master. (341)

SUMMATION

The following Reading was given by Edgar Cayce, August 6, 1933. It was in answer to a Study Group's request that a Reading be given on Jesus the Christ:

Mr. C.: "Yes we have the group as gathered here; and their work, their desires. We will seek that as may be given at this time. . . ."

Then from the sleeping Cayce came another voice. . . .

I, John, would speak with thee concerning the Lord, the Master, as He walked among men. As given, if all that He did and said were written, I suppose the world would not contain all that may be said.

As He, the Christ, is in His glory that was ordained of the Father, He may be approached by those who in sincerity and earnestness seek to know Him—and to be guided by him. As He has given: By faith, all things are made possible through belief in His name.

Believest thou? Then let thine activities bespeak that (which) you as souls, as beings, would make manifest of His love, in the way He will show thee day by day.

As He came into the world—as man knows the world—He became as man; yet in the spirit world He seeks to make manifest that sought by those who do His bidding. For, as He gave, "If ye love me, keep my commandents. These are not new, and are not grievous: that ye love one another—even as the Father loveth me."

The Christ-Consciousness is a universal consciousness of the Father Spirit. The Jesus-consciousness is that (which) man builds in his body as worship. (The body is the Temple of God.) In the Christ-Consciousness, then, there is the oneness of self, self's desires, self's abilities, made in at-one-ment with The Forces that may bring to pass that which is sought by an individuality or soul. Hence, at that particular period, Self was in accord. Hence the physical consciousness had the desire to make it an experience of the whole consciousness of self.

Seek this more often. He will speak with thee, for His promises are true—every one of them. (5749-4)

Certainly this was not Edgar Cayce speaking in the first person. Is this then a direct message from John of the Revelation or how shall we regard it? Or how shall we regard the several references in the Readings concerning John's impending return to the earth?

Throughout history, and to this day, many clairvoyants, psychics and mediums have professed their being contacted or used as a channel by various discarnate spirits or "guides" from "the other side". To these, in all fairness, we must add numerous saints and prophets well-documented within the organized religions of the world. Seemingly, such sensitives can be used as a channel for good or mischievous communications alike—depending on what they set as their ideal, and who or what they attract to their persons. In Cayce's instance, within the Readings, he continually warned against communication with "the dead"—and all such occupations as automatic writing, seances, table tipping, ouija boards, and the like. Additionally, whenever Cayce himself went against the advice of the Readings in any manner—such as by giving information to recipients desiring material gains without spiritually motivated ideals—playing the stock market, or the like—the results were immediate. Cayce would become physically ill—or, though in his clairvoyant sleep-state, he would simply refuse to give the information requested.

However, Cayce did at times exhibit apparent mediumistic capabilities—though not in the usual sense of *attempting* to perform as a medium. The other personages that spoke through him came spontaneously for the most part (and spoke in first person singular). The first more notable example came in 1927.

This psychic reading (5756-5) was volunteered by Edgar Cayce at the beginning of 302-1, a Life Reading, at his office, 115 West 35 Street, Virginia Beach, Va., this 26th day of September, 1927, without a request having been made for it.

E.C.: We have John Drew (the famed actor) here, speaking:

Considering the plans for the outline of the work as being contemplated through the Association as has been formed, why not consider more of those of the (acting) profession? For long have these people sought a way, a plan, or a means whereby these might be taken the more care of when such conditions overtake them, and it is well known that all of the profession are, in a manner, susceptible to suggestions through the psychic—for they are aware that such conditions exist. By play acting, as it were, they come to know more of that of the conscious and subconscious, and superconscious forces, than is ordinarily supposed. Consider this. (5756-5)

9/27/27. E.C.'s letter to Mr. (152) telling of above information: I suppose John Drew is dead—I don't know. With your knowledge of the profession, this possibly will be rather interesting to you.

10/12/27 Mrs. (903)'s answer re. similar letter to her: The John Drew reading is remarkable—he having died only a few months ago. Through that very reading I

shall introduce the "profession". It is certainly true we
(actors) are susceptible.

A message from a recently deceased actor, even a famous
one, is one thing and certainly innocuous enough, but it
hardly prepared Edgar Cayce and his associates for what
was to follow.

In the next such reading (7/15/28) Cayce threads back
to the beginnings of a group Association in Egypt and his
incarnation there as Ra-Ta—especially as it affects the
formation of the then-planned Cayce hospital:

Suggestion: You will have before you the work of the
    Association of National Investigators, Inc. (eventually
    known as A.R.E.) and the Board of Directors govern-
    ing same. You will direct this Board, both individually,
    in regard to each individual's relation to it, and collec-
    tively, in regard to the responsibility of the Board in
    this undertaking of the Association. You will instruct
    Blumenthal and Kahn, and Wyrick, and Bradley, and
    Brown, and Cayce, and each of the rest, just what it is
    that the Forces seek the Association to materialize in
    the work that the Forces shall seek to accomplish
    through the Association. You will then answer ques-
    tions that I will ask you regarding it.

Mr. C.:   Yes, we have those conditions, aims, purposes,
    and the work as set forth in that which has been termed
    Association of National Investigators, Incorporated,
    with its officers, and that which should be accomplished
    through these channels.

(Here follow several pages of organizational advice concerning the Cayce Hospital—Then we resume.)

In the return (to Egypt) in the again establishing of this
priest, (Ra-Ta) in the minor position, yet through the
establishing *of* the priest arose that which became that
study (in Egypt) as is being founded this day (at
Virginia Beach), in a distant land—yet nigh unto those

same shores that washed the shores of the lands of that land—and these call from, and for, the forces of *all* to harken unto that as is being accomplished!

Then, in the activities of those, there arose much, many, and heaps of those same tenets as were given by Him who first gave, "The meek shall inherit the earth".

Those are the tenets upon which *this* foundation must be laid. In that Name, and in Him, shall many find blessings and understandings.

Q. What shall be inscribed upon the cornerstone of the building?
A. Build this in the triangle, and this shall be the inscription: Cayce Hospital—Research and Enlightenment—founded by (the next stone) Association of National Investigators, Inc., 1927. (The next) That we may make manifest the love of God and man.

Then came a sudden announcement from Edgar Cayce. . . . *HARK! There comes the voice of one who would speak to those gathered here:* (Pause)

I AM MICHAEL, LORD OF THE WAY! BEND THY HEADS, OH YE CHILDREN OF MEN! GIVE HEED UNTO THE WAY AS IS SET BEFORE YOU IN THAT SERMON ON THE MOUNT; IN THAT ON YON HILL HIS ENLIGHTENMENT MAY COME AMONG MEN: FOR EVEN AS THE VOICE OF THE ONE WHO STOOD BESIDE THE SEA AND CALLED ALL MEN UNTO THE WAY, THAT THOSE THAT WOULD HARKEN MIGHT KNOW THERE WAS AGAIN A STAFF IN DAVID, AND THE ROD OF JESSE HAS NOT FAILED: FOR IN ZION THY NAMES ARE WRITTEN, AND IN SERVICE WILL COME TRUTH!

We are through. (254-42)

7/17/28. E.C.'s letter to DEK: Morton was here last

weekend, and I think we had one of the most interesting
readings on the work that we have ever had. I'm sending you a copy of it.

Certainly this raised some questions in the minds of those
present. Quite naturally they pursued the phenomenon.
. . .

Q. You will give at this time a discourse on the subject,
"Angels and Archangels, and how they help humanity".
You will also answer the questions which will be asked.
A. Yes. With the bringing into creation the manifested
forms, there came that which has been, is, and ever will
be, the spirit realm and its attributes—designated as
angels and archangels. They are the spiritual manifestations in the spirit world of those attributes that the
developing forces accredit to the One Source, that may
be seen in material planes through the influences that
may aid in development of the mental and spiritual
forces through an experience—or in the acquiring of
knowledge that may aid in the intercourse one with
another.

Then, how do they aid? Under what law do they
operate? The Divine, in its intercourse, influence and
manifestation with that which partakes of the same
forces as they manifest. (5749-3)

Several years later (1933) another message was apparently contributed by Michael, Lord of the Way:

This psychic reading given by Edgar Cayce this 18th
day of June, 1933, before the Second Annual Congress
of the Association for Research and Enlightenment.

Mrs. C.: You will have before you the Association for
Research and Enlightenment, Inc., its officers, members and friends: together with the psychic work of
Edgar Cayce which is being presented by it. You will
give for those assembled at this last meeting of the Second Annual Congress, and for all those who may be

interested in the work to whom it will go, a message on the scope, purposes and ideals of the Association; telling us how we may have a part in making the most of the opportunities and possibilities involved. . . .

Mr. C.: Yes, we have the Association—as an association, the work that is presented by the organization in giving that which may be helpful to those that seek through these channels for that which may aid them in the needs of the present.

As we have given, first there must come to the individuals—through that presented from time to time—that which will supply that lacking in their consciousness, whether in the material, the mental or spiritual approach to the same.

Then there must be drawn by the individuals that parallel as to whether the ideals presented are in accord with that they would endow to the Creative Forces in their experience.

For, as the individual thinketh, as contemplation is made in the material self, there is builded the hope, expectancy, desire, to present or manifest that which is chosen by self as an ideal that the individual would worship in its idea of the Creator.

Hence, as the work of the Association—in its ideals and purposes—is to pass on to others that which has been found to be of help or aid in individuals' experience, so will the leaven be made that will determine—then in groups, then in masses—as to the value of such efforts in this material world.

Thus may the efforts grow, as there is presented through the Association—as individuals, members, friends—that which is truth.

For, the Lord of the Way is as but a growing in understanding and comprehension of those things, con-

ditions and elements that would make for finding
contentment in the service of Truth. Then, the message
that would be given by Him, the Lord of the Way:

BOW THINE HEADS, O YE CHILDREN OF MEN.
FOR THE DAY OF THE LORD IS NIGH AT
HAND! MAKE THINE OWN PATHS STRAIGHT,
IN THAT YE WALK CIRCUMSPECTLY, BEFORE
THINE BROTHER, THAT YE PLACE NOT
STUMBLING-BLOCKS IN HIS WAY NOR CAUSE
HIM TO ERR IN THAT HE IS SEEKING TO FIND
HIS WAY! LET THE LIGHT THOU HAST SHINE
IN A MORE PERFECT WAY: FOR AS THE DAY
DRAWS NEAR WHEN ALL MUST BE TRIED SO
AS BY FIRE, FIND SELF ON THAT SIDE
WHEREIN THINE BROTHER HAS BEEN AIDED!

We are through. (254-66)

On yet another occasion Cayce had been quite ill and was
giving a reading for himself. His voice was barely audible,
weak—when suddenly there was a pause, then out came a
loud and powerful voice from the man who an instant
before could scarcely speak. The words were shouted in
anger, and the very walls seemed to shake. . . .

BOW THINE HEADS, YE CHILDREN OF MEN!
FOR I, MICHAEL, LORD OF THE WAY, WOULD
SPEAK WITH THEE! YE GENERATION OF
VIPERS—YE ADULTEROUS. GENERATION—BE
WARNED!

THERE IS TODAY SET BEFORE THEE GOOD
AND EVIL! CHOOSE THOU WHOM YE WILL
SERVE! WALK IN THE WAY OF THE LORD—OR
ELSE THERE WILL COME THAT SUDDEN
RECKONING, AS YE HAVE SEEN!

BOW THINE HEADS, YE WHO ARE UN-
GRACIOUS, UNREPENTENT! FOR THE GLO-

RY OF THE LORD IS AT HAND! THE OP-
PORTUNITY IS BEFORE THEE—ACCEPT OR
REJECT! (294-100)

It would seem that there had been among the people present a certain degree of ambivalence in purpose concerning the work of Edgar Cayce, plus some additional rather
strained inter-personal relationships.

In the following Reading another of the angels,
Halaliel, is heard from—along with his pronouncement
of John the Beloved's intended return into the earth.

Q. We seek at this time such information as will be of
value and interest to those present, regarding the spiritual, mental and physical changes which are coming to
the earth.

A. *Yes; as each of you gathered here have your own individual development, yet as each seeks to be a channel
of blessings to the fellow man, each attunes self to the
throne of universal information.* And there may be accorded you that which may be beneficial, not only in
thine own experience, but that which will prove helpful,
hopeful, in the the experience of others.

*Many may question you as to the sources, as to the
channel through which such information that may be
given you at this time has come. Know it has reached
that which is as high for each of you in your respective
development as you have merited, and do merit; and
has accorded and does accord to the realm of light that
which may be aidful and helpful in thine own experience, and in the experience of those that ye in your
service to thy fellow man may give unto others.* Hence,
in giving the interpretation, *many are present; many of
those whose names alone would bring to others
awe—discredit, yes—even a wonderment.* For, not only
then must the information be instructive but enlightening; yet it must also be so given that it may be a *practical* thing in the experience of thine own self and in the
experience of life of thine fellow man. Not only must it

be informative in nature, but it must also be that which is constructive; though that which is informative and that which may be enlightening and constructive must at times overlap one another.

First, then: There is soon to come into the world a body; one of our own number here that to many has been a representative of a sect, of a thought, of a philosophy, of a group, *yet one beloved of all men in all places where the uiversality of God in the earth has been proclaimed,* where the oneness of the Father as God is known and is consciously magnified in the activities of individuals that proclaim the acceptable day of the Lord. *Hence, that one, John the Beloved, in the earth—his name shall be John, and also at the place where he met face to face. He comes as a messenger, not as a forerunner, but as a messenger;* for these are periods when mental, material, are to be so altered in the affairs of men as to be even bringing turmoil to those that have not seen that the *Spirit* is moving in His ways to bring the knowledge of the Father in the hearts and lives of men.

When, where, is to be this one? In the hearts and minds of those that have set themselves in that position that they become a channel through which, spiritual, mental and material things become one in the purpose and desires of that physical body!

As to the material changes that are to be as an omen, as a sign to those that this is shortly to come to pass—as has been given of old, the sun will be darkened and the earth shall be broken up in divers places—and *then* shall be *proclaimed*—through the spiritual interception in the hearts and minds and souls of those that have sought His way—that *His* star has appeared, and will point the way for those that enter into the holy of holies in themselves. For, God the Father, God the Teacher, God the Director, in the minds and hearts of men, must ever be *in* those that come to know Him as first and foremost in the seeking of those souls; for He is first the

God to the individual and as He is exemplified, as He is manifested in the heart and in the acts of the body, of the individual, He becomes manifested before men. And those that seek in the latter portion of the year of our Lord (as ye have counted in and among men) '36, he will appear!

As to the changes physical again: The earth will be broken up in the western portion of America. The greater portion of Japan must go into the sea. The upper portion of Europe will be changed as in the twinkling of an eye. Land will appear off the east coast of America. There will be the upheavals in the Arctic and in the Antarctic that will make for the eruption of volcanoes in the Torrid areas, and there will be the shifting then of the poles—so that where there has been those of a frigid or the semi-tropical will become the more tropical, and moss and fern will grow. And these will begin in those periods in '58 to '98, when these will be proclaimed as the periods when His light will be seen again in the clouds. As to times, as to seasons, as to places, *alone* is it given to those who have named the name—and who bear the mark of those of His calling and His election in their bodies. To them it shall be given.

As to those things that deal with the mental of the earth, these shall call upon the mountains to cover many. As ye have seen those in lowly places raised to those of power in the political, in the machinery of nations' activities, so shall ye see those in high places reduced and calling on the waters of darkness to cover them. And those that in the inmost recesses of their selves awaken to the spiritual truths that are to be given, and those places that have acted in the capacity of teachers among men, the rottenness of those that have ministered in places will be brought to light, and turmoils and strifes shall enter. And, as there is the wavering of those that would enter as emissaries, as teachers, from the Throne of Life, the Throne of Light, the Throne of Immortality, and wage war in the air with those of darkness, then know ye the Armageddon is at hand. For with the great numbers of the gathering of the hosts of those that have hindered and would make for man and his weaknesses stumblingblocks, they shall wage war with the Spirits of Light that come into the earth for this awakening; that have been and are being called by those of the sons of men into the service of the Living God. For He, as ye have been told, is not the God of the dead, not the God of those that have foresaken Him, but those that love His coming, that love His associations among men—the God of the *living*, the God of LIFE! For, He IS Life.

Who shall proclaim the acceptable year of the Lord in Him that has been born in the earth in America? Those from that land where there has been born in the earth in America? Those from that land where there has been the regeneration, not only of the body but the mind and the spirit of men, *they* shall come and declare that John Peniel is giving to the world the new *order* of things. Not that these that have been proclaimed have been refused, but that they are made *plain* in the minds of men, that they may know the truth and the truth, the life, the light, will make them free.

I have declared this, that has been delivered unto me to give unto you, ye that sit here and that hear and that see a light breaking in the east, and have heard, have seen thine weaknesses and thine fault-findings, and know that He will make thy paths straight if ye will but live that *ye know* that He will make thy paths straight if ye will but live that *ye know* this day—then may the next step, the next word, be declared unto thee. For ye in your weakness have known the way, through that as ye have made manifest of the *spirit* of truth and light that has been proclaimed into this earth, that has been committed unto the keeping of Him that made of Himself no estate, but who brought into being all that ye see manifest in the earth, and has declared this message unto thee: "Love the Lord thy God with all thine heart", and the second is like unto it, "Love thy neighbor as thyself". Who is thine neighbor? Him that ye may aid in whatsoever way that he, thy neighbor, thy brother, has been troubled. Help him to stand on his own feet. For such may only know the acceptable way. The weakling, the unsteady, must enter into the crucible and become as naught, even as He, that they may know the way. *I Halaliel, have spoken*!

Q. What are the world changes to come this year physically?

A. The earth will be broken up in many places. The early portion will see a change in the physical aspect of the west coast of America. There will be open waters appear in the northern portions of Greenland. There will be new lands seen off the Caribbean Sea, and *dry* land will appear. There will be the falling away in India of much of the material suffering that has been brought on a troubled people. There will be the reduction of one risen to power in central Europe to naught. The young king's son will soon reign.* In America in the political forces we see a re-stabilization of the powers of the peoples in their own hands, a breaking up of the rings, the cliques in many places. South America shall be shaken from the uppermost position to the end, and in the Antarctic off the Tierra Del Fuego *land,* and a strait with rushing waters.

Q. To what country is the reference made regarding the young king?

A. In Germany.

Q. Is America fulfilling her destiny?

A. Rather should the question be sought, my children, are individuals fulfilling those channels to which they have been brought through their own application of the knowledge within themselves to fulfil their position? For each and every one, each and every nation, is led—even as in heaven. For that ye see in earth is a *pattern* of that in the *mind*, as ye well know, and is as a

---

* See 4/61 *Earth Changes* booklet report, p. 30.

shadow of spiritual truth, life and light. Is America as a whole? This is as has been given. *If there is not the acceptance in America of the closer brotherhood of man, the love of the neighbor as self, civilization must wend its way westward—and again must Mongolia, must a hated people, be raised.*

Q. Is there any further counsel or advice for us gathered here, which will enable us to understand better our responsibility?

A. All gathered here in the name of God who is the Father, to those that seek to know His ways—and who is as something outside the veil of their understanding unless sought, even as the counsel of the Father, of that God-Mother in each soul that seeks to know the biddings; not as one that would reap vengeance but rather as the loving, *merciful* Father. For, as ye show mercy, so may the Father show mercy to thee. As ye show the wisdom, as ye show the love of thy fellow man, so may the love be shown, so may the wisdom, so may the guiding steps day by day be shown thee. Be ye joyous in the Lord, knowing that He is ever present with those that seek His face. He is not in heaven, but makes heaven in thine own heart, if ye accept Him. He, God, the Father, is present and manifest in that ye mete to your fellow man in thine own experience.

Would ye know the Father, be the father to thy brother. Would ye know the love of the Father, *show* thy love to thy faltering, to thy erring brother—but to those that seek, not those that condemn.

We are through. (3976-15)

Several individuals, as we have noted before, were indicated to have had blood relationships with the Master in times past. The following are some of the more pertinent excerpts:

Named Uldha, she was the daughter of Uhjltd when the nomads made raids into the north country. She lost in soul development in the first portion of that experience, but gained from the trials of him who first taught her to pray. Uhjltd taught her to pray, and she later became an aide to him in separating various groups for individual healing, and became a leader herself. She was associated with Jesus Christ in his incarnation at that time as her brother, Zend, which was a previous incarnation to that as the Master; for he became the leader in that land, and much is still gained in thought from the Persian philosophy.

Q. Might I receive at this time a message from the Master?

A. *Come, mine daughter, mine sister. In choosing me, as I have chosen you, there comes that beauty of oneness in knowing the way that brings to others peace, joy, happiness, in doing His will; for he that seeks to do His will may in me have that peace, that joy, that understanding, that gives to each in their respective spheres their needs, their desires, as their desires are in me. Be faithful, even as thou wert faithful then.* (993)

Is this not a direct message from the Master, or how then shall we regard it? Or, consider the following . . . given to the entity said to have been Jude.

Q. (Jude). Is this my brother Jesus talking?

A. He speaks with thee often in thy meditations and prayers.

Q. Will I be able to see Jesus?

A. You will.

Q. In John, thou saidest, "after my death, the Comforter will come". Who is the Comforter today?

A. The Comforter is the gift of the Holy Spirit, for it sheds abroad in dark places, and him that keepeth My council is brought to the full understanding, and is brought to remembrance of that walk with Him.

Q. Which of the disciples was the one Jude loved the best?

A. John. Upon this one Jude leaned in days when chains and bonds held thee. Freed with Him and then sent into the wilderness for thy tenderness. He (John) will aid you.

Q. Is John now in the flesh?

A. John yet abides in me.

Q. Will he again come into the flesh?

A. That remains yet to be seen.

Q. Is (5770) Judas Iscariot?

A. Judas Iscariot, betrayer of me.

Q. He is a fine man today.

A. A fine man and leans upon thee. Many have been the trials of this soul in the destruction of many places and cities. Yet, though today with much of what the world calls material bounty, he leans upon thee—yet, this soul leans on thee.

Q. Should he be introduced into the work at Virginia Beach?

A. Yes, the more that are gathered in His name, the greater is the strength thereof.

Q. Am I guided when and in my approach to others regarding this?

A. Thou art. In the hour that thou speakest I put it into thine heart what to say. For oft in prayer do I speak with thee.

Q. Does this demonstrate what you mean when you say "I am with you"?

A. I am and will be with you always, even unto the end. We are through for the present. (137-125)

Within the readings Cayce often quoted the Master—sometimes directly from Scripture, or slightly paraphrased, yet at other times attributing to Him statements that are not found in historical texts. Then, too, as in some of the previous Readings, it is difficult to comprehend that this is merely a flow from Cayce's unconcious mind alone—or someone else, helping with the information.

Mrs. C.: We, the group designated as the healing group, have gathered here to seek through these channels to know the way Thou would have us work in bringing to others help in Thy name. Please clarify our minds as to the method and way for us to proceed in seeking to help others. You will answer any questions that will be asked.

Mr. C.: Yes, we have the individuals and the group as gathered here. *In seeking for understanding, let each harken to what He has to say.*

Come, my children, lift up thine hearts that I may enter in. As ye have chosen me, so have I chosen you, that ye may be a blessing to those who seek in *my* name to *know* the truth as may be magnified in *their* lives through *thine* aid in me. Grace, mercy and peace, is given to those thou asketh for in the proportion as thy trust, thy faith, is *in* me. As ye seek through raising in self that image of love in Him, so *may* thine self be lifted up, and the understanding come *to* him who *seeks* for same.

Q. Is there any danger in trying to heal someone else?
A. (After long pause) Questions—(after) the promise as has been just made?

Q. Should each of us as individuals, after raising the Christ's vibrations in ourselves, send these as individuals or through only one of our group?
A. Where two or three are gathered in My name, *there* I will be in the midst of them, whether in thought or in person.

Q.   Please explain why the Master in many cases forgave sins in healing individuals.

A.   Sins are of commission and omission. Sins of commission were forgiven, while sins of omission were called to mind—even by the Master.

Q.   How should the group make itself known to those whom it might help?

A.   Fear not that thine work will not find an outlet, once there is union of purpose. Has He not said, "Be joyous in that I have chosen *thee,* as *thou* hast chosen me?" and "Ye may be lights in my name"?

We are through. (281-2) 12/16/31

Mrs. C.:   We, the group designated as the healing group have gathered here to seek through these channels to know why and how we are fitted to carry on this special part of the work. Please guide us into the right path, that we may know Thy Will and be used to do Thy Work.

Mr. C.:   Yes, we have the group as gathered here, as designated as a group to carry on that portion in this material world. Each as are gathered here are fitted in their own particular way for a portion of that work designated by the group as the healing group. Hence, when once chosen, and the face set in that direction, that as the warning, as the threat.

Q.   Outline our individual work as we are named, and indicate that which needs to be stressed in our meditations to better fit us for carrying on our part.

A.   Even as there was the call in the past of those that *needed His Love,* His understanding, so may thy part be in making known to others that there *is* that power being made *manifest through* this group, who put *their* trust *in* Him; for the way *ye* know, even as it was given thee—and the place ye know, for ye may make many to know His name, even as I *call* thee by name. *Heed,* as thou didst of old—for this purpose brought I thee into being, that My Love may be known in *this* land. Be *faithful* unto the end. (281-1)

Mrs. C.: You will have before you the group gathered here. Please give them at this time that which they need in continuing their work on the lesson which they are preparing on "What Is Your Ideal?" You will answer the questions which will be asked in regard to this by some of those present.

Mr. C.: We have the group as gathered here. Also that has been given in "What Is Thy Ideal?" As has been given, there will come a sign to the group, or to members of same—will they make the ideal that is as one with Him. *The promise is, as was given of Him; "for I will bring to remembrance all things whatsoever has been my part with you, for in such manifestations is my Father glorified in you".*

Q. Please explain to me how I should proceed in order to attain my true ideal.
A. As is given, in seeking the Father's face, grace, mercy and peace is added in the seeking. Know that thou would worship, and self a part of same, seeing in others then that thou would worship in the Father; *for the prayer was, "May they be one, even as Thou and I are one",* for, as given, a *spiritual insight* brings the *seeing* of the best in each life. There is good in all, for they *are* of the Father, and have been bought with the price, even of the Son, in that flesh may know the *glory of* the Father that may be manifested even in thee!

Q. What can we do as individuals and as a group that we may come to a oneness of purpose, in a cooperative manner, which will then give the group a one IDEAL?
A. This must be found in the Father, for *"Ye I have chosen, as ye have chosen me. He I have called, him did I also predestine—and they hear my voice, and answer by my name."* In that name alone may the *calling* and *election* be sure; presenting selves, each, in a way and manner that is holy and acceptable unto *thee,*

according to thine *own* understanding, doing each day that as thou knowest is in accord with that ideal, and the *way* is shown thee! Be not over hasty in word or deed, for it *is* line upon line, here a little, there a little; for it is the *little* leaven that leaveneth the whole lump, and such compared He to the *kingdom* of God. The kingdom, then, is within. Go. Do. That as I have shown thee, so do ye, and there will be peace, harmony, understanding, light, that saves—even unto the end.

Q. What would be the most important work for the group or individual to do at this time?

A. Each show forth in their own way of manifesting His love day by day. Said He: *"A new commandment give I unto you: Love one another."* In this manner may the greater work, may the greater blessing, *come* to one and all.

Q. In the reading of Feb. 7th, in Knowing Self, please explain what was meant by "Work, work! For the night is coming, and in Him will be that Light that gives rest unto the soul."

A. In this is seen that *as was expressed by Him. "Behold the fields are white unto the harvest, but the laborers are few."* Ye have signified the willingness to be a laborer with Him. Then work, work! For the night, for the shades of those things that bring doubt, darkness, dissimilitude, will come—unless one is busy with that they *know* to do; but with the labor comes that rest as promised in Him.

Q. Just how is it meant that I should give of my best to Him? In what manner may I do that?

A. Study that thou sayest, that thou doest, and reserve *nothing*—in strength of body *or* mind—in service to others, *that is* a reflection of that He would have thee do, as thou knowest how. As was given by Him, let thine works, thine efforts, be *even as was said* by Him, *"If ye will not believe me, ye will believe for the very works sake—for the things I do bespeak that I believe I AM!"* (262-12)

This psychic reading (254-76) was given by Edgar Cayce (without being requested), after entire suggestion had been given for waking him, at the end of 378-50, on 6/11/34.

How beautiful the face of those whom the Lord, the Christ, smiles upon! He would walk and talk with thee, my children, if ye will but put away from thy mind those things and conditions that ye feel are in the way. For, they are as naught compared to the great love that He has bestowed upon His brethren.

How beautiful the face, how lovely the clouds! In His presence abide; ye, *every one* of you are before Him just now. His face is turned toward thee, His heart and hand is offered you. Will ye not accept Him just now? How glorious the knowledge of His presence should awaken in the hearts of you, for He is *lonely* without thee; for He has called each of you by name. Will ye fail Him now?

Let His love, as He gave, be the impelling influence in thine associations one with another; yea, though ye crucify Him in thine activities and words one to another, He was crucified that ye might know Him the better. For *thus* He became the Lord, thy Brother, thy Savior, thy Intermediator with God, the Father.

Count it joy, then, as He, that ye are called by Him in a service—in a *loving* service—to thy fellow man; for through this lowly, weak, unworthy channel (Cayce) has He chosen to speak, for the purposes of this soul (Cayce) have been to do good unto his brethren. Love ye him. Comfort and care, for thy Master has loved him, thy brother, thy neighbor, thy friend! Love God, eschew evil. Speak oft with thy Brother, thy Savior, thy Christ, for He is oft in the midst of thee. He would bless this house, will ye but keep Him near at hand. Turn Him not away with harsh words, unkind thoughts, or belittling acts one to another! If ye are faithful to confess thy faults one to another, He is faithful to forgive;

for He alone can purge thy soul and make it light in His heart, His bosom, His blood. For it was shed for thee, that thou mightest know the love of God, of Christ, in thine day. For the hand of the Lord is upon thee, and upon him that speaks with thee. Do good that He may abide with thee, that the clouds of doubt and fear may be purged every whit from thine experience, from thine consciousness; and know that He is ALIVE in thee, wilt thou but love one another even as He has loved you.

See the glory of His light shine upon him that speaks to thee. Know the Lord is nigh unto thee. Fare ye in the way that brings peace, harmony; for if ye will have peace, make peace with another, make peace with thy self, thy Lord, thy Christ, thine Brother.

Love one another! (254-76)

Cayce then woke up, without a further waking suggestion being given. Strained relations between those present may have been the background which caused the above message to come through at this particular time.

The following reading (1158-9) is noteworthy in that it is one of the very few examples wherein Cayce takes a fellow entity properly to task for negative thinking. Also, the Biblical references alone are worth inclusion.

(In the present, with) the death of the (entity's) father, when in thine own physical purposes there was the reasoning, "If He healed, why did He let Father die? If He is such as so many proclaim, WHY hath He been so long away? WHY does He continue to go here, there? Why do those that are in authority appear against Him?" These are questions then, they are questions ever. Is it not a reciprocal world?

Q. Did I see Jesus after the Resurrection?
A. Saw Jesus upon the Mount, as did many.

Q. Are the children who were born to the entity in this Palestine period known to the entity today, and in what connection?

A. They may be known, as grandchildren.

Q. *Is Peter known to me today?*

A. *Not known. As has been indicated, there are many of the Apostles, or Disciples, that may be known.* There's *Bartholomew* that may be known. There is *Andrew,* there is *Jude* (thy brother) that may be known. There is even *Judas*—don't know him, shouldn't know him; not as a fault in his, but better not. *John may enter,* and will be known—and as one that may be proclaimed by the entity. These come only, to be sure, as conditions—but may become personal experiences. Just as this: How personal is thy God? Just as personal as ye will let Him be! How close is the Christ as was manifested in the physical body, Jesus? Just as near, just as dear as ye will let Him be!

Oft ye may ask, from thy enquiring mind, when I so desire to know Him, why then do I not see, do I not hear?

"How long, O Lord, how long? Look not for a sign, as a SIGN," as He gave, "but BE—and ye *are* as One with Him!"

These become not as trites, not as sayings— they must be *experienced* by self! They may not be experienced by merely being told. Ye live them! "As ye live in me and I in the Father, ask what ye will and it will be done unto thee!"

Ye wait, then, knowing. He knoweth what thou hast need of before ye ask. Then ye say, Why ask?

In the love of thine own children, is it those who ask or those who do not ask that make a response? Not that ye love one more than the other; not for impunity, but a reciprocal reaction!

Those things are as God is. And they that would know Him must *believe* that He is; and most of all ACT that way!

Q. Should I hope and seek for personal experiences or contacts with Jesus as a personality now?

A. As has been indicated, this may be. Not as a desire for self-exaltation, that is, self-proof, self-evidence; but it is evidenced *in* thee when ye *are* (in thy living, in thy thinking, in thy acting) One with Him.

Then, and thus—how hath the angel given? "As ye have seen Him go, so will ye see Him come." Were those just as words? No.

Thou hast seen Him oft in the acts of others and the personality ye called by another name, yet ye may see Him. And when He speaks, "Be not afraid, it is I". Know He is near. And in the breaking of bread ye may know Him!

Q. In my life reading you say, "If ye would know Him, ye must endure". What is meant by Him, and what character of experience must I endure to know Him?

A. This is as has been given again and again, in that as just said. Endure! That is, endure the unkind things that may be said about others. Endure that which is of the world. For as He said, "Ye are in the world but be not *of* the world, even as I am in the world but not of the world".

That is, the imaginative forces that impel the activities are then to be creative—and in so doing, if it requires the self-sacrifice, if it requires this or that experience, *that* is enduring. But we are looking as He gave, "I go to prepare a place—if it were not so I would have told you—that where I AM ye may be—I AM!"

Who shall I say hast sent me?
I AM THAT I AM!

Does it not all remain then as a whole? For without Abraham, without Moses, yea without David what need could there be that Melchizedek, that Enoch, or Joseph, or Joshua, should again come in the flesh? fulfilling all?

Have ye fulfilled all? When ye have, ye are One with Him—are ye not? Is not a reckoning? It IS!

We are through for the present (1158-9)

The following is noteworthy among the Readings because of its obvious first person narrative—

In this present report, these we find conform to many of the ideas and *some* of the ideals. Be sure there is not too much difference made in ideas and ideals, for, as has so oft been given, these must of necessity be for the accomplishment of the purport of teaching, training, and giving to a waiting world the truths as may be exemplified in the individuals' lives, until that or those individuals may become one with that purport as is being set forth—*An idea may be beautiful, may be wonderful, but without the background of an ideal becomes as but sounding brass, or as the gourd without water.*

In these things, then, let each be mindful of that place, that niche, that purport each is to fill, and *fill* that with *all* of the power, might, strength, that lies within that body! *So cooperate with other individuals, working in their individual capacities that the whole purport may be as one, even as the Father and I are one in you. I speak not of myself, but that ye may know the truth, even as delivered in the day when I walked among men and became known as the Son of Man, and the savior of a be-knighted race.* Here, my brethren, ye are come again to fulfil, in this place, a glorious principle, a glorious article of work among the sons of man. Let each, then, in that power that may be gained in that association of the forces as manifest through each, become one in purpose. (254-50)

The following excerpts from the 254 series, or "Work Readings" are extremely important. . . . And with the final paragraphs of 254-92 seem to sum up quite well the entire relationship of spiritual guidance from outside sources.

(254-83) 2/14/35

The members of the Executive Committee of Group 9* of the A.R.E., some of whom are present in this room, salute Thee with greetings of deepest love and thank Thee for again bringing to us the ministry of our kind and helping leader, Edgar Cayce. Realizing that when science investigates the works of God on the higher planes as it has done on the material plane, spirituality will truly come into its own proper place in the consciousness of humanity, we hereby petition your indulgence and cooperation in bringing to us the following information, as the questions are asked, for the more perfect functioning of the work of Edgar Cayce and the Association from this time on, if same meets with your pleasure to do so.

E.C.: *Yes, we—from the source of all knowledge that is promised in Him—salute thee,* and give that which will be helpful to those who seek to be in the ministry of those influences and forces that make for more and more awareness of the divine in each and every soul, that—applied in the experience of each entity, each soul—will bring that day of the Lord that is at hand to those who will hear His voice.

Then, from the heights of those experiences, those hierarchies in the earth and in the air, we come as messengers of truth to those who will hear, and question.

Q. For the better and more rational presentation of the work of Edgar Cayce to the world, will you, if you consider same in order, kindly inform us of Thine Identity

* Group 9 was an A.R.E. group in Washington, D.C. at the time.

and the source or sources from which you bring us the information given in answer to our questions in the Readings other than the Physical? Is it from the Astral——

A. (interrupting) From the universal forces that are acceptable and accessible to those who in earnestness open their minds, their souls, to the wonderful words of truth and light.

Q. To what extent are the Masters of the Great White Brotherhood directing the activities of Edgar Cayce? Who are the Masters directly in charge?
A. Messengers from the higher forces that may manifest from the Throne of grace itself.

Q. Who are the Masters directly in charge? Is Saint Germain—
A. (interrupting) Those that are directed by the Lord of lords, The Kings of kings, Him that came that ye might be one with the Father.

Q. Is Saint Germain among them? Who is Halaliel?
A. These are all but messengers of the Most High. Halaliel is that one who from the beginning has been as a leader of the heavenly host, who has defied Ariel, who has made the ways that have been heavy—but as the means for the *understanding*.

Q. Is Saint Germain among them?
A. When needed.

Q. Please give us Thine Identity?
A. *He that seeks, that has not gained the control—seeks damnation to his own soul! Control thine inner self that ye may know the true life and light! For he that would name the Name must have become perfect in himself!*

Q. If Mr. Cayce is a member and a messenger of the Great White Brotherhood, how do the Masters wish him to proceed and should not his activities henceforth be presented as Their Work?

A.   As the work of the *Master* of masters, that may be
presented when in those lines, those accords, necessary
through the White Brotherhood. This—this—*this*, my
friends, even but *limits*; while in Him is the Whole.
*Would thou make of thyself, of thyselves, a limited
means of activity? Would thou seek to be hindered by
those things that have made of many, contending forces
that continue to war one with another even in the air,
even in the elemental forces?* For He, thy Lord, thy
God, hath called thee by name, even as He has given,
"Whosoever will drink the cup, even as of my blood, he
may indeed be free". While ye labor, let *Him* that is the
author, that is the finisher, that *is* the Life, that is the
bread of life, that is the blood of life, let *Him* alone be
thy guide! Dost He call any soul into service, *then* by
name will He—does He—designate, and to whom it
becomes a charge to keep—even as He has walked with
him, *this body that ye use as a channel of approach to
the Throne; ye make of same oft as a laughingstock to
thy very soul through thine own selfishness!* Let the
light of Him, thy Christ, thy God, IN that it may
cleanse thy body, that it may lighten thy soul, that it
may purge thy mind, that ye will only be just gentle, just
kind; not finding fault with any, for with faults ye build
barriers to thine own soul's enlightenment. *I, thy God,
thy Christ, beseech thee!* (254-83)

Mr. C.: O ye children of light, that come seeking to
know the will of thy God through the light that has been
given thee! In thy activity let thy light shine, *in thee,*
that others may know, may see—*in thee*—that thou
hast been in close communion with Him who *is* the
light. For in Him is no darkness at *all*! So, let thy
thought, thy acts, thy conversation one with another, be
so permeated with that love as He gave, that ye may
know that there is no approach save through that
awareness within thine own self that makes ye one with
Him.

Let thy ways be His ways. Let that which prompts thee
be not of thyself, but He—thy Lord, thy God—working

in and through thee. For thou hast been called unto a service in Him. Then let thy prayer, thy meditation, be "Not my will but Thine, O Lord, be done in and through me".

Q. Would it meet Thy Will and the Will of the Father, if, henceforth, the readings given by Edgar Cayce should be designated as pronouncements of Thee and the Father, given as is justified by the merit of those asking?

A. *This is the condition; this is the activity.* Yet be ye all things to all men; thereby ye may save the more. For he that declares as a name, in a name, save in the universality of the Father, limits the ability of the seeker, of the channel through which that glory may come to any.

Learn, rather, that given: By what name shall I say that I am sent? "I AM THAT I AM." That rather than in any name of this, that or the other manner. The I AM that seeks may gain, then, that access to the I AM that brought, brings, holds, the worlds in their place.

Q. May we ask with propriety by what name Thou didst call Thy servant Edgar Cayce during Thine Incarnation on earth?

A. *Lucius.*

As has been given, ye have in thine own hands, thine own minds, that which is unexcelled in manifestations of His at-oneness with the Creative Forces manifesting in the earth. *Yet man, in his miscomprehension, misunderstanding, makes same either that glorious effect or become the laughingstock of him that passeth by.*

Look upon those that were called into service as was Saul, the son of Kish; as was Jeroboam, the son of Nebat. These came by the Divine call from out of their own brethren, and were endowed with that which would make for such a manifestation as had not before been seen in the earth. Yet counsellors of these made them but laughingstocks to the nations roundabout.

So, in thine choosing channels, in choosing way, in choosing means, be thou very slow; yet make haste. For the day of the Lord is at hand and the reckoning of many is nigh unto their own door. (254-85)

(254-92) 12/16/36

Work and plans of the Association for Research & Enlightenment, Inc., in studying and presenting the psychic work of Edgar Cayce. We seek counsel and guidance in carrying forward this work. You will consider the affairs of the Association under the general heads which will be presented and answer the questions that will be asked.

Mr. C.: Yes, we have the work of the Association for Research and Enlightenment, Incorporated; and its plans and its endeavors in presenting the work, the psychic information as may be given through Edgar Cayce.

First, as we would give, for general information and for study of those who may undertake in any way to present information of a psychic source or where it may be an influence in the lives of individuals:

First, as a corporation, as an organization, the Association for Research & Enlightenment, Inc., presents a problem for consideration in itself.

Know that all the laws as pertain to the activities are the same, and that what has come into materialization first has had its inception in the mental and the spiritual realm, and is as perfect a body in those realms (or the more perfect, dependent upon the basis of the inception or the desire that has brought it into being) as it is in the material plane.

And, as has ever been given, those influences are the same in applying or in relationships to such organizations as about any individual or any individual organization. And the same laws apply in same.

Thus in seeking information as to the conducting of the affairs and of carrying forward the ideals and purposes of such an organization, consider the sources from which such information may come and as to what and as to how they apply toward what is set as the ideal. *And know there is only* ONE IDEAL!

But as has been given as respecting individuals, "He hath given His angels charge concerning thee, lest at any time ye dash your foot against a stone". It's just as applicable in any group organization as it is in an individual entity. *Yet there becomes in the practical application more of a confusion unless the ideals and the purposes that are of a spiritual nature are held to.*

This is not intended to indicate there are individual souls or entities that have been set aside or appointed by a hierarchy of another realm to look after the affairs, as some would have others believe. Not that they do not, or cannot, but is that thy ideal? Is that thy purpose, that it shall become a personal thing? Or is it rather that it shall be a channel through which only the fatherhood of God, the brotherhood of man, the universal Christ-Consciousness may be applied in the lives and the affairs of individuals in every way and manner?

For do not consider for a moment (for this might be carried on to an indefinite end) that an individual soul-entity passing from an earth plane as a Catholic, a Methodist, as Episcopalian, is something else because he is dead! He's only a dead Episcopalian, Catholic or Methodist. And such personalities and their attempts are the same; only that IDEAL! For all are under the law of God equal, and how did He say even as respecting the home? "They are neither married nor given in marriage in the *heavenly home but are* ONE!"

Hence the ideals and the purposes of the Association for Research & Enlightenment, Inc., are not to function

*as another schism or ism. Keep away from that! For
these warnings have been given again and again. Less
and less of personality, more and more of God and
Christ in the dealings with the fellow man.*

To be sure, those phases of the activity of the Association, in the material plane, must take concrete
evidence and present concrete evidence of its being
grounded in mental and spiritual truth. But not that it is
to build up any organization that is to be as a schism or
a cult or ism, or to build up money or wealth or fame,
or position, or an office that is to function in opposition
with *any* already organized group.

How did thy Master work? In the church, in the
synagogue, in the field, in the lakes, upon the sands and
the mountains, in the temple! And did He defy those?
Did He set up anything different? Did He condemn the
law even of the Roman, or the Jews, or the Essenes, or
the Sadducees, or any of the cults or isms of the day?
All, He gave, are as ONE—under the law! And
grudges, schisms, isms, cults, must become as naught;
that thy Guide, thy Way, thy Master, yea even
Christ—as manifested in Jesus of Nazareth—may be
made known to thy fellow man!

So in thy considerations, seek ye to know more and
more of how each organization has its counterpart
bodily, mentally, spiritually, and guidance may be given
thee.

Ye have an organization then with a physical being,
with a mental being, with a spiritual concept. *And only
that which is not merely idealistic, but in keeping with
God's, Christ's precepts, Jesus' anointings, may be that
which may grow and become as a LIVING thing in the
experience, in the bodies, in the minds; yea to the very
awareness of the souls of men whom such a group, such
an organization would serve.*

In the bodily functioning, then, the activities are to have

due and proper consideration, to be sure. *But let each phase of the Work present how not only mentally but spiritually there is a grounding in TRUTH, as is set forth in the Christ-Consciousness as exemplified by Jesus, as has been proclaimed by many of the saints of old.*

And then ye may be very sure that all of those influences from the spiritual realm are as ONE. FOR WHETHER IT BE AS YE HAVE SEEN AT TIMES, THE LORD OF THE WAY OR THE CHRIST HIMSELF AS JESUS, OR OTHERS BE SENT AS AN AID, *depends upon whether ye hold that ideal that is One with the Universal Truth for and to man.* (254-92)

In closing we have included this OPEN READING given on WORLD AFFAIRS at the Thirteenth Annual Congress of The Association for Research and Enlightenment, Inc. June 22, 1944, six months prior to Edgar Cayce's death.

Mrs. C.:   It has been indicated through this channel that much might be given regarding what the vibrations of nations, as individuals, might mean. You will give such information concerning these vibrations and their relations to the spirit of the various nations, particularly in connection with the seven sins and twelve virtues in the human family, which will be helpful to us as an organization and as individuals in our attempt to be channels of blessing to our fellow men. You will then answer the questions which may be submitted, as I ask them.

Mr. C.:   When there came about the periods of man's evolution in the earth, what was given then as to why man must be separated into tongues, into nations, into groups? "Lest they in their foolish wisdom defy God." What is here then intimated? That man, seeking his own gratification of the lusts of the flesh, might even in the earth defy God. With what, then, has man been endowed by his Creator? All that would be necessary for each individual soul-entity to be a companion with God. And that is God's desire toward man.

Thus when man began to defy God in the earth and the confusion arose which is represented in the Tower of Babel—these are representations of what was then the basis, the beginnings of nations. Nations were set up then in various portions of the land, and each group, one stronger than another, set about to seek their gratifications.

As ye will recall, it even became necessary that from one of these groups one individual, a man, be called. His ways were changed. His name was changed. Did it take sin away from the man, or was it only using that within the individual heart and purpose and desire even then, as man throughout the periods of unfoldment put—in his interpretation—that of material success first? It isn't that God chose to reserve or save anything that was good from man, so long as man was, is, and will be one who uses that living soul as a companion with God. That's God's purpose. That should be man's purpose.

In the application of this principle, then, in the present day what has come about? Each nation has set some standard of some activity of man as its idea, either of man's keeping himself for himself or of those in such other nations as man's preparation for that companionship with God. For remember, there are unchangeable laws. For God is law. Law is God. Love is law, Love is God. There are then in the hearts, the minds of man, various concepts of these laws and as to where and to what they are applicable. Then, just as in the days of old, the nature of the flesh, human flesh and its natures, has not changed, but the spirit maketh alive. The truth maketh one free. Just as man has done throughout the ages, so in the present, as one takes those of the various nations as have seen the light and have, through one form or another, sought to establish as the ideal of that nation, of that people, some word, some symbol that has and does represent those peoples in those days of the fathers of the present land called America.

What is the spirit of America? Most individuals proudly boast "freedom". Freedom of what? When ye bind men's hearts and minds through various ways and manners, does it give them freedom of speech? Freedom of worship? Freedom from want? Not unless those basic principles are applicable throughout the tenets and lines as has been set, but with that principle freedom. For God meant man to be free and thus gave man will, a will even to defy God. GOD has not willed that any soul should perish, but hath with every trial or temptation prepared a way of escape.

There have come, through the various periods of man's unfoldment, teachers proclaiming, "This the way, here the manner in which ye may know", and yet in the Teacher of Teachers is found the way, He who even in himself fulfilled the law. For when God said, "Let there be light" there came Light·into that which He had created, that was without form and was void and it became the Word, and the Word dwelt among men and men perceived it not. The Word today dwells among men and many men perceive it not.

Those nations who have taken those vows that man shall be free should also take those vows "He shall know the truth and the truth then shall make him free".

Then what is this that would be given thee today? Here is thy lesson: Hear ye all! Beware lest ye as an individual soul, a son, a daughter of God, fail in thy mission in the earth today; that those ye know, those ye contact shall know the truth of God, not by thy word, bombastic words, but in long-suffering, in patience, in harmony, that ye create in thine own lives, for it must begin with thee. God has shown thee the pattern, even one Jesus, who became the Christ that ye might have an advocate with the Father, for the Father hath said, "In the day ye eat or use the knowledge for thine own aggrandizement, ye shall die". But he that had persuaded the spirit, the souls that God had brought into being, to push into matter to gratify desire for self-expression, self-indulgence, self-satisfaction, said, "Ye shall not surely die", or what were then the activities of man—for as had been said, "A day is a thousand years, a thousand years as a day".

What was the length of life then? Nearly a thousand years. What is your life today? May it not be just as He had given, just as He indicated to those peoples, just as He did to the law-giver, just as He did to David—first from a thousand years to a hundred and twenty, then to eighty? Why? Why? The sin of man is his desire for self-gratification.

What nations of the earth today vibrate to those things that they have and are creating in their own land, their own environment? Look to the nations where the span of life has been extended from sixty to eighty-four years. You will be judge who is serving God. These are judgments. These are the signs to those who seek to know, who will study the heavens, who will analyze the elements, who will know the heart of man, they that seek to know the will of the Father for themselves answer "Lord, here am I, use me, send me where I am needed".

Just as have been those principles of your present conflict. "Send help, for man's heritage of freedom would be taken away." By whom? He that hath said, "Surely ye will not die". There are those two principles, two conflicting forces in the earth today: the prince of this world, and that Principle that says to every soul, "Fear not, I have overcome the world and the prince of the world hath nothing in me". Can ye say that? Ye must! That is thy hope; that "The prince of this world, Satan, that old serpent, hath no part in any desire of my mind, my heart, my body, that I do not control in the direction it shall take." These are the things, these are the principles.

What then of nations? In Russia there comes the hope of the world, not as that sometimes termed of the Communistic, of the Bolshevistic; no. But freedom, freedom! that each man will live for his fellow man! The principle has been born. It will take years for it to be crystallized, but out of Russia comes again the hope of the world. Guided by what? That friendship with the nation that hath even set on its present monetary unit "In God We Trust". Do ye use that in thine own heart when you pay your just debts? Do ye use that in thy prayer when ye send thy missionaries to other lands? "I give it, for in God we trust"?

In the application of these principles, in those forms and manners in which the nations of the earth have and do measure to those in their activities, yea, to be sure, America may boast, but rather is that principle being forgotten when such is the case, and that is the sin of America.

So in England, from whence have come the ideas—not ideals—ideals of being just a little bit better than the other fellow. Ye must GROW to that in which ye will deserve to be known, deserve to receive. That has been, that is, the sin of England.

As in France, to which this principle first appealed, to which then came that which was the gratifying of the desires of the body—that is the sin of France.

In that nation which was first Rome, when there was that unfolding of those principles, its rise, its fall, what were they that caused the fall? The same as at Babel. The dissensions, the activities, that would enforce upon these, in this or that sphere, servitude; that a few might just agree, that a few even might declare their oneness with the Higher Forces. For theirs was the way that seemeth right to a man but the end is death. That is the sin of Italy.

The sin of China? Yea, there is the quietude that will not be turned aside, saving itself by the slow growth. There has been a growth, a stream through the land in ages which asks to be left alone to be just satisfied with that within itself. It awoke one day and cut its hair off! And it began to think and to do something with its thinking! This, here, will be one day the cradle of Christianity, as applied in the lives of men. Yea, it is far off as man counts time, but only a day in the heart of God—for tomorrow China will awake. Let each and every soul as they come to those understandings, do something, then, in his or her own heart.

Just as in India, the cradle of knowledge not applied, except within self. What is the sin of India? SELF, and leave the "ish" off—just self.

Then apply in thine own life truth. What is truth? It might have been answered, had an individual entity who stood at the crossways of the world waited for an answer. Yet That Soul had purified itself and had given the new commandment that "ye love one another".

What is it all about then? "Thou shalt love the Lord thy God with all thine heart, thine soul, thine mind, thine body, and thy neighbor as thyself." The rest of all the theories that may be concocted by man are nothing, if those are just lived. Love thy neighbor as thyself in the associations day by day, preferring as did the Christ who died on the cross rather than preferring the world be his without a struggle.

Know, then, that as He had His cross, so have you. May you take it with a smile. You can, if ye will let Him bear it with thee. Do it.

We are through for the present. (3976-29)

APPENDIX A

MY LIFE AND WORK

by Edgar Cayce

(This brief account by Mr. Cayce is one of his few written documents. It was written in 1935 for the purpose of giving people who requested a reading some understanding of the nature of his work.

We reproduce it here not only because it gives the principal biographical facts of his life, but also because it reflects so faithfully the attitude Mr. Cayce had toward his work and the people who came to him asking for help.)

I am asked so often to tell my experiences leading to the development of the phenomena as manifested through me that I feel the need of presenting the facts here in a simple manner. This is no attempt to write an autobiography, nor even set down in chronological order the curious happenings which have impelled me to accept psychic phenomena as natural experiences of my everyday life. If I could sit down with you for a quiet conversation, I would tell you this story.—

I was born and reared on a farm in western Kentucky. I attended the schools in the district and was considered rather dull until I began to read. A woodcutter told me the first Bible story that made a lasting impression. He told me that he was "strong as Samson". He said that the night before the preacher talked about this strong man who was somebody in the Bible. I went to my mother with the story and asked her to tell me about him. Later I asked my father to procure a Bible for me, for my own, that I might read it.

By the time I was fourteen I had read the Bible through several times, understanding little, yet to my developing mind this book seemed to contain that something which my inner self craved. As I read its promises and the prayers of those who sought to commune with the One God, I felt that it must be true. I had a religious experience, a vision and a promise (a promise that to me is still very sacred). As I have read this Book throughout the years, its promises become more and more real, and I have better understood the need for faith and prayer if we would make these promises our own.

However, the promise received at that time did not prevent my missing my lessons in school, as usual, the following day. In the evening I had the same hard time in preparing my spelling lesson. I studied it and each time felt that I knew it, yet when I handed the book to my father and he gave me the words to spell I couldn't spell them. After wrestling with it for two or three hours, receiving many rebuffs for my stupidity, something inside me seemed to say, "Rely on the promise". I asked my father to let me sleep on my lesson just five minutes. He finally consented. I closed the book, and leaning on the back of the chair went to sleep. At the end of five minutes I handed my father the book. I not only knew my lesson, but I could then spell any word in the book; not only spell the words but could tell on what page and what line the word would be found. From that day on I had little trouble in school, for I would read my lesson, sleep on it a few minutes, and then be able to repeat every word of it.

I could not explain this ability. It was a wonder to my parents, my associates, and my teachers. I did not attempt to reason why this happened. Today, my life is a combination of literally thousands of such experiences. Although I understand many of the laws associated with these phenomena, my understanding is born of experience, and I leave the technical explanations to others.

I do not make any claims for myself. I do feel from experience that through the readings, as may be obtained through me from time to time while in an unconscious state, those lessons, those suggestions are presented which if applied in the inner life of the individual to whom they are directed, will give a clearer, a more perfect understanding of physical, mental and spiritual ills. But you must judge for yourself. Facts and results are the measuring rods.

At fifteen I left school and began to work on the farm. I loved to read, but I had access to few books, therefore my Bible and Sunday School literature constituted my library. For two years I labored on the farm. One day I decided to seek work in town. I went to various shops, finally deciding that a book and stationery store looked the best to me. I went in and informed the man I was going to work for him. He said he did not need anyone, but I was sure he did, so Monday I reported for work. Two brothers owned this store, both wonderful men, but a little incident that happened the second morning I was there has been a lesson to me.

I was busy dusting off the stock when one of the brothers walked through the store. He said, "Good morning. I see you are busy. Be careful though; don't fall off and break something." He passed on into his office. In a few minutes the younger brother came through. He spoke, "Good morning. I see you are busy. Be careful—don't fall and hurt yourself." Just a little difference, but my! what a difference! We are all prone to think first of ourselves and when we find an individual interested in us we are interested in him, but if he is interested in himself first, seldom do we find him interesting. Then, how it must come home to us, "Know ye not that I must be about my Father's business?" if we would have Him interested in us.

I remained in the employ of these brothers for four or five

years. Finally I decided to make a change. Selecting a wholesale book and stationery house, I wrote these people for their catalogue. This I memorized word for word until I was able to repeat the whole through. I did this much in the same way as I learned my lessons in schools, by reading over sections of the catalogue and then sleeping. I applied to this firm for a position. They wrote me their regular stereotyped letter—did not need anyone, but would put my application on file, when they did they would let me know, etc. I proceeded, however, to get letters of recommendation from every firm in our little city that bought goods from these people, then I began to mail these so they would get at least two in each mail. The third day I received this wire: "Stop sending recommendations and report for work at once".

A short time after this I began suffering from severe headaches. My physician seemed unable to locate the cause. Then one day I had a very severe attack and became unconscious. A friend found me wandering about the streets and carried me home. For days I knew nothing. When I became conscious again I had no control whatever of my voice and for twelve months or more I could scarcely speak above a whisper. Everything we knew of was tried, but I continued to fail in health.

Among those who treated me was a hypnotist—not a physician, not a highly educated man—just a plain business man who was interested in the phenomenon of hypnotism. While under this influence, it was said, I was able to speak, yet when brought from under it, I could not. Successive attempts to hypnotize me seemed to "get on my nerves". I was unable to sleep, so this was discontinued for the time. As the experiments were witnessed by many, I received a good deal of newspaper publicity. A noted physician of New York visited me. Hypnotism was tried again, but at this time with no results. Then I told him of my experiences as a child, and that I felt sure that I could make myself unconscious for I felt within me the same condition taking place when being hypnotized as felt when putting myself to sleep. He suggested that this was why the hypnotist was unable to give me post-suggestion, but if I would put myself in the unconscious condition and have someone talk with me, I would be able to tell them the trouble and how to get rid of it. Can you imagine what that meant to my mind? When I think this over now I wonder why I haven't been called more names than I have.

My parents, having little faith in hypnotism, were afraid to try this physician's suggestion. After several months I was unable to even whisper, and many declared I had galloping consumption. I pleaded with my mother and father to at least let the man who had first hypnotized me try the experiment the specialist had suggested. They finally agreed. So on a Sunday afternoon, March 31, 1901 this man came to our home. No one was present except my mother, father, and this gentleman. I lay on the couch and gave the first of what is now called a "reading". In a few minutes I lost consciousness. They told me I said (after this man's suggestion that I could see myself):

"Yes, we can see the body. In the normal physical state this body is unable to speak, due to a partial paralysis of the inferior muscles of the vocal cords, produced by nerve strain. This is a psychological condition producing a physical effect. This may be removed by increasing the circulation to the affected parts by suggestion while in this unconscious condition."

I am told that in five to ten minutes I said, "It is all right." Then the man told me to wake up at a given time. When I was conscious again I knew that I could speak.

That was my first reading.

Since that time I have given more than fifteen thousand individual readings. The gentleman who assisted in this first reading believed that if I could describe what was wrong with myself I might also help others. He asked me to try and so I began spending much of my time in an unconscious state giving information for those who, hearing of this unusual power, sought help.

I was still ashamed to talk about these readings. People thought me odd and I resented for a time the little slights and slurs of my associates who took pleasure in laughing at me. It is hard to be "different". I finally selected photography as a life work and gave only my spare time and evenings to the increasing number of requests for readings. It was only when I began to come in contact with those who received help from following the suggestions given in readings that I began to realize the true nature of the work which lay before me. Indeed, I did not even decide to give my whole time to this work until results in my own family brought me face to face with facts.

One day a man phoned me at my studio: "I have heard of what you, with the assistance of a certain man, have been able to do for those who are very sick. I have a little girl whose condition is said to be hopeless. Won't you come and see what you will say about her condition?"

I will never forget my feelings on that occasion. I journeyed to the little city where this professor lived. He met me at the train with his carriage, drove me to his home, introduced me to his wife, then asked me if I would like to see the little girl and examine her. How foolish I felt! I didn't know whether I wanted to or not. I knew that of myself I could tell nothing. I knew I had never studied anything of the kind and didn't know what it was all about. I told him, "Yes, but I do not suppose it makes any difference." They led me into a room where the little girl was sitting on the floor rolling blocks. A nurse was attending her. She looked as well as any child I had ever seen, and I couldn't imagine what in the world would be said regarding such a perfect looking little girl.

I entered another room, lay on a couch and went through the same proceedings I had previously done for myself.

When I was conscious again I saw the father and mother in tears. The mother gripped me by the hand and said, "You have given us the first hope we have had in years respecting Amie's condition."

Here is the father's affidavit, secured later for research purposes:

"Personally appeared before Gerrit J. Raidt, a notary public in and for said county, C. H. Dietrich, and after being duly sworn, deposes and says that:

"Amie L. Dietrich, born January 7, 1897, at Hopkinsville, Ky., was perfectly strong and healthy until February, 1899, when she had an attack of LaGrippe, followed by two violent convulsions, each of twenty minutes' duration. Dr. T. G. Yates, now of Pensacola, Florida, was the attending physician. Convulsions returned at irregular intervals with increasing severity. She would fall just like she was shot, her body would become perfectly rigid, the spells lasting from one to two minutes.

"This went on for two years, or until she was four years old. At this time she was taken to Dr. Linthicum in Evansville, Indiana, and Dr. Walker, also of Evansville. They said a very peculiar type of nervousness was all that ailed her and proceeded to treat her accordingly, but after several months' treatment, with no results, the treatment was stopped.

"In a few months, Dr. Oldham, of Hopkinsville, Kentucky, was consulted and he treated her three months, without results. Later he took her for four months more treatment, making seven months in all, but without results. She was now six years old and getting worse, having as many as twenty convulsions in one day. Her mind was a blank, all reasoning power entirely gone.

"March 1st, 1902, she was taken to Dr. Hoppe, of Cincinnati, Ohio, who made a most thorough examination. He pronounced her a perfect specimen physically, except for the brain affection, concerning which he stated that only nine cases of this peculiar type were reported in medical records, and every one of these had proved fatal. He told us that nothing could be done, except to give her good care, as her case was hopeless and she would die soon in one of these attacks.

"At this period our attention was called to Mr. Edgar Cayce, who was asked to diagnose her case. By auto-suggestion he went into a sleep and diagnosed her case as one of congestion at the base of the brain, stating also minor details. He outlined to Dr. A. C. Layne, now of Griffin, Ga., how to proceed to cure her. Dr. Layne treated her accordingly, every day for three weeks, using Mr. Cayce occasionally to follow up the treatment, as results developed. Her mind began to clear up about the eighth day and within three months she was in perfect health, and is so to this day. This case can be verified by many of the best citizens of Hopkinsville, Kentucky, and further deponent saith not.

"Subscribed and sworn before me this 8th day of October, A.D. 1910.

(Signed) C. H. Dietrich.

"Gerrit J. Raidt, Notary Public
Hamilton County, Ohio."

Following the Dietrich case there came a growing demand from all classes and kinds of people for readings on every possible subject. I was still skeptical and entered only half-heartedly into giving readings under all kinds of circumstances. Some of my experiences during this period were most trying, and as I look back it seems a wonder that I did not destroy the effectiveness of the readings.

In 1910 and 1911 a series of unusual cases were brought to the attention of the newspapers of the country through reports made to one of the research societies in Boston, Massachusetts. A great deal was written in the papers throughout the country, some very glowing accounts, some very scathing, and I was called everything from a prevaricator and a charlatan to a second Messiah.

The time came when the true nature of the readings was brought home to me. I had given hundreds and hundreds of readings for other people through the years, but none for my own family. My wife became very ill. After several months under the care of three or four physicians, the one in charge of the case called me to his office one morning and said, "Cayce, I am sorry to tell you, but your wife cannot possibly live another week. Everything possible that I know has been done. One lung is choked. No air has been going through it for months. The other is now affected and you must know from the hemorrhages it is bleeding. With the high temperature, with the little resistance, she can not hold out. I will come whenever she wants me, but if there is anything in this monkey business you are doing you had better try it."

Will anyone ever understand what it meant to me to know that I was taking the life of one near and dear to me in my own hands, and that the very force and power I had been wishy-washy in using for years must now be put to a crucial test? Imagine how I felt when I was conscious again after the reading, when the physician who had been called especially on the case said, "Cayce, that was the most beautiful lecture I ever heard on tuberculosis, and I have lectured both here and abroad on the subject. You say there is hope, but with my examination and experience, I can not see how there can be." There were suggestions made in the reading for her improvement. One of the physicians in the case followed these suggestions very closely. Many, many years have passed since then, and my wife is in better health today than she has ever been in her life.

It was during my wife's illness that a very famous psychologist from Harvard University visited our city to investigate my work. In a very gruff manner he told me that he had come to expose me. He said, "I have exposed more fake mediums than any man in this country, and there has been too much written recently about you in the papers. Where is your cabinet? What is your modus operandi?"

I did not know what the man was talking about. I explained to him no special preparations were necessary, that I had just as soon lie on the street or the roadside as in an office. I said, "Doctor, the preparations evidently must be in the minds and hearts of those who seek information. Here is my wife. Just a few days ago she was given up by doctors in charge of her case. Information was given through a reading. Today there is hope. Here is the reading. Here is the patient. Examine her. Read this. Go and ask Professor Dietrich, or Mrs. Dabney, about their experiences. Then explain the work to me. Tell me if I am fooling myself, for I claim nothing."

The following day this psychologist came and listened to information which was given for some man who sought aid. For several days he talked with those who came for readings, listened to the information as it was given and talked with people in our city about me and the work. Finally he came to me and said, "Cayce, this is no fake. You are mixed up with the wrong type of people. Keep your feet on the ground. Always be sincere. Do not attempt to force anything. If you never do another case than that of the little Dietrich girl, your life will not have been in vain."

Since that time practically every member of my own and my wife's family has had readings. Is the information through these readings a cure-all? No. For, some years ago my mother, the most wonderful mother a man ever had, passed on. During the last few hours of her illness, she called me to her bed. I will always remember her words: "Son, your mother is going now. You have kept her alive for years through your work. Now she must go, but you must so live your own life that you may bring to others that comfort, that ease, which has so often come to your mother through those readings in which God speaks to those who will listen."

Even after these experiences I could not make up my mind to give my whole time to these readings. I moved to another state and set about to build up a business as a photographer. But the stories of the readings followed me to Alabama and finally to Selma, a small town near Montgomery, where I settled with my family.

The information which has come through my readings has always stimulated me to greater studies of the Scriptures and applications of the truths which they contain. It was in Alabama that I became very active in Sunday School, Church and Christian Endeavor work. During ten happy years my young men's classes and groups of Junior Christian Endeavor Experts made fine records. Indeed, as I look back over many years of church work there were few periods during which I did not have a Sunday School class, but the years in Selma, Alabama, brought greater opportunities to work with young people.

Our files contain the following report from one of the finest Christian gentlemen I have ever known.

"State of Alabama
Jefferson Co.
"Before me the undersigned authority, Notary Public in and for said County and State, personally appeared Wm. K. Schanz who is known to me, and who, being first duly sworn, deposeth and saith as follows:

"In the five years that I have known Mr. Edgar Cayce, of Selma, Alabama, it has been to my great personal pleasure and benefit; meeting him through Christian Endeavor, he being Superintendent of the best Junior C.E. Society it has been my pleasure to meet and talk to, I being State Treasurer of the Alabama C.E. Union and Field Worker. I first came to know him as a deep, earnest, sincere Christian man. Naturally we met at different times and talked about Christian Endeavor work, and religion, until we became close friends. Visiting in Selma quite frequently, I came to hear, from others, of the great work Mr. Cayce had done in Selma and other places with his psychic power, and it has been my pleasure to meet quite a few people who have benefitted by Readings given by Mr. Cayce, and who have personally told me of the good Mr. Cayce has done for them. I, however, do not wish to speak from hearsay, but from personal knowledge, it having been my pleasure to be present at the following Readings, where, as Court Reporter, I reported verbatim every word uttered during these Readings, and which I afterwards transcribed, a copy being given to Mr. Cayce of each Reading, and a copy of which I have here in my office, and which I will forward, if necessary.

"While on a vacation to my mother's home in Reading, Pa., this summer just past, I had the misfortune, while bathing, to get water in both my ears, which later resulted in abscesses forming and making me wretched. I consulted and was treated by a doctor in Atlantic City, N.J., and also by a doctor at Reading, Pa.; the abscesses opened and left me with running ears. From this trouble my nose and throat became affected, and through taking treatment from an ear, nose and throat specialist in Bessemer, Alabama, upon my return South, I got gradually worse, until in the middle of October I could hardly hear and had great difficulty in breathing and speaking. I got in touch with Mr. Cayce, and he came to Birmingham and gave me a Reading upon his arrival here. Mr. Cayce knew very little of my trouble in my head, but in the Reading went thoroughly into the trouble, explained where the trouble was, and how it could be cured, telling me to stop treatment with the ear specialists and take up osteopathy and electric violet ray treatment. I have followed his advice as closely as it was possible for me, and am still following the treatment, and today my hearing is entirely restored, my ears have stopped running since the beginning of December, and I have again started singing; with the exception of a little trouble with my nose (which I know will disappear in time), I am perfectly well.

"During Mr. Cayce's stay in Birmingham I was present and reported verbatim Readings on the following persons: Oct. 15, Mrs. Fannie Kahn; Oct. 19, Louis Halbert Tinder; Oct. 20, Mrs. Lorena Tinder; Nov. 2, a second Reading on myself, the first having been given on Oct. 15; Nov. 3, Phillip Pendleton, and Nov. 5, Mrs. Willie Vandefrig. All of these Readings were on diagnosis and given in the Hotel Tutwiler, Birmingham, Alabama; however, Mrs. Fannie Kahn was in Lexington, Kentucky, when the Reading was given for her; Louis Halbert Tinder was sitting in an automobile in front of the Tutwiler Hotel while his Reading was given; and Mrs. Lorena Tinder was visiting at Irvine, Kentucky, at the time the reading on her was given. The others were present in the room. At most of these Readings the room where the Reading was given was full of spectators, and at nearly every one there were from one to three doctors present and asking questions. I know personally that all of the above mentioned people have been greatly and wonderfully helped by following the diagnosis and treatment given in the Readings by Mr. Cayce, and all are loud in their praise of Mr. Cayce and the help he has given them. I know also that the doctors and professional and business men present at the Readings were amazed at Mr. Cayce's revelations, but one and all have confessed that there was no doubt but that Mr. Cayce had a power that few, if any, possess; and that his practice of using his power for the benefit of humanity was noble and princely.

"For myself, I believe in Mr. Cayce and his power, for seeing and experiencing is believing. I know not whence comes his power, but I do know that he is using it for good, hence it must come from good, the All Good, which is God. May he never lose his power.

(Signed) Wm. K. Schanz.

"Subscribed and sworn to before me this 22nd day of January, 1921.

(Signed) G. P. Benton,
Notary Public."

Far from discouraging my work in giving readings my studies of the Bible have given me greater understanding of the true meaning and significance of my experiences, and I certainly believe that the information contained in hundreds of readings in our files helps to clarify and explain my Bible for me. I consider the Bible the greatest of all records of psychic experiences.

Individuals continually sought me out asking that I try to help them through my readings. I began to realize that my greatest field of service for fellow men lay in trying to be of assistance to those who desired help. It was then that I began to seek the help of others who believed the readings worthy of study and the first attempts were made to form an organization to preserve and examine the daily readings which were given.

Ignorant of the laws governing the whole vast realm of the "psychic" we made many mistakes. Holding to an ideal does not insure an individual's being protected from the hard knocks of experience, especially when that ideal involves studies in advanced fields of thought.

Upon repeated attempts to establish a hospital the information that came through continued to insist upon Virginia Beach, Virginia, as the best place from which to conduct the work. Finally, where readings could be followed carefully, I moved in 1925, with my family, to this little coastal town, then only a small, insignificant resort. It is here that we have lived and worked since that time.

A hospital was built under our first organization, the Association of National Investigators, Incorporated. During the few years of its operation, some remarkable cases were handled and some unusual records secured.

I must pause here to give you one brief report from the complete case histories of individuals who received aid in the hospital.

This is the story of a man who was brought to the hospital after he had followed readings given for him while in a very serious condition. Let him tell his own story:

"Since returning to my duties as Superintendent of the Carolina Wood Products Company at Asheville, N. C., I felt it my duty to write and thank you for the courteous treatment that I have received at your institution, to which I owe my life.

"It might be interesting for me to review just what happened to me. We work nearly one thousand men and owing to the stress of my duties, I was in a very run-down condition. I became very ill, which led to unconsciousness for several days. My associates obtained the best doctors possible in the South under the direction of Dr. Bernard Smith, of Asheville, who is reputed to be one of our leading men.

"Some of the doctors felt I had a strange fever. A very prominent Atlanta doctor took an X-ray which showed a clear case of advanced tuberculosis. My family wired you for a reading. The diagnosis came back that I had bacilli in the blood stream. Upon further examination it proved to be streptococci. The doctors had given me a transfusion of one quart of blood which the reading said would save my life provided certain other medicines were taken and certain treatment followed out.

"The doctors had given me up to die, but one week later when Dr. Paullin from Atlanta arrived again for the second examination, upon examining the plates of the X-ray he agreed with Dr. Murphy, the X-ray physician, that it was a mild case of bronchitis, if the plates were to be believed. Three weeks later I was taken on a cot to your hospital where daily readings were given and their suggestions followed. Soon I was strong enough to sit on the sand at Virginia Beach.

"Later I was permitted to go in the water and five weeks from the day I arrived at the Beach I was permitted to return to New York to report to the president of our firm for duty.

"I have never felt better in my life than I have felt in the past eight months and I agree with Dr. Smith who in a letter to me stated that I was out of the hands of the doctor and in the hands of God, and you no doubt have been the means for the information to come from God Himself to save my life and to you again I say I owe my thanks. I certainly enjoyed the personal attention received from you, your doctors and nurses at the institution and if at any time I can be of service to you or yours, you have but to command.

"I am, with kindest personal regards,
"Very sincerely,
(Signed) L. Francis."

Complete records of this case along with hundreds of others are in the files of the Association for Research and Enlightenment, Inc., which is now making a study of my work. I make no claims or promises. It is my earnest desire to be of help whenever and wherever possible. I could go on and on with records of case after case; for, indeed, the work of my life is written plainer in others' experiences, in others' results from following the information given in readings, than in any achievements of my own. You who desire to study it further must seek it there.

Many questions must arise in your minds. Let me see if by past experience I can answer some of them. First, "If this is true, why haven't I heard of it long ago?" This, I believe, is the reason, my friends: for several years there were a great many papers that carried articles concerning the phenomena, especially at the time they were reported to the research society, and more recently in New York when I was accused of "attempting to tell fortunes", but most of these have been of such a nature that one could not blame people for not believing them or for feeling that the whole thing was a lot of "bunk". You must remember, also, that for years, even while many of these articles were being written, I did not myself believe in the "work" (as

we now call it). For as has been said, "Man will deign to
make of it a pageant, stage its directions as follows:

> "Enter the king.
> Fanfare of trumpets.
> The army marches by.
> Array of great ones."

Man's pageant must pass and fade, but God works in
slower and more secret ways His wondrous works to perform. He blows no trumpet, He rings no bell. He begins
from within, seeking His ends by quiet growth. There is a
strange power that men call weakness, a wisdom mistaken
for folly. Man has one answer to every problem—power,
but that is not God's way. Then, why shouldn't I dread
publicity?

You ask, I am sure, "Have there been failures?" If there
were not failures, friends, I would be afraid there was
something supernatural about me. I am only human.
Humanity is doomed to failure when it trusts in its own
weak self, and most of us have that failing.

Besides giving two readings every day and talking with
hundreds of people who came asking for readings and inquiring about the hospital, I attempted to handle for a
time much of the business details of the institution. Yet as
I look back over the turmoils and tribulations, the disappointments and periods of despair, the good which was accomplished stands out above everything else.

In February, 1931, with the increasing economic pressure,
the Association of National Investigators, Incorporated,
through some of its directors, felt it necessary to close the
hospital and discontinue the program of the organization.
I tried to take stock of myself and the work. Even then I
wondered, "Am I all wrong?"

A few weeks later individuals from every walk of life who
had had experience with readings gathered in my home.
They came from all parts of the country and crowded into
every available space extending onto the porch and lawn.

There were literally hundreds of letters and telegrams from those who could not be present. To them I said as I say to you today:

"Friends, I have nothing to sell. I am not attempting to spread propaganda. Each one here has had personal experience with the information, or phenomena, as manifested through me; some of you know of my own shortcomings, as well as shortcomings of others. It isn't a question as to whether I want to go on, but the question is, do you, as a group, as individuals, want to see a study of phenomena, or the information, continue? Is it worth while? My position is this: Some years ago, when through the information my wife's life was spared, a little later my boy's eyes received their sight and the younger boy was healed also, I could only say, 'God, I don't understand, but for the good that has come to me, may I be able to help others when they ask'. You all know from your own experiences whether this is worth while. Do not consider my experience, but your experience."

Each and every one gave testimony of their personal experience, indicating a desire to see the work go on. From this meeting there was organized the Association for Research and Enlightenment, Incorporated, a philanthropic organization, chartered under the laws of the State of Virginia, to carry on "psychical research". There are no barriers to prevent any individual from taking part in the work of this Association.

Today we are able to keep more complete records than ever before. A number of case studies are available in pamphlet form for those desiring to know something of the results obtained in following readings given within the last few years.

My friends, the life of a person endowed with such powers is not easy. For more than forty years now I have been giving readings for those who came seeking help. Thirty-five years ago the jeers, scorn and laughter were even louder than today. I have faced the laughter of ignorant crowds, the withering scorn of tabloid headlines, and the cold smirk of self-satisfied intellectuals. But I have also known the wordless happiness of little children who have been helped, the gratitude of fathers and mothers and friends. There are few mails that do not bring me expressions of appreciation for new life, new hope, new ability, stimulated through the readings which have been applied in some individual's life. Trouble and worry and criticism mean very little at such times.

I believe that the attitude of the scientific world is gradually changing toward these subjects. Men high in their respective fields are devoting time and effort to studying the laws that govern all kinds of psychic phenomena. Universities in this and other countries are carrying on advanced experiments. Psychical research must have open-minded, intelligent cooperation from scientists in many fields in order to be ultimately of lasting value in human experience. Our Association hopes to have some part in bringing about such cooperation.

There must be many questions in your minds, questions that can only be answered by a more thorough study of the readings themselves. Indeed, the final answers must come from your own experiences.

Readings devoted to questions regarding the study and presentation of this information have stressed certain ideas that should be considered carefully by anyone interested in this work. These may be expressed briefly as follows:

(1) Make sufficient study of the readings and experiences of others to determine if the information is in keeping with your highest ideals. Does the application of the information make individuals better husbands, wives, sons, daughters, citizens, friends? Deeds, thoughts, standards that build toward a better life, mental and spiritual enlightenment and understanding are measuring signs. Do the principles expressed in the readings bear the stamp of Divine approval in the light of His standards?

(2) Do not seek a reading to satisfy some emotional whim or idle curiosity. To be of real value the information must strike a vibrant chord within your inner being, ringing true to your spiritual desire.

(3) Determine that you will follow the suggestions given in the readings without being moved by the criticisms or scorn of others who cannot understand your point of view.

(4) That which an individual seeks, that he will find. Those that seek only that which is of the earth earthy may only find such; they that seek to bring a whole, well-rounded life, may find it.

Under the Association for Research and Enlightenment, Incorporated, we are attempting to make a careful study of the phenomena of the readings and at the same time ever pass on to others that which is proved helpful in each member's experiences. I give myself to these studies and experiments knowing that many have been helped, and hoping that I may be a "channel of blessing" to each individual who comes with some physical, mental or spiritual burden. This is my life.

EDGAR CAYCE

APPENDIX B

Metaphysical Concepts—
As Stated In Three Pertinent Readings.

Given by Edgar Cayce at the Seventh Annual Congress of
the A.R.E. 6/27/38:

Q. In all Life Readings given through this channel there
are references to sojourns of the soul-entity between incarnations on the earth plane, in various planes of consciousness represented by other planets in our solar
system. You will give at this time a discourse which will
explain what takes place in soul development in each of
these states of consciousness in their order relative to
the evolution of the soul; explaining what laws govern
this movement from plane to plane, their influence on
life in this earth plane and what if any relationship
these planes have to astrology.
A. Yes, we have the information and sources from
which same may be obtained as to individual experiences, sojourns and their influence.

As we find, in attempting to give a coherent explanation
of that as may be sought, or as may be made applicable
in the experience of individuals who seek to apply such
information, it is well that an individual soul-entity, the
record of whose astrological and earthly sojourns you
have, be used as an example.

Then a comparison may be drawn for those who would judge same from the astrological aspects, as well as from the astrological or planetary sojourns of such individuals.

What better example may be used, then, than this entity with whom you are dealing (Edgar Cayce)?

Rather than the aspects of the material sojourn, then, we would give them from the astrological.

From an astrological aspect, then, the greater influence at the entrance of *this entity that ye call Cayce was from Uranus.* Here we find the extremes. The sojourn in Uranus was arrived at from what type of experience or activity of the entity? *As Bamebridge,* the entity in the material sojourn was a wastrel, one who considered only self; having to know the extremes in the own experience as well as of others. Hence the entity was drawn to that environ. Or, *how did the Master put it?* "As the tree falls, so does it lie". Then in the Uranian sojourn there are the influences from the astrological aspects of EXTREMES; and counted in thy own days from the very position of that attunement, that tone, that color. For it is not strange that music, color, vibration are all a part of the planets, just as the planets are a part—and a pattern—of the whole universe. Hence to that attunement which it had merited, which it had meted in itself, was the entity drawn for the experience. That form, that shape.

The birth of the entity into Uranus was not from the earth into Uranus, but from those stages of consciousness through which each entity or soul passes. It passes into oblivion as it were, save for understanding, there have been failures and there are needs for help. Then help CONSCIOUSLY is sought!

Hence the entity passes along those stages that some have seen as planes, some have seen as steps, some have seen as cycles, and some have experienced as places.

How far? How far is tomorrow to any soul? How far is yesterday from thy consciousness?

You are IN same (that is, all time is one time), yet become gradually aware of it; passing through, then, as it were, God's record or book of consciousness or of remembrance; for meeting, being measured out as it were to that to which thou hast attained.

Who hath sought? Who hath understood?

Only they that seek shall find!

Then, born in what body? That as befits that plane of consciousness; the EXTREMES, as ye would term same.

As to what body—what hast thou abused? What hast thou used? What hast thou applied? What hast thou neglected in thy extremes, thy extremities?

These are consciousnesses, these are bodies.

To give them form or shape—you have no word, you have no form in a three-dimensional world or plane of consciousness to give it to one in the seventh—have you?

Hence that's the form—we might say—"Have You?"

What is the form of this in thy consciousness? It rather indicates that everyone in questioned, "Have you? —Have You?"

That might be called the form. It is that which is thy concept of that being asked thyself—not that ye have formed of another.

With what sojourn then the entity finds need for, as it were, the giving expression of same again (the answering of "Have you?") in that sphere of consciousness in which there is a way in and through which one may become aware of the experience, the expression and the manifesting of same in a three-dimensional plane.

Hence the entity was born into the earth (as Edgar Cayce) under what signs? Pisces, ye say. Yet astrologically from the records, these are some two signs off in thy reckoning!

Then from what is the influence drawn? Not merely because Pisces is accredited with an influence of such a nature, but because it IS! And the "HAVE YOU" becomes then "There Is", or "I Am" in materiality of flesh, or material forces—even as He who has passed this way!

The entity *as Bamebridge was born in the English land* under the SIGN, as ye would term, *of Scorpio; or from Venus as the second influence.*

We find that the activity of the same entity in the earthly experience before that, in a French sojourn, followed the entrance into Venus.

What was the life there? How the application?

A child of love! A child of love—the most hopeful of all experiences of any that may come into a material existence; and to some in the earth that most dreaded, that most feared!

(These side remarks become more overburdening than what you are trying to obtain! but you've opened a big subject, haven't you?)

In Venus the body-form is near to that in the three-dimensional plane. For it is what may be said to be rather ALL inclusive! For it is that ye would call love—which, to be sure, may be licentious, selfish; which also may be so large, so inclusive as to take on the less of self and more of the ideal, more of that which is GIVING.

What is love? Then what is Venus? It is beauty, love, hope, charity—yet all of these have their extremes. But these extremes are not in the expressive nature or manner as may be found in that tone or attunement of Uranus; for they (in Venus) are more in the order that they blend as one with another.

So the entity passed through that experience, and on entering into materiality abused same; as the wastrel who sought those expressions of same in the loveliness for self alone, without giving—giving of self in return for same.

Hence we find the influences wielded in the sojourn of the entity from the astrological aspects or emotions of the mental nature are the ruling, yet must be governed by a standard.

And when self is the standard, it becomes very distorted in materiality.

Before that we find the influence was drawn for a universality of activity from Jupiter; in those experiences of the entity's sojourn or activity as the minister or teacher in *Lucius*. For the entity gave for the gospel's sake, a love, an activity and a hope through things that had become as of a universal nature.

Yet coming into the Roman influence from the earthly sojourn in Troy, we find that the entity through the Jupiterian environment was trained—as we understand—by being tempered to give self from the very universality, the very bigness of those activities in Jupiter.

For the sojourn in Troy was as the soldier, the carrying out of the order given, with a claim for activities pertaining to world affairs—a spreading.

What form, ye ask, did he take? That which may be described as in the circle with the dot, in which there is the turning within ever if ye will know the answer to thy problems; no matter in what stage of thy consciousness ye may be. For "Lo, I meet thee WITHIN thy holy temple," is the promise.

And the pattern is ever, "Have you?" In other words, have you love? or the circle within, and not for self? but that He that giveth power, that meeteth within, may be magnified? Have you rather abased self that the glory may be magnified that thou didst have with Him before the worlds were, before a division of consciousness came?

These become as it were a part of thy experiences, then, through the astrological sojourns or environs from which all take their turn, their attunement.

And we find that the experience of the entity before that, as Uhjltd, was from even without the sphere of thine own orb; for the entity came from those centers about which thine own solar system moves—in Arcturus.

For there had come from those activities, in Uhjltd, the knowledge of the oneness, and of those forces and powers that would set as it were the universality of its relationships, through its unity of purpose in all spheres of human experience; by the entity becoming how? Not aliens, then—not bastards before the Lord, but sons —co-heirs with Him in the Father's kingdom.

Yet the quick return to the earthly sojourn in Troy, and the abuse of these, the turning of these for self—in the activities attempted—brought about the changes that were wrought.

But the entrance into the *Ra-Ta* experience, when there was the journeying from materiality—or the being translated in materiality as *Ra-Ta*—was from the infinity forces, or from the sun; with those influences that draw upon the planet itself, the earth and all those about same.

Is it any wonder that in the ignorance of the earth the activities of that entity were turned into that influence called the sun worshippers? This was because of the abilities of its influences in the experiences of each individual, and the effect upon those things of the earth in nature itself; because of the atmosphere, the forces as they take form from the vapors created even by same; and the very natures or influences upon vegetation.

The very natures or influences from the elemental forces themselves were drawn in those activities of the elements within the earth, that could give off their vibrations because of the influences that attracted or drew away from one another.

This was produced by that which had come into the experiences in materiality, or into being, as the very nature of water with the sun's rays, or the ruler of thy own little solar system, thy own little nature in the form ye may see in the earth!

Hence we find how, as ye draw your patterns from these, that they become a part of the whole. For ye are RELATIVELY related to all that ye have contacted in materiality, mentality, spirituality! All of these are a portion of thyself in the material plane.

In taking form they become a mental body with its longings for its home, with right and righteousness.

Then that ye know as thy mental self is the form taken, with all of its variations as combined from the things it has been within, without, and in relationship to the activities in materiality as well as in the spheres or various consciousnesses of "Have you—love, the circle, the Son?"

These become then as the signs of the entity, and ye may draw these from the pattern which has been set. Just as the desert experience, the lines drawn in the temple as represented by the pyramid, the sun, the water, the well, the sea and the ships upon same—because of the very nature of expression—become the PATTERN of the entity in this material plane.

Draw ye then from that which has been shown ye by the paralleling of thy own experiences in the earth. For they all bear a relationship one to another, according to what they have done about, "The Lord is in His holy temple, let all the earth keep silent!"

He that would know his own way, his own relationships to Creative Forces or God, may seek through the promises in Him; as set in Jesus of Nazareth—He passeth by! Will ye have Him enter and sup with thee?

Open then thy heart, thy consciousness, for He would tarry with thee!

We are through. (5755-1)

Reading given by Edgar Cayce 6/19/41, pursuant to request of those present at the Tenth Annual Congress of A.R.E.:

Q. It has been given through this source that souls become entangled in cosmic systems similar to the solar system, where conditions are like those presented in this system. For the enlightenment of those gathered here, it is requested that you now take up the implications of this statement, in so far as it is possible to do so in terms of language and human experience. You will discuss the questions which have been prepared, as I ask them, using, wherever possible, parallels with life as it is on this earth.

A. Yes, we have the implications that have been indicated through these channels; as to how souls may be entangled in systems or influences similar in nature to human experience in matter.

In answering many of those questions presented here, or that may be in the minds of those gathered here, it is well that the premise be given from which such answers would be made.

Thus in the answers we may find that, though there may be worlds, many universes, even much as to solar systems, greater than our own, that we enjoy in the present, this earthly experience or this earth is a mere speck when considered even with our own solar system. Yet the soul of man, thy soul, encompasses ALL in this solar system or in others.

For, we are joint heirs with that universal force we call God—if we seek to do His biddings. If our purposes are not in keeping with that Creative Force, or God, then we may be a hindrance. And, as it has been indicated of old, it has not appeared nor even entered into the heart of man to know the glories the Father has prepared for those that love Him. Neither may man conceive of destruction, even though he is in the earth a three-dimensional awareness. Neither may he conceive of horror, nor of suffering, nor even of what it means to be in outer darkness where the worm dieth not.

Then in considering those conditions, those experiences as may be a part of the soul's awareness—in the beginning was the Word, and the Word was God. THAT is the premise.

Q. May we assume that the term "entangle" means a soul's participation and immersion in a form or system of creative expression which was not necessarily intended for such participation and immersion, as the earth?

A. To be sure, there are those consciousnesses or awarenesses that have not participated in nor been a part of earth's PHYSICAL consciousness; as the angels, the archangels, the masters to whom there has been attainment, and to those influences that have prepared the way.

Remember, as given, the earth is that speck, that part in creation where souls projected themselves into matter, and thus brought that conscious awareness of themselves entertaining the ability of creating without those forces of the spirit of truth.

Hence that which has been indicated—that serpent, that satan, that power manifested by entities that, created as the cooperative influence, through will separated themselves.

As this came about, it was necessary for their own awareness in the SPHERES of activity. Thus realms of systems came into being; as vast as the power of thought in attempting to understand infinity, or to comprehend that there is no space or time.

Yet in time AND space, in patience, you may comprehend.

Q. In systems where conditions for expression parallel those in the solar system; is entanglement a parallel experience to entanglement in this system, so that a soul is apt only to become immersed in one of these systems, and after working out of it, be immune to the attractions of others?

A. No. No two leaves of a tree are the same. No two blades of grass are the same. No two systems have the same awareness, neither are they parallel.

There ARE those awarenesses that are relative relationships, yes. But hast thou conceived—or canst thou conceive—the requirements of the influence to meet all the idiosyncrasies of a SINGLE soul? How many systems would it require? In thyself ye find oft one friend for this, another for that, another for this relationship, another for the prop, another to arouse. Yet all are the work of His hand, are thine to possess, thine to use—as one with Him.

Q. Can you describe, by similes or comparison, what it is in other systems which attracts the souls?
A. Take what has just been given; that there are conditions that may meet every idiosyncrasy of the INDIVIDUAL soul! Then consider the millions, and how much is required of thee!

There are centers through which those of one solar system may pass to another, as we have indicated in information for individuals. There are also those experiences in which individual souls may seek a change. As He gave, "As the tree falls so does it lie." This is not only material, it is also mental and spiritual. Is God's hand short, that there would not be all that each soul would require? For it is not by the will of God that any soul perishes, but with every temptation, with every trial there is prepared the way of escape.

GOD, the Father, then, is the Creator—the beginning and the end. In HIM is the understanding, BY and through those influences that have taken form—in universes—to meet the needs of each soul—that we might find our way to Him.

Q. Do these other systems have a planet, like earth, which is a focal point for the meeting and material expression of its forces and principles?
A. Relatively so, in that dimension of consciousness or awareness necessary to meet that arousing of the soul to its need—its awareness of the Maker, the Word, the Spirit; and the influences therein answer to that within the individual soul.

For, an individual soul here finds itself a body, a mind, a soul. Ye may sin in mind, ye may in body. Do ye answer only in spirit?

As He has given, every SOUL shall give account of the deeds done in the body. What body? That body of mind, that body of physical manifestation, that body of spirit; each in its own sphere, its own realm.

Earth, in this solar system, merely represents three dimensions. Then, how many dimensions are in this solar system? Eight! What position does the earth occupy? Third! What position do others occupy? That relative relationship one to another.

Who is the author and the finisher of same? The Word. Who is the Word? He that made Himself manifest in the flesh. Who is the beginning, the end? Ever Jesus, the Christ!

We are through for the present. (5755-2)

Given by Edgar Cayce 11/15/31 in accordance with request made by self:

Mrs. C.: You will have before you the body and the soul-mind of Edgar Cayce, present in this room, and the experience or vision had by him on October 30 while teaching the Sunday School lesson at the First Presbyterian Church, Virginia Beach, Va., in which he saw a number of the Jewish faith apparently enter the church and listen at the discourse. You will please tell this body if this was a true vision, and just what, if anything, he is to do about it.

Mr. C.: Yes, we have the body, the enquiring mind and the soul-body Edgar Cayce, present in this room, and the experience, the vision had by the body while discoursing on the lesson.

As should be understood by the body, this was an experience, real, literal, in the sense that we as individuals are ever encompassed about by those that are drawn to us by the vibration or attitude concerning conditions that are existent in the experience of entities or souls seeking their way to their Maker.

As this particular discourse dealt with the activities of a peculiar or individual people, so there was gathered mostly those that had held in common a faith and desire in this particular phase of experience.

The carnal eye was then lifted for Cayce, so that he saw; even as the servant of Elisha saw those that camped between those that would hinder Elisha in his service to his people.

As the visions as a child, then, Cayce is again entering that phase of development or experience where there may be in the physical consciousness periods when there may be visioned those that are seeking in the spirit realm for that which will aid them to understand their relations with the whole.

It should be understood that Life is One, that each soul, each entity is a part of the Whole, able, capable of being one with the Source, or the Universal Power, God, yet capable of being individual, independent entities in their own selves. *As He has given, to those whom He calls does He give the power to become the Sons of God.*

As has been given to this body Cayce, to this peculiar people has he been sent; as one—one—that may aid many to come to a better understanding of their relationships to the Creator and their relationships to their fellow man.

Then, as indicated from that visioned, they that are seeking, though they be in another dimension, or phase, or plane of experience, are listening, harkening, gathering, that they may gain the better concept of what is to be done.

Naturally there arise such questions as these: How does a disincarnate entity hear carnally that spoken from a material mind? With what eyes do they see? With what ears do they hear? With what bodies do they appear? Wherewithal are they clothed?

As given, "Know, O Israel, the Lord thy God is *One!*" and the hearing that is come, and does come to an entity is with that whereunto the body-entity has builded; hence by the very nature are drawn together as *one*, the eyes as with the visions that are one, whereunto such entities, such souls have seen in their sojourn through the material plane. They are clothed with that body, that clothing which is in its essence from the very source of that builded through the power given them by their relationships to the Creative Forces that are manifest in a material world.

That a man's ideas have changed because he has passed from the material plane into the unseen, how can one conceive of this being different? From whence is the lily clothed? From whence comes the clothing that man may wear? From whence comes the power of differentiation in the ability of an individual man to see or to hear? Wherewithal are they given the power to disseminate speech in its various intonations or incantations, for their communications one with another?

One that has been endowed with an understanding of a peoples known as the Indian, that may by grunts, incantations, or in the various forms of expression to convey that which is being sought of the relations of one to another, is not understood by one who has been endowed with an understanding of the other environs; as in France or in the U.S.A. Not understood, no; but when that language that bespeaks of faith, hope, kindness, love, is manifest, it expresses, it conveys to the heart and soul of all a *universal* language; as does music, as does the beauty of a rose, as does the music of the spheres partake of that which is the closer to that relation as the soul, whether occupying this or that body, has with that Creative Force from which it emanated.

So, as in the vision that is shown here, as in the visions that may come to the body, to the soul-mind of the body, honor and reverence same, that the language of the spheres, that the Voice of the Creative Forces are being manifest; but do not abuse same by *thinking,* acting, speaking or *feeling* that self *has* been exalted or raised to any particular position other than of being of greater service to thy fellow man.

Remember that, "He that would be the greatest among you will be the servant of all". He that will humble himself shall be exalted. He that remains true shall be lifted up, even as He gave; "And I, *if* I be lifted up will draw all *men* unto me".

Know, then, that there is being shed some of that glory that was in Him, and that is given thee in this carnal body, this weakened flesh, through the insight of the glories that await man if he will remain true to those lessons that are set before him; that self is being lifted up with the greater abilities, the greater opportunity to reach the more.

He that is called to service must indeed obey. Know also that it is true in thy experience as it was in His experience, "Though He were the Son, yet learned He obedience by the things which He suffered".

As the carnal forces, the carnal mind with its desires, its necessities for the satisfying of those conditions that are created as habit, as desires of the flesh, as desires of the attributes of the physical or material mind are suffering under the strain that comes in the various periods of the manifestations of the glory, know that the body is being given more and more the opportunity then to minister to not only those in the material things in the material life, but these as seen who are seeking in the Borderland, those that are to many a loved one in the spirit land they are seeking—seeking. . . .

Give then of thyself in the strength that He gives to thee, for thou hast been called and chosen as one through whom—*bodily*—there may come a channel who may speak face to face with his peoples.

Keep the faith. Keep the body clean. Look up, *lift* up thine eyes unto the hills from whence the help comes; for God is in His holy temple. Keep, then, thy body clean, thine temple of thine body in such a state, *mentally, spiritually*, that He may come and lodge with thee, that He may oft speak with thee as Father to Son.

As thine Elder Brother may He walk with thee in thy going in, thine coming out among men; for that thou hast seen is holy—HOLY; and thou must conduct thine self in such a manner that is *worthy* of these visions, those helps coming to thee the more often.

Do not become self-important, nor self-exalting. Be rather selfless, that there may come to all who come under the sound of thy voice, to all that come in thy presence, as they look upon thine countenance, the knowledge and feeling that, indeed this man has been in the presence of his Maker; he has seen the visions of those expanses we all seek to pull the veil aside that we may peer into the future. As ye may become a teacher to those that are "beyond the veil" also, how glorious must be thy words even then to those that falter in their steps day by day!

In patience know thy soul may go out and minister to others. *As, as thy presence brings that faith, hope and confidence in men's lives, so may the words of thy mouth be acceptable in the sight of thy Redeemer, so may He indeed give thee the abilities to speak even as the oracles of the fathers, as the oracles of God Himself who sits in His Throne and has given to His Son that ability to quicken the hearts of men* that they may know His Face also.

Be, then, patient, my son. Keep in the ways that He has gone. Know that Mother stands near oft, and will guide in the ways that will aid in coming—coming—nearer to the closer walk with him.

We are through. (294-155)

EDGAR CAYCE

World Renowned Psychic

__EDGAR CAYCE'S STORY OF ATTITUDES AND EMOTIONS ed. and arr. by Jeffrey Furst 0-425-10601-2/$5.50

__EDGAR CAYCE'S STORY OF KARMA ed. and arr. by Mary Ann Woodward 0-425-10246-7/$5.99

__EDGAR CAYCE'S STORY OF THE ORIGIN AND DESTINY OF MAN ed. and arr. by Lytle Robinson 0-425-09320-4/$5.99

__EDGAR CAYCE'S STORY OF JESUS ed. and arr. by Jeffrey Furst 0-425-10327-7/$7.99

Payable in U.S. funds. No cash accepted. Postage & handling: $1.75 for one book, 75¢ for each additional. Maximum postage $5.50. Prices, postage and handling charges may change without notice. Visa, Amex, MasterCard call 1-800-788-6262, ext. 1, or fax 1-201-933-2316; refer to ad #276a

| Or, check above books and send this order form to: The Berkley Publishing Group P.O. Box 12289, Dept. B Newark, NJ 07101-5289 | Bill my: ☐ Visa ☐ MasterCard ☐ Amex _____ (expires) Card#_____ Daytime Phone #_____ ($10 minimum) Signature_____ |

Please allow 4-6 weeks for delivery.   Or enclosed is my: ☐ check ☐ money order
Foreign and Canadian delivery 8-12 weeks.

Ship to:

Name_____	Book Total	$_____
Address_____	Applicable Sales Tax (NY, NJ, PA, CA, GST Can.)	$_____
City_____	Postage & Handling	$_____
State/ZIP_____	Total Amount Due	$_____

Bill to: Name_____

Address_____   City_____

State/ZIP_____

PENGUIN PUTNAM INC.
Online

Your Internet gateway to a virtual environment with
hundreds of entertaining and enlightening books
from Penguin Putnam Inc.

*While you're there, get the latest buzz on
the best authors and books around—*

Tom Clancy, Patricia Cornwell, W.E.B. Griffin,
Nora Roberts, William Gibson, Robin Cook,
Brian Jacques, Catherine Coulter, Stephen King,
Ken Follett, Terry McMillan, and many more!

**Visit our website at
www.penguinputnam.com**

PENGUIN PUTNAM NEWS

Every month you'll get an inside look at our upcom-
ing books and new features on our site. This is an
ongoing effort to provide you with the most
up-to-date information about
our books and authors.

Subscribe to Penguin Putnam News at
www.penguinputnam.com/newsletters